VICTIMS' STORIES AND THE ADVANCEMENT
OF HUMAN RIGHTS

VICTIMS' STORIES AND
THE ADVANCEMENT
OF HUMAN RIGHTS

Diana Tietjens Meyers

OXFORD
UNIVERSITY PRESS

OXFORD
UNIVERSITY PRESS

Oxford University Press is a department of the University of Oxford. It furthers the University's objective of excellence in research, scholarship, and education by publishing worldwide.Oxford is a registered trade mark of Oxford University Press in the UK and certain other countries.

Published in the United States of America by Oxford University Press 198 Madison Avenue, New York, NY 10016, United States of America.

Library of Congress Cataloging-in-Publication Data
Names: Meyers, Diana T., author.
Title: Victims' stories and the advancement of human rights /
Diana Tietjens Meyers.
Description: New York : Oxford University Press, 2016. | Includes
bibliographical references and index.
Identifiers: LCCN 2015031692| ISBN 978–0–19–993038–8 (hardcover : alk. paper) |
ISBN 978–0–19–993040–1 (pbk. : alk. paper) | ISBN 978–0–19–993039–5 (ebook) |
ISBN 978–0–19–049010–2 (online content)
Subjects: LCSH: Human rights advocacy. | Victims of crimes—Civil rights.
Classification: LCC JC571 .M455 2016 | DDC 362.88—dc23 LC record available at
http://lccn.loc.gov/2015031692

1 3 5 7 9 8 6 4 2
Printed by Sheridan, USA

For Lewis

CONTENTS

ACKNOWLEDGMENTS

I owe a great debt of gratitude to the University of Connecticut Human Rights Institute for awarding me a fellowship and the Dean of the College of Liberal Arts and Sciences for awarding me a sabbatical in 2006–2007. This funding and time free from teaching enabled me to start the research and writing that evolved into this monograph. I'm also indebted to the University of Connecticut faculty members and guest conveners who participated in the Narrative, Humanity, and Humanitarianism Workshop sponsored by the University of Connecticut's Foundations of Humanitarianism Program. Our monthly conversations were a source of insight and inspiration for me.

Friends and colleagues have given me immensely valuable feedback on my work leading up to this book. They include Cheshire Calhoun, Claudia Card, Lori Gruen, David Ingram, Catriona Mackenzie, Samuel Martinez, Lewis Meyers, Serena Parekh, and Lisa Tessman. I am grateful to all of them, and I very much hope I have not omitted anyone. Thanks, too, to the research assistants who unstintingly aided me with this project over the many years it was incubating—Asha Bhandary, Kristina Grob, Allan Breedlove, Caitlin

Purvin-Dunn, and Sarah Babbitt. As well, I have presented parts of this project at conferences and colloquia too numerous to mention, but I am grateful for many useful suggestions that I received from participants in those events. Last but of the utmost importance, I thank Lucy Randall, my editor at Oxford University Press, for her generous support and expert guidance.

Versions and pieces of a couple of the chapters in this book have previously appeared in journals or edited collections. I think of these earlier publications as intimations of the line of thought I present here, and I thank the publishers of these predecessors for the opportunity to publish my developing ideas and for permission to use parts of them or revised versions of them in this work. For Chapter 1, I thank *Humanity: An International Journal of Human Rights, Humanitarianism, and Development*, where I published "Two Victim Paradigms and the Problem of 'Impure' Victims" (Vol. 2, No. 2, Fall 2011: 255–275, Copyright © 2011 University of Pennsylvania Press), and *Law, Culture, and Humanities*, where I published "Recovering the Human in Human Rights" (March 31, 2014; doi 1743872114528440). For Chapter 2, I thank Springer, where I first published "Narrative Structures, Narratives of Abuse, and Human Rights" in *Feminist Ethics and Social and Political Philosophy: Theorizing the Non-Ideal*, edited by Lisa Tessman (2009).

VICTIMS' STORIES AND THE ADVANCEMENT OF HUMAN RIGHTS

Introduction

Whereas recognition of the inherent dignity and of the equal and inalienable rights of all members of the human family is the foundation of freedom, justice and peace in the world,

Whereas disregard and contempt for human rights have resulted in barbarous acts which have outraged the conscience of mankind [sic], and the advent of a world in which human beings shall enjoy freedom of speech and belief and freedom from fear and want has been proclaimed as the highest aspiration of the common people,

. . .

Now, Therefore THE GENERAL ASSEMBLY proclaims THIS UNIVERSAL DECLARATION OF HUMAN RIGHTS as a common standard of achievement for all peoples and all nations, to the end that every individual and every organ of society, keeping this Declaration constantly in mind, shall strive by teaching and education to promote respect for these rights and freedoms and by progressive measures, national and international, to secure their universal and effective recognition and observance, both among the peoples of Member States themselves and among the peoples of territories under their jurisdiction.

Preamble, *Universal Declaration of Human Rights**

Just as I was completing the final arguments of Chapter 5 of this volume, news came of the publication of Mohamedou Ould Slahi's

* http://www.un.org/en/documents/udhr/#atop (accessed February 7, 2015).

Guantánamo Diary. Slahi's book is unquestionably the most important victim's story of human rights abuse in recent US history. And it may be the premiere victim's story of our time, if only because those responsible for the abuse he recounts acted as agents of one of the world's oldest and strongest constitutional democracies.

Regrettably, Slahi's book attests to the persistent relevance—indeed, the urgency—of my topic. Despite the official founding of the human rights regime in 1948—the year the *Universal Declaration of Human Rights* was adopted by the UN General Assembly—people continue to be victimized for "reasons" that beggar the imagination. Patterns vary in different parts of the world. But people worldwide remain vulnerable to violations of their human rights on account of ancient prejudices centering on religion, race, ethnicity, gender, sexuality, and disability. Moreover, new kinds of victims are proliferating. Shifting distributions of geopolitical power and surging ideological extremisms furnish novel rationales for abusing other human beings, while burgeoning technological developments provide ever more ingenious and potent means to do so.

As a transnational moral community, our collective record in the post-World War II, post-Holocaust era is surely cause for shame and self-reproach. Some might add despair. Nevertheless, this book seeks to give cause for hope—the hope that facing terrible truths can foster mutual recognition of our common humanity and gradual fulfillment of the promise of human rights. We need, I maintain, to hear the stories of victims—to learn who these individuals are and to grasp the moral significance of what they have to tell us. I do not exaggerate the importance or overestimate the potential influence of victims' stories. There is no single remedy for the tenacity of human rights abuse. However, I am convinced—and I'll endeavor to convince you—that victims' stories can make a substantial contribution to eradicating the hatred and contempt that slick the slope that descends to flagrant abuse.

The line of thought I develop in this book takes a cue from the work of philosophers who maintain that the basic form of a moral problem is a story (Cavell 1979; MacIntyre 1984; Rorty 1986; Walker 1998). The idea is that organizing the subjective states and behaviors of individuals into intelligible relationships and interconnected occurrences creates a story-until-now, which in turn poses a question: What next? Because the protagonists are agents, the answer—the next episode—is up to them, and so they must decide how to go on. Because they are moral agents, they must decide how to continue in a mutually acceptable—that is, morally commendable—way.

The stories victims tell about human rights abuse raise the question of how we as a moral community can carry on together at two levels. On the micro level, the question of what comes next concerns the particular victim or group of victims. What do we owe to this individual (these individuals)? A sincere apology? An honest accounting? Commensurate recompense? Punishment of the malefactors? These are questions of the utmost importance, but they are not the focus in this project.[1] Rather, I'll focus on the macro level and ask how victims' stories can contribute to building a culture of human rights—a transnational moral community in which human rights are fully realized and enjoyed by all persons, a community in which the dignity of every person is secure. My aim here is to show that victims' stories can lend support to interpretations of human rights that augment the protections they afford and can fortify non-victims' commitment to human rights norms.

There has been ample philosophical discussion of some issues that victims' stories raise—for example, respect for victims, their standing to speak and credibility, and their need to reconstruct their selfhood and agency. However, a number of key topics have been neglected:

- Paradigms of victimhood and unjustifiable exclusions from the category of victim;

- Narrative structures as constraints on victims' stories and as vehicles for articulating human rights norms;
- The role of emotional responses to victims' stories in discerning their normative significance;
- Empathy with victims' stories as a pathway to moral understanding and human rights commitment;
- The need for an institutional framework through which victims' stories can be ethically obtained and disseminated for the purpose of advancing human rights.

I address these concerns by analyzing the rhetorical resources for and constraints on victims' ability to articulate their stories and by clarifying how their stories can contribute to enlarged understandings of human rights protections and deepened commitments to realizing human rights. I theorize the normative content that victims' stories can convey and the bearing of that normative content on human rights. In short, I mobilize philosophical theory to illuminate victims' stories, and I appeal to victims' stories to enrich the philosophy of human rights. To give you a preliminary idea of the nature of human rights abuse and the normative power of victims' stories, I analyze some salient themes in *Guantánamo Diary*. After that, I sketch the development of my argument chapter by chapter.

This book does not supply a compendium of victim types. The diversity of post-1948[2] victims is far too great to compass in a single volume, let alone a volume that aspires to propound a philosophical view. Nor are the stories I excerpt[3] as illustrations of or support for my philosophical claims a representative sample of the experiences of victims or the stories they tell. Victims' stories are as various as the individuals who tell them and the abuses they recount. Moreover, the stories I've elected to discuss are not typical of victims' stories in style or structure. Victims tell their stories in a wide variety of contexts and media—in courts, truth commissions, support groups; to journalists, talk show hosts, social scientists, clinicians, human rights practitioners; in books, newspapers, magazines, videos, films; on Internet websites, radio programs, television, and so forth. With all these outlets and their disparate purposes and audiences, it is impossible to generalize confidently about the form or content of victims' stories. Nevertheless, a number of recurring themes surfaced over the course of my research into victims' stories. None of these themes appears in every victim's story, but previewing them here will give you a taste of the meanings of victimhood and the density of the stories that victims tell.

I'll introduce these themes by looking into Slahi's *Guantánamo Diary*. Strictly speaking, his book isn't a diary. It's a memoir detailing Slahi's abduction in Mauritania as a suspected terrorist, followed by his fourteen-year incarceration and interrogation, first in Jordan, then in Afghanistan, and finally at the US prison at Guantánamo Bay, Cuba. As well, the handwritten text that Slahi produced in detention has, as the credited editor puts it, been edited twice—censored by the US government before the manuscript was released to Slahi's attorneys, and grammatically corrected and to some extent reorganized for readability by Larry Siems.[4] Still, Slahi's distinctive voice and his remarkable personality shine through.

Before I take up the themes concerning victimization that I wish to highlight, I need to provide a little biographical background about Slahi.[5] A native Mauritanian with a talent for science and mathematics, the eighteen-year-old Slahi won a scholarship to study electrical engineering at the University of Duisburg in Germany. A devout Muslim, he interrupted his education in 1991 to join the US-backed Mujahedeen then battling the Soviet occupiers of Afghanistan. After returning to Germany and completing his education, he lived, worked, and practiced his religion in Germany for most of the 1990s.

Slahi's first terrorism-related detention came in 2000. He was traveling from Canada, where he had become dissatisfied with his employment, and was en route to Mauritania, where he planned to stay. He was questioned about a plot to bomb the Los Angeles airport hatched by someone who prayed at the same mosque in Montreal where Slahi had been worshipping. As no reason to keep him in custody turned up, Slahi was released. In the fall of 2001, he was living among his family and working as an electrical engineer in Nouakchott, Mauritania.

Because Slahi was trained by al-Qaeda in Afghanistan, because his brother-in-law was for a while a confidant of Osama bin Laden, and because he worshipped at mosques in Germany and Canada attended by several known terrorists, Slahi came to the attention of US intelligence operatives. Shortly after the attack on the World Trade Center in New York City on September 11, 2001, Slahi got snared in the US security dragnet. Under pressure from Washington, D.C., Mauritanian officials turned Slahi over to a CIA rendition team that flew him to Amman, Jordan. Despite seven and a half months of intensive interrogation, he failed to incriminate himself or anyone else. Nevertheless, another US rendition team picked him up and flew him to the Bagram Air Base in Afghanistan. Two weeks later, he was flown to Cuba, where he has been held at the Guantánamo Bay detention facility since August 2002.

At Guantánamo, Slahi was questioned at all hours of the day and night and was subjected to stress positions, sexual molestation, sleep deprivation, frigid cold, and threats to his family.[6] When these torture techniques failed to extract any confession or actionable information, Slahi, shackled as always, was beaten to within an inch of his life and treated to a "Birthday Party" involving two lengthy speedboat rides (Slahi 2015, 241, 250–261, 265). On the first, he was forced to drink gallons of salt water. On the second, sharp-edged, stinging ice cubes were forced into his prison uniform from his neck to his ankles and replenished whenever the ice began to warm and soften.

When he eventually recovered his ability to move and speak, he began confessing to anything his interrogators wanted to hear and implicating anyone his interrogators wanted to link to anti-US terrorism. His confessions and finger-pointing ceased, though, when he took a polygraph test in which he denied any involvement in terrorism, as he consistently had done until the "Birthday Party" broke his resolve to answer honestly. He passed the test.[7]

In 2005, Slahi petitioned for habeas corpus. Four years later, US District Court Judge James Robertson heard his case. On March 22, 2010, Judge Robertson granted Slahi's petition and ordered his release. Nevertheless, Slahi's case is stranded in legal limbo. Although he has never been charged with any crime, the Obama administration appealed Judge Robertson's decision, and the Appeals Court sent Slahi's petition back to the District Court for rehearing. At the time of this writing, that rehearing has yet to take place, and Slahi is still imprisoned at Guantánamo.

During the summer of 2005, after the escalating violence of his "special interrogation plan" had subsided, Slahi wrote the 466-page manuscript that has been published as *Guantánamo Diary*.[8] In contrast to the bare-bones case history I have just laid out, his story describes his interaction with his captors, along with his subjective responses to the treatment he was receiving. We are invited to listen in on his speculations about what is happening to him and why, to vicariously experience his eddies and attacks of affect, and to follow the twists and turns of events as he remembers them. We are vouchsafed, in other words, one victim's experience of extreme human rights abuse and the layers of meaning that experience had for him.

What does he want us to understand about who he is and what he went through? A great deal more than I can review here. However, I'll endeavor to identify some features of Slahi's narrative that will find echoes in victims' stories that I'll discuss later.

Slahi offers many insights into the quality of human rights abuse. Many victims' stories pivot on humanly inflicted, life-threatening danger that the author experiences as fated yet normatively unintelligible. Slahi captures his plunge into the post-9/11 sinkhole of arbitrariness in this bizarre exchange:

> INTERROGATOR: "There is no innocent detainee in this campaign."
>
> . . .
>
> SLAHI: "But I've done no crimes against your country."
>
> INTERROGATOR: "I'm sorry if you haven't. Just think of it as if you had cancer!"
>
> (Slahi 2015, 20–21; attributions of the statements added)

Shortly after this passage, Slahi describes the pain inflicted for the ostensible purpose of concealing the identities and employers of the people transporting him to Guantánamo. Blindfolding goggles were tied so tightly around his head that they caused agonizing pain for the forty-hour trip from Afghanistan to Cuba (Slahi 2015, 26–27). To make this suffering palpable, he invites readers to tie a pair of goggles tightly around their hands and keep them tied for a couple of hours—to try for themselves an approximation of what we will discover is a comparatively minor cruelty in his long captivity. Later in the text, however, he seems to give up on readers' empathy, and he denies that those of us who have never been prisoners can understand what prison life means (Slahi 2015, 232, 319). Despite his explicit doubts about readers' comprehension, Slahi's story makes every effort to penetrate our comfort, complacency, and obtuseness. He does his best to make us understand, and his best is extraordinarily good. In support of this praise, I'll examine two types of response to abuse that Slahi depicts—symptoms of victimization that he suffered, and the survival of his humanity despite victimization.

Slahi's story catalogues a symptomology of victimization. His descriptions of what I think of as terrorization syndrome are ghastly to read. Here is a sample:

> I started to have nausea. My heart was a feather, and I shrank myself so small to hold myself together. I thought about all the kinds of torture I had heard of, and how much I could take tonight. I grew blind, a thick cloud built in front of my eyes, I couldn't see anything. I grew deaf . . . all I could hear was indistinct whispers.
>
> (Slahi 2015, 77–78)

> I started to shake, my face got red, my saliva got as bitter as green persimmon, my tongue as heavy as metal.
>
> (Slahi 2015, 182–183)

> My mouth dried up, I started to sweat, my heart started to pound . . . and I started to get nausea, a head-ache, a stomach-ache.
>
> (Slahi 2015, 216)

> I drowned in sweat, got dizzy, and my feet failed to carry me. My heart pounded so hard that I thought it was going to choke me and fly off through my mouth.
>
> (Slahi 2015, 265–266)

> Every move behind my door made me stand up in a military-like position with my heart pounding like boiling water. My appetite was non-existent. I was waiting every minute on the next session of torture.
>
> (Slahi 2015, 272)

Can anyone read these passages impassively? No shiver of fear? No constriction in the throat? Just in case these somatic phenomenologies of terror bypass a reader's sensibilities, Slahi switches to the third-person perspective and remarks on his appearance: "I looked like someone who was going through an autopsy while still alive and helpless" (2015, 266).

In addition to these affective and corporeal symptoms of victimization, Slahi depicts cognitive symptoms. Most of the time, Slahi displays astounding self-possession and cognitive acuity regardless of what is visited upon him. However, his wits sometimes fail him. The strangest cognitive lapse he describes occurred when he first arrived at Guantánamo. He forgot his wife's name and gave an incorrect one (Slahi 2015, 212–213). The unreliability of trauma victims' recall, especially under pressure, is well documented in the medical literature.

In the clutches of the US rendition program, he generates wild fantasies and contemplates them as if they were realistic possibilities. While shackled to a seat in the rendition plane that's refueling on a tarmac in Cyprus on the way to Jordan, he "drowned in [his] daydreams"—he fancies that the local police will search the plane, arrest him for, of all things, stopping in Cyprus without a transit visa, and deport him home to Mauritania (Slahi 2015, 146). Perhaps most preposterously of all, he cooks up a "neuroscientific" theory of the function of the sound-cancelling headsets the rendition squad fastened to his ears. Despite his expertise in telecommunications technology, he becomes fearful that the headsets will electrocute him while extracting information directly from his brain (Slahi 2015, 143). His imagination sometimes plays the friend, sometimes plays the enemy. One moment it gives him hope; the next moment it intensifies his fear. Alas, it conspires with his captors to keep him affectively and cognitively off balance.

Contortions of victims' sense of humor are also symptomatic of their plight. Slahi is subject to uncanny bursts of laughter. Absurdity

in the midst of moral outrage tickles his funny bone, and the weird-
ness of this response is not lost on him:

> All I could hear was moaning. Next to me was an Afghani who
> was crying very loudly and pleading for help [redacted]. He was
> speaking in Arabic, "Sir, how could you do this to me? Please
> relieve my pain, Gentlemen!" But nobody even bothered to check
> on him. . . . I felt so bad for him. At the same time, I laughed. Can
> you believe it, I stupidly laughed! Not at him; I laughed at the
> situation. First, he addressed them in Arabic, which no guards
> understood. Second, he called them Gentlemen, which they
> were most certainly not.
>
> (Slahi 2015, 33; also see 281)

It seems to me that the episodes of amusement Slahi recounts can be
construed both as symptoms of the extremity of his suffering and as
expressions of his irrepressible humanity. Symptomatic of his victimization because, as Slahi well knows, the agonies of his fellow prisoner
really should take precedence over the ironies of the situation. Expres-
sive of his humanity because he could neither miss the incongruities of
the situation nor jam the eminently human relief valve of laughter.

I now focus on the theme of retained humanity despite human
rights abuse, which takes several forms in Slahi's narrative. The first
comes at the outset of his rendition to Jordan. It's a naked affirmation
of his existence as a self-reflective human consciousness deserving
of moral consideration—an affirmation of his dignity. To explain a
remark he had just made to the Mauritanian intelligence officer who
is betraying him, Slahi tells us, "I was eager to let my predator know
I am. I am" (2015, 142). I am not merely a victim, I take him to be
saying. I am like you a person, a bearer of human rights. "Tell them
not to torture me," he implores (2015, 142).

Agency is the second way in which Slahi's humanity is expressed despite his victimization. His capacity for intelligent choice and action is evidenced in two main ways—his religious observance and his conduct under interrogation.

Religious observance is a ubiquitous motif is Slahi's story. When he can, he prays according to prescribed ritual (2015, 91, 140, 346). When guards withhold information about the time of day or the direction of Mecca or when they prohibit prayer altogether, he follows others' lead in praying, prays spontaneously, or "prays in his heart" (2015, 11, 17, 77, 205, 216, 231, 235, 246, 247, 265, 272, 273, 299). He resourcefully devises methods for estimating the time of day and keeping track of the days of the week in order to pray appropriately on a daily basis and on the holy day, Friday (2015, 286). He knows the Koran by heart, but he is pleased and comforted when he is allowed to keep a copy of the sacred text (2015, 17, 39, 159, 345).

Slahi is a man of faith and an intellectual. Near the end of his book, when his interrogators have finally relented, a relatively friendly interrogator takes charge of him. She (usually the genders of Guantánamo personnel are redacted, but there's an occasional slip-up in the censorship) dispenses with the by now unmistakably futile intelligence-gathering-through-brutality gambit. Instead, she helps Slahi plant an herb garden, orders that the nutritional content of his diet be improved, and gives him a copy of the Bible to read (2015, 351–355). A sophisticated and amusing philosophical dialogue about religion ensues. Slahi and his interrogator discuss Christian and Islamic theological positions, such as the cogency of the doctrine of the Trinity and the fairness of condemning non-Christians to hell (Slahi 2015, 355–359). In light of Slahi's curiosity and intellect, not to mention his clever scheme to outwit his captors and worship according to Islam's hourly and daily mandates, I am reluctant to explain his devotion to his religion while he was being tortured as superstition or as a knee-jerk reflex. Rather, I am inclined to see it as an expression of his agency—his enacting of the values and beliefs to which he is profoundly committed.

Here is an earlier episode in his story that also argues for interpreting his worship as an expression of his agency. After his "Birthday Party," guards and medics wearing Halloween-like masks attended Slahi (2015, 271). Kept awake around the clock, starved, occasionally given food that he can't swallow, forced to drink nearly a gallon of water as punishment for not eating, and then ordered to run in his shackles, he begins to have aural hallucinations (2015, 270–273). He diagnoses his own problem. He's going insane, and he knows that no one will allow him to receive psychological treatment (2015, 273). Alone and without any hope of aid from others, he needs to gain distance from his torments and figure out how to stop the voices in his head. Under the circumstances, turning to prayer is clearly a rational step. When he is finished, he knows what to do, and he requests an appointment with a relatively trusted interrogator (Slahi 2015, 273).

At this point, his cooperation with his interrogators veers in a new direction. Throughout his incarceration, he cooperated by steadfastly telling the truth. All available public records vindicate his professions of personal innocence and ignorance of terrorist plots. He persisted on this course despite the evident exasperation of his interrogators and ill treatment by his guards. Occasionally, he insouciantly takes issue with the injustice of his situation or jousts with an interrogator who is following a nonsensical line of questioning or advancing obviously unfounded claims (Slahi 2015, 175, 192, 194, 212, 309–310). Clearly, he was in command of his capacity for choice and action. After his "Birthday Party" and the psychopathology that then besieged him, Slahi shifts gears (Slahi 2015, 275–283, 290). He pumps his interrogators to ascertain what they believe he has done, and he confesses to those crimes. He prods his interrogators to reveal what they need to know to convict other people, and he testifies to their wrongdoing. "I allowed myself to say anything to satisfy my assailants" (Slahi 2015, 278). It is undeniable that Slahi is acting under duress. However, his compliance is not automatic or mindless.[9] It is a coping strategy that he correctly predicts will bring an end to his torture (Slahi 2015, 276). It is an expression of his capacity for choice and action based on reasons. Further evidence that Slahi retained his agentic capacities despite his suffering comes when one of his interrogators begins to doubt the veracity of the evidence Slahi is supplying and suggests that Slahi take a polygraph test (Slahi 2015, 297). Although understandably anxious about submitting to the test, Slahi jumps at the chance to prove his innocence and reverts to his original story while the test is being administered (2015, 297–300). As I've already mentioned, the results of the test corroborated his story. It seems clear, then, that Slahi's capacity to grasp reasons and act accordingly remained intact.

The third way in which Slahi's humanity is expressed is through his sociability. Sometimes his sociability comes through in disturbing ways. For example, at Bagram Air Base, as the guards are preparing the prisoners for transport to Guantánamo, Slahi describes a scene in which one by one prisoners are blindfolded, shackled, and shoved out a gate. Each prisoner falls on top of the one before. The callousness of this scene notwithstanding, Slahi notes that the warmth of the bodies piling up on and around him comforted him (Slahi 2015, 25)—a paltry comfort, to be sure, but also the comfort of a social being who has not lost his humanity. Human connection, even when attenuated as much as it is here, remains valuable to Slahi.

Most amazing of all, Slahi makes friends everywhere he is forced to go. Although the guards in the detention centers are forbidden to talk with the prisoners, Slahi befriends guards in Jordan and at Guantánamo. In Jordan, guards teach him about their culture, gossip about goings-on in the prison, and bring him books from the prison library (Slahi 2015, 175–176). Nor can Slahi bring himself to hate his

Guantánamo abusers. After his torture regimen has collapsed, Slahi describes the change in his relations with his guards:

> Now the guards discovered the humorous guy in me, and used their time with me for entertainment. . . . We slowly but surely became a society and started to gossip about the interrogators and call them names.
>
> (2015, 326–327)

The guards bring him books, which he eagerly devours (Slahi 2015, 318, 322, 343). One of them teaches him to play chess, and he quickly becomes a champion player, beating the guards (Slahi 2015, 327). He repairs the guards' DVD players and PCs, and in return they give him movies to watch (2015, 319, 326, 336, 345). Slahi's comment on his taste in cinema is telling. He reports that "in his real life" he didn't care for fictional movies, but that in prison, he likes any depiction of life outside Guantánamo. "I just want to see some mammals I can relate to," he declares (Slahi 2015, 337). Guantánamo couldn't torture the sociability out of Slahi.

Indeed, it is touching, though by no means excusing, to read that a number of the people who viciously abused Slahi at Guantánamo came to respect and like him. A number of interrogators and guards bring him parting gifts when they're posted elsewhere (2015, 347, 368–369). Slahi accepts them in the spirit in which they're offered, and he reflects that he might have been friends with these people had they met under different circumstances (2015, 369). Yet, on the same page, he demands justice—war crimes trials. Slahi is an amiable individual who prizes human companionship *and* a self-respecting moral subject who has not forgotten the heinousness of the wrongs committed against him.

No victim's story is identical to that of any other victim, but there are family resemblances among victims' stories. Although each of the stories I invoke in subsequent chapters recounts a different type of abuse—persecution of political dissent, genocide, child soldiering, and mass rape during armed combat—the themes I've identified in Slahi's narrative recur in many of them.

Before I outline my philosophical agenda in this book, I want to spotlight an additional issue bearing on victims and their stories that Slahi's work puts on unusually conspicuous, graphic display. There are black bars covering text and signaling redactions on almost every page of *Guantánamo Diary*. Many of the redactions protect the identities of the persons who abducted and tortured Slahi. Given that the US government refuses to prosecute any of these individuals, it is unsurprising, though highly problematic, that we are prevented from learning who they are. Although the legitimacy of these name redactions is debatable, two other redactions are blatantly egregious. Slahi's entire description of his polygraph test—material that presumably would exonerate him once and for all—is redacted (2015, 301–307). Likewise, several pages that are preceded by "One of my poems went" are blacked out (2015, 359–361). His poem—presumably a deeply personal statement concerning subject matter of great importance to him—has been censored.

Victims of human rights abuse are routinely silenced. Their stories are told, if they are told at all, only in private settings. Consequently, they do not come to the attention of the public. Suppressing victims' stories is a form of revictimization. It compounds the harms that victims have already endured by condemning them to isolation from the larger moral community. Because suppressing their testimony entails refusing to enter into dialogue with them, it further insults their dignity. Not only that, silencing victims deprives other moral agents of knowledge they need in order to conduct themselves in accordance with their principles. If people don't know about human rights abuse, they can't take action to protest it and bring it to a halt. Thus, silencing victims authorizes practices of abuse with impunity and endows a class of abusers with immunity. Breaking the silence of victims and attending to their stories are necessary steps toward realizing human rights.

Victims' Stories and the Advancement of Human Rights takes on a set of questions suggested by the prevalence of victims' stories in human rights campaigns, truth commissions, and international criminal tribunals:

1. What conceptions of victims are presumed in contemporary human rights discourse? How do these conceptions impede progress in recognizing victims and realizing human rights, and how should these conceptions be modified to better mesh with a twenty-first century human rights agenda?
2. How do conventional narrative templates fail victims of human rights abuse and resist raising novel human rights issues? What alternatives are available?
3. How does the interplay between a reader's emotions and a victim's story contribute to interpreting the text, and how can victims' stories ward off disgust and/or moral revulsion?
4. What is empathy, and how can victims frame their stories to overcome empathetic obstacles and promote commitment to human rights?
5. How is it possible to ethically use victims' stories in the service of human rights? How can individual consumers of these stories avoid victim blaming? How can human rights professionals ethically acquire and publicize victims' stories? How can outraged responses to victims' stories be channeled in morally desirable and practically effective ways?

These are the topics of the chapters to come.

Chapter 1 critically analyzes two current paradigms of victims of human rights abuse. Pathetic victims are marked by passivity and helplessness in the face of overpowering force and unspeakable humanly inflicted suffering. Heroic victims face off against the repressive power of the state to fight injustice using nonviolent tactics. These paradigms, I argue, encode polarized conceptions of innocence that are out of keeping with well-established social practices regarding the acknowledgment of victims. Worse, they block recognition of certain victims of human rights abuse. Finally, I challenge the stigmatization of pathetic victims and the veneration of heroic victims. Pathetic victims, such as Mohamedou Ould Slahi, are not passive and helpless. They retain their agency—their capacity for intelligent choice and action. Heroic victims need not be paragons of virtue. Liao Yiwu, who was incarcerated and tortured by Chinese authorities for protesting the 1989 events at Tiananmen Square, writes not only about his righteous rage against state repression but also about his plentiful discreditable behavior before and during his imprisonment.

In light of the mismatch between the victim paradigms and actual victims of human rights abuse, I propose an overhaul of the paradigms. Human rights violations are not actions that dehumanize pathetic victims or super-humanize heroic victims. They are systematic, unnecessary, and severe humanly inflicted harms.[10] The innocence criteria embedded in the two paradigms are misguided. A burdened agency criterion must replace them. The conception of a victim that I advocate better aligns with a realistic understanding of human subjectivity and agency and allows for a more inclusive understanding of who is a bearer of human rights and under what conditions right-holders become victims of rights abuse.

By formulating a cogent account of victims of human rights abuse, I set the stage for the rest of this book. In the succeeding chapters, I explicate some ways in which the stories that victims tell can help to promote human rights.

Chapter 2 explores relationships between structural features of victims' stories and normativity. Since there is no scholarly consensus on the nature of narrative, I treat it as a variegated form of representation. Conventional victims' stories, structured according to the template Anthony Amsterdam and Jerome Bruner set out in their work on narrative and law (2000), depend on societal norms to define the trajectory of the plot—acceptable starting points, unacceptable disruptions, and appropriate remedies. In addition, they conform to the traditional aesthetic value of unity by presenting material chosen to ensure completeness and continuity. Stories cast in this mold can work very well as legal testimony or in memoirs, and I examine the emotional power of a conventional autobiographical victim's story in Chapter 3. Yet, because many victims' stories can't fit comfortably into this mold, I consider alternative approaches to narrative.

Hayden White distinguishes full-fledged narratives from annals and chronicles and claims that moral summation is necessary for narrative closure (1987). However, I point out that in addition to moral closure there are several other kinds of narrative closure—equilibrium, emotional, and epistemic—and that these possibilities create pitfalls for victims of human rights abuse who want their stories to make the connection between their suffering and the urgency of respect for human rights. Elizabeth Spelman's reading of *Incidents in the Life of a Slave Girl, Written by Herself* supplies a number of useful pointers for crafting victims' stories that effectively communicate their moral implications. *Incidents in the Life of a Slave Girl, Written by Herself* qualifies as a full-fledged narrative by White's criteria. However, many victims' stories fail to satisfy White's criteria for annals, chronicles, or full-fledged narratives, which in my view helps to clarify what is at stake in the relationship between victims' stories and moral closure.

In defense of the normative significance of victims' stories, I propose an account of the relation between normativity and a salient type of victim's narrative that seems especially resistant to integration into human rights discourse. Many victims' stories are hybrids that resemble annals in some respects, chronicles in other respects. Hybrid victims' stories present incomplete, disjointed sequences of events and employ figurative language to express the horror of victimization. I illustrate my conception of hybrid narratives with passages from victims' stories of the 1994 Rwanda genocide that journalist Jean Hatzfeld recorded in the late 1990s. Victims often tell these stories in the hope of attaining emotional closure and healing. Yet, I argue that there is a form of moral closure that is compatible with hybrid victims' stories. A victim's story that at first seems to represent nothing more than what the narrator has endured may on closer inspection represent a moral void, together with an implicit moral imperative that has been systematically disregarded. In voicing a moral demand for protection, such stories achieve a kind of moral closure—namely, a fully formed appeal to conscience. If I am right, hybrid narratives also resemble White's full-fledged narratives inasmuch as they reach moral closure. I return to the topic of hybrid victims' stories in Chapter 4, where I discuss such a story in relation to empathy.

Whereas Chapter 2 explores the structure of narrative, Chapter 3 explores the kind of understanding that narrative imparts. Some students of narrative claim that narrative imparts causal or moral knowledge; others accuse narrative of purveying normative disinformation or of tempting people to mistake feelings for truth. After critically examining the views of Noël Carroll (2001), Hayden White (1987), and J. David Velleman (2003), I defend and adapt Jenefer Robinson's account of how affective engagement with great novels can be morally instructive (2005). To make my case for the value of emotionally understanding victims' stories, I sift through some problems that Ishmael Beah's *A Long Way Gone: Memoirs of a Boy Soldier* raises for Robinson's affective/normative account. There are hazards associated with emotionally understanding his story, for, as with many victims' stories, some of the incidents he recounts are emotionally staggering, and these intense responses tend to overpower other feelings aroused by other parts of his story. Through a discussion of corrective rhetorical devices and a discussion of imaginative resistance, I show that victims' stories can curb such emotional excess and prevent readers' interpretations from going awry.

I contrasted victims' stories that explicitly appeal to human rights with stories that make more oblique reference to human rights in Chapter 2. I take up a closely related, but subtly different topic in Chapter 3. As illustrated by an incident in Jean-Jacques Rousseau's *Emile*, a victim's story can explicitly invoke not only the normative content of a right, but also the very concept of a right. I grant that this type of story can be useful. However, in the spirit of Robinson's thought, I urge that structuring victims' stories to mirror human rights theory is less productive overall from a moral point of view. If I am right about the downside of authorial moralizing and superintendence over interpretation, it follows that victims' stories that leave the concept of a right implicit have the greatest potential for moral generativity. But a disadvantage of such stories is that they are especially susceptible to readings that are hostile to human rights. Open as they are to individual readers' interpretations, they may or may not prompt readers to draw on human rights norms to conceptualize their affective responses. Although this indeterminacy exposes these victims' stories to misinterpretation, I urge that it awakens readers' affective capacities and their powers of imagination to better understand the meanings of human rights in human lives and perhaps to identify shortcomings in current conceptions of human rights.

Chapter 4 considers the role of empathy in our knowledge of human rights. Many contemporary moral philosophers dispute empathy's contribution to moral knowledge (Goldie 2000, 2011; Goldman 1992; Mackenzie and Scully 2007; Prinz 2011a, 2011b).

Yet others defend empathy as a moral power (Darwall 1998; Gruen 2015; Nussbaum 2001; Sherman 1998). A major reason that it's difficult to get a philosophical purchase on empathy's role in moral life is that this term is used in so many different ways in different contexts. Coined for purposes of aesthetic theory, the term *empathy* subsequently found homes in clinical psychology, social psychology, philosophy of mind, and ethics. Moreover, *empathetic* is firmly ensconced in colloquial speech as a term of approbation.

In view of these disparate, sometimes conflicting usages, clarity about empathy demands a certain amount of stipulation. The account of empathy that I advocate blends key elements from ordinary speech with helpful distinctions that can be traced back to David Hume and Adam Smith. I develop and defend my account in the context of Peter Goldie's incisive work on empathy and kindred concepts. Goldie denies that empathy is a moral response (2000). I agree with him that empathy does not necessarily lead to moral behavior. However, much hinges on Goldie's characterization of empathy, which, I argue, needs amplification. Moreover, it is one thing to deny that empathy motivates moral action; it is another to deny that empathy is a morally significant epistemic capability. After reviewing Nancy Sherman's (1998) and Stephen Darwall's (1998) work linking empathy to altruistic action and Catriona Mackenzie and Jackie Leach Scully's (2007) critique of the claim that empathy enables you to grasp the viewpoints of people whose embodiment and social circumstances differ significantly from your own, I urge that empathy enables you to glimpse values and disvalues as another person experiences them.

Sonia Kruks's account of sexed/gendered embodiment and visceral empathy stands in opposition to my claim that victims' stories can mediate corporeal differences and enable differently embodied individuals to grasp alternative normative realities (2001). To show that different forms of embodiment do not prevent people from different social groups from understanding one another's experiences of value and disvalue, I analyze passages from a published text that is more polished than many hybrid testimonial outpourings but that fits best in this category of victims' stories—the anonymously published diary of the Red Army's mass rape campaign at the end of World War II, *A Woman in Berlin: Eight Weeks in the Conquered City*.[11] This eloquent diary illustrates how a victim's story (1) can induce visceral empathy with attacks on features of our common humanity while also (2) providing sufficient personal detail to support empathy with the particular victim's unique experience of suffering as a result of the attacks.

Finally, I argue that empathetic engagement with a victim's story can heighten the empathizer's awareness of just how bad it is to be subjected to human rights abuse. By dispelling ignorance of or confusion about victims' moral claims, empathy with victims' stories can erode indifference to them. Empathetically processed, the gravity of human rights violations, the moral void that a hybrid victim's story depicts, and the demand that it issues for a moral response are viscerally encoded. As a result, empathy can transform your value system—enabling you to grasp values that might previously have been opaque to you and consolidating your commitment to the value of respect for human rights.

Chapters 2, 3, and 4 explicate ways in which victims' stories can help to build a culture of human rights. Chapter 5 confronts some ethical questions raised by projects that use these highly personal stories to promote human rights. I consider the ethics of using victims' stories from the standpoint of individual consumers, from the standpoint of professional users, and from the standpoint of civil society actors.

One of the major problems that arises in connection with using victims' stories to advance human rights is that individual consumers—readers, auditors, and viewers—are prone to indefensible victim derogation and blaming, especially when they feel powerless to do anything effective to help (Ross and Miller 2002). After reviewing psychological studies of this malign phenomenon, I identify strategies that organizations that publicize victims' stories ought to employ to blunt this response, as well as measures that individual consumers ought to take to counteract the moral distortions this defense mechanism produces.

Professional users of victims' stories are a highly diverse group—journalists, academic researchers, truth commissioners, the officials of international and domestic courts, the staffs of UN agencies and nongovernmental organizations (NGOs)—and their projects are diverse as well. Yet, all of them gather victims' stories to gain firsthand knowledge of human rights abuse, and all aim to use that knowledge to promote a human rights agenda. Consequently, all of these professionals owe it to their informants to resolve the ethical question of how to respect these individuals while also using their stories in the interest of human rights. To ensure respect for victims, human rights professionals must obtain informed consent to use their stories, and they must takes steps to protect victims from retraumatization. Still, living up to these obligations varies depending on the project a professional is pursuing. Thus, I divide human rights projects into three types—justice, aid, and research projects—and I develop guidelines for each of these types.

Some of the organizations that employ human rights professionals are civil society actors, but civil society is broader than those professionalized organizations. In addition to professionally staffed NGOs, civil society includes grassroots associations and social movements. I conclude my inquiry into the ethics of using victims' stories by specifying the responsibilities of participants in more informal, volunteer-based human rights projects, by defending professionalized human rights NGOs against charges that they are undemocratic and anti-participatory, and by advocating greater cooperation across the spectrum of human rights advocacy organizations. To keep faith with the countless victims of human rights abuse, present and past, who have shared their stories, human rights organizations must stop competing with one another and start welcoming collaboration on the vital goal of advancing human rights.

Chapter 1

Two Victim Paradigms and the Problem of "Impure" Victims

The contempt we always feel for losers—Jews in the thirties, Muslims now—combines with our disgust at the winners' behavior to produce the semi-conscious attitude: "a plague on both your houses."

Rorty (1993, 113)

In this passage, Richard Rorty is commenting on the failure of the United States and its European allies to take effective military action to stop the massacres and genocidal rape camps that Serbians launched against Muslims during the 1990s wars in the former Yugoslavia. Instead of construing the problem as a question of what we owe to distant others or a question about the limits of national sovereignty, Rorty frames it in terms of moral psychology. "We" perceive victims as contemptible losers.[1] "We" perceive victimizers as disgusting brutes. Both are morally tainted and hence unworthy of "our" moral attention and response.

Stated baldly, this seems undeniably true and utterly bizarre. People shy away from trouble and extra responsibilities. So it's no surprise that "we" would stick our collective head in the sand during the Holocaust and the "ethnic cleansing" in the Balkans. Lost in this orgy of "there's blame all around"-ism is John Locke's firm distinction between wrongdoers and victims.

"In transgressing the law of nature," Locke avers, "the offender declares himself to live by another rule than that of reason and common equity" ([1690]1980, Chap. 2, Sec. 8). Such an individual "so far becomes degenerate, and declares himself to quit the principles of human nature, and to be a noxious creature" (Chap. 2, Sec. 10). By injuring another person—a right-holder—the perpetrator becomes an enemy of the entire human species, more like a rogue elephant running wild and causing indiscriminate harm than an adult human being.[2] In taking leave of reason, offenders forfeit their rights, which clears the way for others to punish them (Chap. 2, Sec. 10 and 11). In sum, Locke divides people into three rights-centric categories: (1) bearers of rights who deserve protection from harm; (2) offenders who deserve to be punished for violating someone's rights; and (3) victims who deserve compensation because someone has violated their rights.

Admittedly, Rorty is discussing a far more complicated situation with very high stakes—military intervention in another state's treatment of its own citizens. However, Rorty does not comment on the niceties of international law, nor does he speculate about the possibility that intervening might cause greater loss of life and aggravate the trauma. Instead, he focuses on why humanitarian intervention is pretty much a nonstarter in the popular imagination—why "we" do not conceptualize the victims' peril and suffering, on the one hand, and their assailants' cruelty and brazen flouting of human rights, on the other, in Locke's crystalline moral terms. According to Rorty, "we" perceive the people caught up in the crisis through schemas that render all of the parties despicable, thereby freeing us to guiltlessly ignore their plight.

In Locke's moral world, a one-to-one correspondence obtains between recognized rights and cognizable violations of rights, and between recognized bearers of rights and cognizable victims of rights violations. However, if Rorty is right about how onlookers frame human rights crises, these seemingly straightforward correlations have broken down. Indeed, I am skeptical that they ever held in practice. Yet, the philosophical literature on victims is spotty. The main topics that grab philosophers' attention are defending and interpreting human rights, proposing policies to recompense victims of rights violations or otherwise repair the damage wrought by rights violations, and demonstrating that social policy and legal institutions systematically occlude the victimization of members of historically subordinated social groups. Ignoring the question of how to conceptualize victims, philosophers implicitly adopt Locke's view that victims are just people whose rights have been violated. I believe that things aren't so simple—that prevalent conceptions of victims adversely affect our capacity to recognize violations of human rights and to secure the respect we owe to victims.

My argument proceeds in four stages. First, I analyze two victim paradigms that emerged in the late twentieth century, along with the initial iteration of the international human rights regime—the pathetic victim paradigm and the heroic victim paradigm.[3] Although I derive the paradigms from Amnesty International's (AI's) conceptualization of victims, I offer evidence that these paradigms have gained popular acceptance (at least in Western democracies). Second, I show that AI's own activism provides grounds for skepticism about the paradigms. AI regards sex trafficking and the death penalty in all their forms as human rights abuse, and the organization extends support to women trafficked into sex work and prisoners on death row, although neither of these groups of victims fit into the bifurcated paradigms. In other words, AI does not let these paradigms get in the way of pursuing a broad human rights agenda. Nevertheless, the popular hegemony of the two victim paradigms produces social and legal blind spots that close off debate about the justice of deporting trafficked women and the justice of executing convicted criminals. Third, I probe the concept of innocence in human rights discourse.

Noting that the heroic victim paradigm countenances innocent agentic victims, whereas the pathetic victim paradigm demands the passivity of victims as a guarantee of innocence, I argue that both paradigms are out of sync with established social practices regarding the acknowledgment of victims. Finally, I propose an alternative to the two victim paradigms' criteria of innocence. In particular, I endorse greater attention to how different kinds of systematic, severe, and unnecessary humanly inflicted suffering constrains right-holders' agency. Moreover, I urge that the innocence criteria embedded in the two paradigms be replaced by a burdened agency criterion. These modifications better align the concept of a victim with a realistic understanding of human subjectivity and agency and with the value of human dignity at the core of human rights. As a result, they allow for a less rigid, more capacious understanding of the conditions under which right-holders become victims of human rights abuse.

1. TWO VICTIM PARADIGMS

Although rooted in over two centuries of philosophical inquiry and institutional reform, the present-day system of human rights got started in the aftermath of World War II. Amid the international community's horrified response to the atrocities committed under the Nazis, the *Universal Declaration of Human Rights* was adopted by the United Nations General Assembly in 1948.[4] A series of international treaties that encoded human rights in the corpus of international law ensued.

It is not surprising, given the politics of human rights and the cross-purposes of the nation-states participating in building a culture of human rights, but it is nonetheless troubling that human rights covenants are strong on moral fanfare and weak on legal enforcement. By and large, they make no reference to the concept of a victim and do not concern themselves with enforcing the rights of individuals. Instead, each covenant sets up an oversight committee with two mandates: (1) to receive reports from States Parties regarding their progress in realizing a particular group of human rights, and (2) to prepare reports that assess the progress being made and that document stasis or backsliding. The Convention Against Torture and Other Cruel, Inhuman, and Degrading Punishment (1987) is a rare exception to this rule, but still quite toothless. Like other human rights treaties, this one calls on States Parties to submit progress reports to the oversight committee. But, in addition, Article 22 grants victims the right to bring charges to the UN Committee Against Torture, provided that the state(s) that allegedly victimized them have acknowledged the authority of the committee to receive such charges. The committee's powers to adjudicate these cases are puny—confined to weighing the victim's accusations against the state's rejoinder and reporting its conclusions to the claimant and the state.

More in line with the *Universal Declaration*'s "recognition of the inherent dignity and of the equal and inalienable rights" of persons, and with the Holocaust fresh in the minds of representatives of the community of nations, the 1951 Geneva Convention Relating to the Status of Refugees defines a quintessential type of victim of human rights abuse—namely, the refugee. Refugees are persons fleeing persecution "for reasons of race, religion, nationality, membership of a particular social group, or political opinion."[5] In other words, they are fleeing the infliction of severe harm or a credible and wrongful threat of severe harm in their homeland, and they have been targeted for this treatment because of their positioning in a social hierarchy or their opposition to the state. According to an influential human rights account of persecution, the harm that moves refugees to travel to a foreign land is a state-sponsored or state-condoned practice of "sustained or systemic denial of core human rights" (Hathaway 1991, 108). At their destination, refugees apply for asylum in the hope of gaining a safe haven. The right to asylum numbers among the very few remedies available to victims of human rights abuse, and it is recognized by three-quarters of the world's states.

Of course, the class of refugees is a small subset of the class of victims of human rights abuse. For a variety of reasons, most victims of persecution are trapped without recourse to flight. Since its inception in 1961, AI has been a vital force in defending these victims. AI introduced its mission by coining the resonant phrase "prisoner of conscience," which the organization still uses to identify victims of a broad range of human rights violations. AI's characterization of these victims overlaps with the Geneva Convention's definition of refugees:

> People who have been jailed because of their political, religious or other conscientiously-held beliefs, ethnic origin, sex, color, language, national or social origin, economic status, birth, sexual orientation or other status, provided that they have neither used nor advocated violence.
>
> (http://www.amnestyusa.org/our-work/issues/prisoners-and-people-at-risk/prisoners-of-conscience, accessed 10/9/2015)

This definition of prisoners of conscience is both confusingly inclusive and curiously exclusionary. It includes both people persecuted for their beliefs and people subject to persecution merely because of their membership in an ethnic, racial, sexual, linguistic, or other unjustly despised social group. But whereas the label *prisoner of conscience* makes sense with respect to people under detention for their beliefs, issues of conscience are beside the point when people are persecuted for their ethnic origin, sex, color, language, or membership in another unjustly despised social group. Before her release in 2010, Nobel Peace Laureate Daw Aung San Suu Kyi clearly qualified as a prisoner of conscience, as did the socialists who were targeted by the Nazi Holocaust. However, it is misleading to regard the Jews, Roma, gays and lesbians, and people with disabilities who were targeted by the Nazi Holocaust as prisoners of conscience, for they were in fact casualties of murderous bigotry. In this section, I extract two salient paradigms of victimization—the pathetic paradigm and the heroic paradigm—from the two groups of persecuted individuals that AI picks out.

A. The Pathetic Victim Paradigm

The starving Jews, Roma, and gays and lesbians whom Allied soldiers found when they reached Hitler's concentration camps epitomize the pathetic victim paradigm.[6] Hunted down by the Gestapo and then denied every necessity and sometimes singled out for additional torment, those inmates of the camps who survived were reduced to bare survival. Holocaust victims share several characteristics that are typical of pathetic victims:

1. They were innocent of any wrongdoing relevant to their treatment;
2. They were utterly helpless in the face of insuperable force; and
3. Other people subjected them to unspeakable suffering.[7]

Notable as well from the standpoint of the cognizability of these victims, the evidence for this severe, humanly inflicted harm is indisputable.

This sketch of pathetic victims coincides with the conception of a victim that Rorty says connotes being a loser—a conception that often rationalizes moral indifference. One reading of Rorty's observation would reduce his point to a psychological truism about human defense mechanisms. Easily triggered defense mechanisms function to deflect awareness of moral responsibilities (1993, chap. 5, sec. 1). To be sure, NGOs must overcome these psychological obstacles to mount successful human rights campaigns. Still, I think there's a philosophical point buried in Rorty's rhetoric.

I call this class of victims pathetic because the term *pathetic* is ambiguous in a morally significant way. It is ascribable to persons whose attributes or circumstances move you to compassionate or contemptuous pity (http://www.merriam-webster.com/dictionary/ pathetic; accessed 3/20/2009). Rorty's diagnosis of moral psychopathology notwithstanding, finding Holocaust victims or, for that matter, victims of the Srebrenica massacre contemptible would be unforgivably obtuse. Still, because contempt is not always a morally indefensible response to a sorry state of affairs, conscientious subjects need guidelines to help them differentiate (1) people who are legitimately claiming to be pathetic victims and who therefore deserve a compassionate response, from (2) imposters who deserve indignation, if not contempt.

The pathetic victim paradigm requires claimants to have undergone severe, documentable, humanly inflicted harm that they are not responsible for incurring.[8] The irreproachable innocence of pathetic victims is crucial. Otherwise they can be accused of provoking their own suffering, whether because it is a foreseeable consequence of their actions or because it is a penalty for their wrongdoing. So important is the innocence of victims to those who might help them that charitable donors often resort to a crude sorting device. To ensure that their beneficiaries are innocent, they opt to help victims of natural disasters, leaving victims of human rights abuse in the lurch (Zagefka et al. 2010).

In a related vein, current discourse regarding the innocence of pathetic victims has taken a troubling turn. In ostensible cases of human rights abuse, subjection to force so overwhelming as to have reduced you to passivity has come to stand in for non-responsibility and hence innocence. In other words, victimization and agency are construed as incompatible categories. Thus, psychologist Teufica Ibrahimefendić's testimony at the Tribunal for the Former Yugoslavia regarding the trauma incurred by the Bosnian women who were present at Potočari, the site of the genocidal massacre of boys and men orchestrated by Serb forces in the environs of Srebrenica in 1995, invokes this view of innocence to certify their victimization:

> This all took place in an atmosphere which was beyond their control; there was nothing they could have done. They were completely helpless.
>
> (Leydesdorff 2011, 204)

Similarly, Jayashri Srikantiah observes that the political rhetoric surrounding the passage of the US Trafficking Victims Protection Act of 2000 repeatedly underscored the meekness, helplessness, and passivity of trafficking victims in order to distinguish them from reviled undocumented economic migrants (2007, 160). Commenting on the same piece of legislation, Wendy Chapkis emphasizes that it counters the "expectation that all migrants are guilty by creating an utterly passive, entirely pure, and extremely vulnerable victim who is above reproach" (2003, 930). Gudrun Dahl points out that the "Agent NOT Victim" trope is pervasive in Swedish policy statements on immigration and development aid and in Swedish broadcast radio bromides (2009, 391–392). Joanne Baker presents interview data demonstrating the lengths to which young Australian women (ages 18–25) from diverse backgrounds will go to avoid the "victim" label and project an agential self-image (2010).

In each case, being victimized is understood as excluding agency— that is, as entailing shameful, albeit blameless, passivity.[9] Conversely, affirming agency is understood as proudly and knowingly taking responsibility for yourself. Pathetic victims, then, are people whose capacities for choice and action have been so completely neutralized that there can be no doubt that they are innocent.[10] I return to this perversion of the pathetic victim paradigm in section 2, but first I set out a contrasting victim paradigm.

B. The Heroic Victim Paradigm

The *prisoner of conscience* tag best fits victims who exemplify the heroic paradigm. Daw Aung San Suu Kyi was a prime case of a prisoner of conscience before her release in 2010 because she was held under house arrest for over a decade as a result of her nonviolent opposition to the Myanmar military dictatorship and her demands for democracy and human rights. Unless the Chinese authorities change their mind before this book appears, Liu Xiaobo continues to epitomize this category of victim, as he is serving an eleven-year sentence in a Chinese prison for nonviolently advocating democracy and human rights. Heroic victims, such as Daw Aung San Suu Kyi and Liu Xiaobo, are particularly interesting to me because they disturb a key assumption of the pathetic victim paradigm—namely, that you must in no way be complicit in your suffering to count as a victim.

Heroic victims are idealistic and courageous. They take it upon themselves to face off against the police power of the state in the name of a just cause. They may stand up for democracy and human rights, resist the subjugation of a social group singled out for oppression, or protest the misuse of military might. What heroic victims have in common isn't a single political agenda but rather a commitment to peace and justice. The governments they resist are often authoritarian police states like Myanmar and China. However, liberal democracies are not always loath to detain people for their beliefs. Some heroic victims act alone. Others act as members of a movement or political party. Some engage in civil disobedience. Others confine themselves to "working within the system." Whatever their particular cause or methods, political officials regard them as sufficiently threatening to national stability or their own grip on power to deploy repressive tactics aimed at silencing them and defeating their cause.

The justice of the heroic victim's cause is indispensable, for states are plainly acting within their rights when they arrest, prosecute, and punish ordinary criminals. Fraudulent investigative methods, torturing people to extract testimony favorable to the prosecution, rigged trial procedures, and inhumane conditions of incarceration are widespread and abrogate human rights under the pretense of legitimate law enforcement. But imprisoned individuals whose rights have been violated in these ways are pathetic victims, not prisoners of conscience.

To qualify as a heroic victim, it is all-important that your agency not be morally compromised. It is undeniable that heroic victims are not passive. In fact, they are quite stunningly agentic figures. They freely choose to engage in public dissent for the sake of their beliefs. Moreover, in persisting despite the known risk of persecution, they goad the state's repressive apparatus. Although it might seem that their crusading capacities for choice and action are all but crushed once they have been incarcerated, persecuting heroic victims sometimes endows them with an indirect form of agency—that is, the symbolic power of their personal sacrifices and their steadfast refusal to abandon the values they stand for may inspire others and fortify their resolve to uphold the cause. Such transitive, paradoxically enhanced agency has been the bane of government officials of many stripes.

Arguably, then, heroic victims knowingly act in ways that in effect court their own victimization. Yet, both in virtue of acting peacefully and in virtue of acting in support of a just cause, the heroic victim's agency is beyond reproach—inoculated against the charge of complicity in bringing on her or his own suffering. Put another way, heroic victims exercise their rights to free expression and, depending on their strategies of advocacy, freedom of association and peaceful assembly as well. Despite the fact that these rights may not be recognized by the regimes they oppose, acting within the bounds of internationally recognized human rights sanitizes the agency of heroic victims in the eyes of those who see the justice of their causes. Thus, the nonviolent activism of heroic victims secures their innocence and justifies the charge that their right not to be arbitrarily imprisoned is violated when they are detained.

Heroic victims are routinely subjected to solitary confinement, if not to torture, in many parts of the world. Even so, they are not pictured in agony or broken down. Heroic victims are admired for their strength of character, especially their allegiance to their followers and their courage, despite the abuse they are known to endure. Their resolute commitment to their beliefs secures their integrity and preserves their dignity. Abused for their supererogatory self-sacrifice, they are honored as moral exemplars.

All of the elements of the heroic victim paradigm are present in Kwame Anthony Appiah's 2010 letter nominating Liu Xiaobo for the Nobel Peace Prize. I quote at some length from his letter:

> On December 25, 2009, when the Chinese government believed that the world would not be paying attention, a Beijing court sentenced Liu to 11 years in prison and an additional two years' deprivation of political rights for "inciting subversion of state power."
>
> . . .
>
> Liu has been a leading figure in the Independent Chinese PEN Center (ICPC), our sister center, whose 250 members are doing courageous, on-the-ground advocacy work for freedom of expression in China despite constant pressure from Chinese authorities.
>
> . . .

Liu's writings express the aspirations of a growing number of China's citizens; the ideas he has articulated in his allegedly subversive writings, ideas that are commonplace in free societies around the world, are shared by a significant cross section of Chinese society.

. . .

While he was a young university professor, Liu was a major protagonist in the final days of the Tiananmen Square protests, and . . . he is widely credited with preventing far greater bloodshed when government troops moved into the square. Liu admonished the students to make their own movement more democratic; he disarmed a group of workers who appeared with guns to protect the student demonstrators (there is stirring news footage of him seizing a rifle and smashing it at a Tiananmen rally shortly before the crackdown); and he helped persuade students to evacuate the square in the final hours. Deeply committed to non-violence and democracy, Liu has been able both to articulate and to channel the frustrations of the Chinese people for more than two decades.

. . .

Liu Xiaobo stands in the company of Andrei Sakharov, Shirin Ebadi, and Dr. Martin Luther King, brave proponents of civil and political rights who have stood up to systematic repression in their own countries and practiced principled, non-violent resistance to bad laws and policies. In fact, the year before my countryman Dr. King was awarded the Nobel Peace Prize in 1964, he wrote in his seminal letter from a Birmingham jail, "An individual who breaks a law that conscience tells him is unjust and who willingly accepts the penalty of imprisonment in order to arouse the conscience of the community over its injustice, is in reality expressing the highest respect for the law." Ten days after Liu Xiaobo was sentenced, he was able to release a statement through his lawyers. In it, he echoed Dr. King when he declared, "For an intellectual thirsty for freedom in a dictatorial country, prison is the very first threshold. Now I have stepped over the threshold, and freedom is near."

. . .

Liu Xiaobo is one of some 45 writers currently imprisoned in China in violation of Article 19 of the UDHR and the International Covenant of Civil and Political Rights, and honoring him with the Nobel Peace Prize would be a powerful way to underscore the fact that the rights that are enshrined in international human rights law—values that China has acknowledged and endorsed—are the non-negotiable entitlements of every man and woman.

(http://www.foreignpolicy.com/articles/2010/10/08/why_i_nominated_liu_xiaobo, accessed 9/6/2014)

Appiah's stirring text underscores Liu's courage in the face of repression, his active but strictly nonviolent agency, his commitment to a just cause, his inspiring refusal to back down, and his exercise of internationally recognized human rights.[11] Liu was awarded the Nobel Peace Prize in absentia in 2010.

2. CONTROVERSIAL—"IMPURE"—VICTIMS

AI's definition of a victim notwithstanding, the organization's human rights mission is not confined to clear instances of the two paradigmatic types of victims.[12] AI advocates for trafficked sex workers. But it is a stretch to maintain that all of them fit the pathetic victim paradigm, and they bear scant resemblance to heroic victims. As well, AI defends death row inmates, including those who cannot qualify as pathetic or heroic victims because they committed the crimes of violence for which they were sentenced to die. In this section, I do not argue that all trafficked sex workers and death row inmates should count as victims of human rights abuse.[13] My point is that AI does so classify them, even though they do not satisfy the passivity criterion of the pathetic victim paradigm or the honorable dissidence criterion of the heroic victim paradigm. In view of the conflict between AI's victim paradigms and AI's human rights agenda, I urge caution in adopting the pathetic and heroic victim paradigms as vehicles for advancing human rights.

A. Trafficked Sex Workers

Many trafficked sex workers don't fit the pathetic victim profile.[14] They aren't naïve country girls, and they aren't duped about their employment prospects abroad (Kara 2009, 7; Waugh 2007, xiv, 63). Rather, they are desperately poor women who have no avenues of economic betterment in their home countries (Daley 2010; Kara 2009, 7, 23–30, 115, 142; Waugh 2007, 3, 73). Echoing the women she interviewed, Louisa Waugh characterizes them as "forced migrant labour" (2007, xv; also see Kara 2009, 16). They are driven to seek out traffickers by their utter hopelessness—their entirely reasonable belief that there is no other way to alleviate their own and their children's extreme deprivation.[15] Immigration quotas rule out getting work visas, and there are no adequately remunerated jobs in the LDDW (Large Deficit of Decent Work; I take this conception from the UN Millennium Development Goals) economies of their own countries. Their options are few, and they are uniformly grim.

Still, these women do not describe themselves as victims (Jacobsen and Skilbrei 2010, 197–201; Waugh 2007, xv). Rather, they see themselves as "migrants who'd been brutalized because they'd had to resort to desperate measures, or else had believed they were being offered genuine legal jobs abroad" (Waugh 2007, xv).[16]

The latter women—those who were convinced by false promises of good jobs—are victims of fraud. Because of this initial deceit and because handlers not only force them to work as prostitutes after escorting them to foreign countries but also threaten to harm their families if they try to escape, these women neatly fit the pathetic victim paradigm. Anti-trafficking laws aim to bring the people who buy, sell, rape, beat, and exploit these women to justice. However, the former group of women—those who knowingly allow themselves to fall into the clutches of traffickers in order to immigrate—is excluded from the category of trafficked women. In Britain and the United States, they are considered "smuggled" women; their self-narratives of attempted migration are summarily dismissed; and they receive none of the (meager) benefits that anti-trafficking laws confer on victims.

Although both "smuggled" and trafficked sex workers typically suffer abuse so severe and prolonged that it causes grave physical and psychological damage, the so-called smuggled women do not fit the pathetic victim paradigm because they initially cooperated with the people who subsequently abused them (Daley 2010; Kara 2009, 115, 143; Waugh 2007, 25, 33, 80–81). Some choose to play along with the charade of counterfeit passports and tourist visas, while others pay to be taken by clandestine routes to more affluent countries. All know that they are destined for sex work (Waugh 2007, 37, 50, 63, 80, 142; Kara 2009, 7). When they are deported or caught trying to cross the border, they think of themselves as "failed migrants" (Waugh 2007, 39; also see Peach 2006, 107). Plainly, these women insist on affirming their own agency.

In what follows, I seek to respect the agency that they rightly claim while also clarifying what conceptual changes would be required to classify them as pathetic or heroic victims. Assimilating their predicament to the pathetic victim paradigm would necessitate a reconsideration of our understanding of coercion in relation to the human right not to be held in slavery or servitude and the human rights to work, to remuneration compatible with human dignity, and to a decent standard of living (*UDHR*, Articles 4, 23, and 25). Assimilating their predicament to the heroic victim paradigm would necessitate a reconsideration of what counts as nonviolently pursuing a just cause.

Before I continue, I'd like to make it clear that I reject a view that some feminist human rights advocates adopt. I do not favor sex work abolitionism—the view that because freely agreeing to do sex work is a contradiction in terms, sex work should be wiped out (Srikantiah 2007, 15). It seems possible that in a non-patriarchal, non-heterosexist society in which sex workers enjoyed the same legal safeguards as anyone else, some people would be willing to sell sexual services and others would want to purchase them for a fair price. If so, it is a mistake to condemn sex work as inherently degrading just because virtually all sex workers presently labor under abominable conditions and pimps confiscate their earnings. Agnostic as I am about how sex work might be structured in future, I won't address the problem posed by allegedly smuggled sex workers by invoking an inalienable right not to perform sexual services for pay.[17]

Instead, I explore the relations between allegedly smuggled sex workers and the two victim paradigms. It is arguable that these "smuggled" sex workers resemble pathetic victims inasmuch as their economic circumstances are coercive. Some of these women also resemble heroic victims because they are willing to sacrifice themselves for the sake of superordinate values. That all of them are sold into sexual bondage and forced to perform sexual services at their destinations adds weight to classifying them as pathetic victims who deserve the full protection of the law.[18] Yet, standard interpretations of the victim paradigms rule out this conclusion.

Liberty rights and economic rights commingle in the *Universal Declaration of Human Rights*. Attacking both the right to work and the right to a decent standard of living (*UDHR*, Articles 23, 25), LDDW economies inflict inescapable individual poverty together with concomitant insupportable hardships. Like the decisions of street crime victims to hand over their valuables, the coping measures people take in the midst of economic collapse are amalgams of rational choice and "no other choice"—instances, as it were, of coerced free agency.[19]

Reports on the financial rewards that migrant sex workers reap are anecdotal. It seems clear, however, that wage bondage is pervasive. Some women use their paltry wages to buy back their freedom, but it is impossible to say how many succeed in sending money home.[20] Yet, the prospect of achieving so little by risking so much is not a bad bargain for women who make themselves available to operatives known to traffic in women. They regard the alternative of downwardly spiraling, annihilating poverty as worse. It would seem, then, that the coercive force that obliges these women to act is poverty in the context of an LDDW national economy.[21] However, according to liberal theory, a government can be an offender in Locke's sense— a perpetrator of wrongdoing—but a national economy cannot. Moreover, in crossing borders without mandatory legal documents, "smuggled" women compromise their innocence, for they were not passive victims in the recruitment and transport phase of their migration. If these considerations stand up to scrutiny, migrants who avail themselves of irregular channels seeking relief from the depredations of LDDW economies cannot count as pathetic victims.

The stories that "smuggled" women tell feature alcoholic or absent husbands, children to support, jobs lost, deep debt, and rent payments in arrears (Waugh 2007, 15–16, 31–32; Pheterson 1989, 227–230).[22] What they aim to accomplish in handing themselves over to known thugs is to save themselves, their children, and sometimes their extended families from homelessness, chronic hunger, and other privations. Although their motives aren't base, these women do not have grand visions of justice, nor do they pursue political solutions like those that heroic victims characteristically fight for. They rely entirely on personal initiative to solve their problems. By regnant standards, these differences disqualify them as heroic victims.

To be a hero, you must wage a public battle on behalf of the oppressed or campaign against large-scale suffering. Struggling to care for your family, even at great personal cost, doesn't qualify as heroic.[23] Yet, many of these women live by a moral code that is analogous to the just cause and self-sacrificial ethic of the heroic victim. They stand for the worth and dignity of their children, and they are willing to risk unimaginable abuse to try to give their children decent lives. In light of these morally significant similarities between so-called smuggled women and uncontroversial examples of heroic victimization, you might infer that sexist presuppositions about heroism should be expunged from the heroic victim paradigm and that these women should be regarded as heroic victims. Yet, as long as the heroic victim paradigm prizes public political action over private familial care, it must deny "smuggled" sex workers standing as heroic victims, thereby justifying the use of immigration policies to brand them as criminals, not victims.[24]

B. Death Row Inmates

Among human rights attorneys, it is agreed that the rights of prisoners, especially candidates for execution, are a very hard sell (Banner 2000/2001, 20; Schaffer and Smith 2004, 160–162). The victims of the crimes for which they were convicted are in the spotlight, and any abridgments of the prisoners' rights are likely to be sidelined as trivial by comparison. That the crimes punishable by death are among the most heinous compounds the difficulty of securing the rights of the subset of prisoners who occupy death row. As well, there is little public support in the United States for AI's contention that capital punishment is the "ultimate denial of human rights"—a violation of both the right to life and the right forbidding cruel, inhuman, or degrading treatment or punishment (Articles 1 and 5, *UDHR*; http://www. amnesty.org/en/death-penalty, accessed 1/1/2009).[25] For proponents of the death penalty, the reason why death row inmates do not qualify as victims is simply that no one is violating their rights. Due in no small part to sensationalistic media portrayals, these prisoners are widely viewed as irremediably vicious monsters whose testosterone-fueled aggression ran fatally amok.

I set aside claims for the deterrent effect of the death penalty, which in my view have no basis in fact. Nor do I confront the vexed question of the scope of Articles 1 and 5 of the *Universal Declaration of Human Rights* head-on. Instead, I ask how the victim paradigms that frame thinking about the death penalty interfere with acknowledging persons sentenced to die as victims. If the logic of prevalent American victim concepts precludes considering these individuals to be victims, it is no wonder that affirming that execution is a violation of their rights seems absurd.[26]

The contrast between AI's position on capital punishment and the Innocence Project's is instructive. AI "opposes the death penalty in all cases without exception regardless of the nature of the crime, the characteristics of the offender, or the method used by the state to kill the offender" (http://www.amnesty.org/en/death-penalty, accessed 1/1/2009). The Innocence Project is a US NGO founded in 1992 that seeks to redress "wrongful convictions" (http://www. innocenceproject.org/about/Mission-Statement.php, accessed 1/2/ 2009). Some of the organization's most celebrated cases have spared mistakenly convicted individuals from execution, and the organization's success in demonstrating the frequency of wrongful convictions in capital cases is credited with influencing former Illinois governor George Ryan to declare a moratorium on executions in 2000 (Baumgartner et. al. 2008, 64).[27] Yet, the organization's webpage does not endorse abolishing the death penalty, never mind couch the injustice of this practice in the language of human rights.[28] As its name implies, the Innocence Project undertakes to exonerate people who didn't commit the crimes for which they were convicted and imprisoned, including but not exclusively or primarily those who have been sentenced to death.

The Innocence Project's revelations about miscarriages of justice in the United States have outflanked supporters of capital punishment and have scored a number of successes for abolition. As a matter of expediency, it makes a lot of sense for death penalty opponents to undermine public confidence in the reliability of US trial procedures, for no one wants to be associated with killing demonstrably innocent people. Although I applaud the Innocence Project's achievements, it troubles me that their program implicitly endorses the absolutist version of the innocence criterion embedded in the pathetic victim paradigm.

To be pathetic victims, recall, persons must be innocent of any wrongdoing relevant to the harm that befalls them, and passivity in the face of force, fraud, or coercion ensures innocence. No one could be more at odds with this criterion, it seems, than a person who has correctly been judged to be guilty of a capital offense and who compounds her crime by withholding any expression of regret or plea for forgiveness.[29] These individuals once exercised their agentic powers to commit the vilest crimes, and they now refuse to acknowledge the grievous harm they have caused. However badly they have misused their agency, they are by no means passive. Rather than challenging the liabilities of the pathetic victim paradigm, however, the Innocence Project reinforces its authority by abandoning death row's unrepentant, "recalcitrant guilty."[30]

What the Innocence Project's framework mistakenly rules out is the possibility that someone who deserves to be punished nevertheless is a pathetic victim in virtue of the nature of the punishment to be inflicted.[31] Because the assumptions that underwrite AI's opposition to capital punishment countenance this possibility, they are more in keeping with robust human rights theory and morally grounded advocacy. To be sure, arguing that the death penalty is a violation of human rights, regardless of whether the person sentenced to die is guilty, has failed to rouse a surge of anti-death penalty sentiment in the United States. Be that as it may, the conceptual foundations of this approach are solid.

Sadly, one of AI's most outstanding achievements—namely, formulating the heroic victim paradigm and mobilizing sympathy and support for heroic victims—may magnify the negative impact of the pathetic victim paradigm on death row inmates. By singling out a morally "pure" set of prisoners as deserving of concern, the heroic victim paradigm squeezes the rights of other prisoners and any abuse they may be subjected to out of the picture. As a result, the only way to show that a person awaiting execution is a victim is to prove that the individual did not commit the crime, which is exactly what the Innocence Project attempts to do, leaving other death row inmates without moral or legal recourse.

What I am suggesting is that the salience and rigidity of the pathetic and heroic victim paradigms render the idea of a victim of a human rights violation who has rightly been convicted of violating someone else's rights nonsensical.[32] The combined effect of the two victim paradigms is to divert attention from the moral import of the treatment meted out to prisoners. Most pernicious of all, these paradigms deny the intelligibility of a death row inmate who is guilty as charged and who is also a victim of human rights abuse.[33] Although I'll argue later that in actual legal practice innocence is an elastic concept, it plainly cannot be stretched enough to include those prisoners on death row who did what they were condemned for. If this is so, and if the death penalty violates the human rights of people sentenced to die at the hands of the state, the victim paradigms developed in the aftermath of World War II are inadequate to conceptualize today's human rights agenda. A conception of a victim that gives due weight to capitulation to overwhelming power used to inflict severe, unnecessary suffering and that acknowledges that some pathetic victims aren't altogether blameless is sorely needed if prisoners' rights, including those awaiting execution, are to be taken seriously.

3. PARAMETERS OF INNOCENCE

To count as a victim at the mercy of a malign human power, both victim paradigms demand that you be innocent—that is, nothing you have done could reasonably be construed to imply consent to the harsh treatment you've endured. Although the conceptions of innocence that underwrite the two victim paradigms nicely fit some victims of human rights abuse, we have seen that there may be—indeed, AI maintains that there are—victims of human rights abuse that the paradigms exclude. In this section, I explore the theoretical implications of "impure" victims—that is, victims whose innocence, if they are innocent, can't be captured by the victim paradigms.

For starters, there is an asymmetry between the innocence requirement of the heroic victim paradigm and that of the pathetic victim paradigm. Whereas nonviolent pursuit of a just cause—honorable dissidence—confers innocence on the heroic victim, helpless passivity confers innocence on the pathetic victim. For heroic victims, acting within their rights rules out complicity in incurring the harms of imprisonment, torture, and so forth. For pathetic victims, de-agentification rules out complicity in incurring the various harms that human rights violations inflict. Although the heroic paradigm is flawed in other ways, it rests on standard understandings of innocence and non-consent. In contrast, I argue, the pathetic victim paradigm's passivity criterion departs radically from familiar ways of thinking about victims. Moreover, in view of the patent implausibility of the pathetic victim paradigm and the weakness of the heroic victim paradigm, I propose an alternative view of the innocence of victims.

A. Getting Real about Innocence

There are a number of ways to analyze non-consent and noncomplicity. One approach appeals to a species of rights. Inalienable rights place moral limits on what you can freely agree to do. Specifically, possession of an inalienable right rules out divesting yourself of the right itself and, with very few exceptions, eliminates your option to forgo the benefit to which the right entitles you (Meyers 1986, 23–37, 51–52). Relying on the claim that inalienable rights limit the scope of morally cognizable choice and action, some opponents of sex trafficking argue that there is an inalienable right not to sell sexual services (see section 2A of this chapter). Consequently, no woman working in the sex industry could have consented to sex work, and all women in this line of work are victims of sex trafficking (Srikantiah 2007, 15).[34] If human rights are inalienable rights, they deny that anyone can meaningfully consent to perform certain acts or undergo certain types of treatment. By constraining agency, these rights guarantee the non-complicity and innocence of anyone found to be engaging in activities or undergoing types of treatment that the rights prohibit.

Another approach to explicating the impossibility of consent and the absence of complicity in certain outcomes focuses on the incapacities of certain types of agents. Individuals who have serious cognitive impairments or who are under age are not considered competent to choose for themselves. Thus, there is broad agreement that cognitively impaired or immature individuals who have committed violent crimes should not be subject to the same legal penalties as responsible adults. Similarly, cognitively impaired or immature individuals who have cooperated with sexual abusers are nonetheless regarded as innocent victims of sexual assault, for they lack the capacities needed for autonomous choice and hence are not in a position to give valid consent.

One more approach to making sense of non-complicity in incurring humanly inflicted harm spotlights the circumstances in which an agent acts. When force, fraud, or coercion wrongfully constrains an agent's options, it nullifies consent. In addition to the exculpatory youth of child soldiers, for example, there are reliable reports that captors drug the abducted children to ensure their obedience or threaten to kill children who refuse to perform grisly acts.[35] Likewise, there is plentiful evidence that international prostitution rings use strategies that combine deception and coercion. To lure targets abroad, traffickers often assure poor women that they will get respectable, well paid jobs. Afterward, they confiscate their captives' passports, take photographs of them being raped, and threaten to send the pictures to their families.[36] Although the traffickers' lies are transparent to many of their targets, their intimidation tactics are highly effective. Consequently, the women they ensnare submit to sex work, often under abhorrent conditions.

Each of the analyses I have canvassed locates controversy about whether a claimant is a pathetic victim of a human rights violation in a different place. The inalienable rights analysis raises questions about whether any or all human rights are inalienable and, if some are inalienable, what to make of people whose behavior contravenes their rights. Because there is neither agreement about the grounding of inalienable rights nor agreement about which rights are inalienable, I won't rely on this approach. The cognitive impairment/immaturity analysis raises issues about what capacities are constitutive of responsible agency and what degree of development is necessary for a person to be considered a responsible agent. These are important questions. However, I set them aside because I believe that it will be possible to develop a better understanding of the victimization of these subsets of individuals with their distinctive vulnerabilities once we have in hand an adequate understanding of a victim who is a responsible adult. The force/fraud/ coercion analysis raises issues about what counts as overwhelming force, impenetrable fraud, and irresistible coercion. In other words, what applications of power, deceptive schemes, and threats of harm are agents allowed to submit to without falling into complicity in their own misfortune and forfeiting their status as cognizably innocent victims? For purposes of explicating the concept of a victim of human rights abuse, I find the force/fraud/coercion analysis most promising because it speaks directly to norms that underpin social expectations about individual agency as well as the psychodynamics of agency.

It is useful to start by noting that everyday understandings about victims of rights violations are predicated on a broad presumption of innocence in the event of aggression. Thus, there are countless measures you need not take to prevent or halt an attack on your rights. For example, it may be imprudent for a frail elderly person to walk alone late at night in a crime-ridden neighborhood, but extra vulnerability and imprudence would not exclude her from the class of victims if she were beaten and robbed. We do not expect such individuals to stay home or to hire armed bodyguards to accompany them if they go out. Nor do we expect them to overcome their fear and risk life and limb trying to resist muggers in order to gain entry into the class of victims. In this case and countless others, the self-protective measures someone could take are considered too costly—beyond most people's means or terribly dangerous.[37] Consequently, failing to take them doesn't entail sacrificing your standing as a victim should your rights be violated. Paradoxical as this may seem, custom and law grant people a good deal of latitude to "cooperate" with possible violations of their rights without excluding themselves from the class of morally and legally cognizable victims of force, fraud, or coercion.[38]

Conceptions of force, fraud, and coercion take into account how reasonable people can be expected to cope with attacks on their rights, and they endow right-holders with considerable discretion as to how they address potential or occurring rights violations. By specifying precautions and risks that people aren't obligated to take in order to qualify as victims, conceptions of force, fraud, and coercion delineate action spaces—spheres of freedom and permissible agency. Acting within the bounds of these action spaces ensures that right-holders' non-complicity and innocence are not in jeopardy. Whatever harms may befall them, they have not forfeited their status as cognizably innocent victims.

More specifically, a conception of force sets limits on obligatory self-protection—options you need not forgo and dangers of interpersonal aggression you need not take every possible step to thwart in order to be considered a victim of wrongfully imposed control. A conception of fraud sets limits on due diligence—suspicions you need not entertain and inquiries you need not make to be considered a victim of wrongful deception. A conception of coercion sets limits on tolerable risk—threats you need not defy and harms to which you need not acquiesce in order to be considered a victim of wrongful manipulation. Each of these norms specifies how right-holders may exercise their agency—what they need not do and by implication what they are at liberty to do—without calling their innocence into doubt. It would take us too far afield to furnish general accounts of force, fraud, and coercion here.[39] Instead, I'll deploy my observations regarding the innocence-preserving functions of each of these concepts to further illuminate the two victim paradigms and to develop a better conception of innocence.

B. The Victim Paradigms Revisited

The heroic victim paradigm describes an idealized figure whose shining integrity vanquishes persecutors' nefarious designs. In contrast, the pathetic victim paradigm describes an objectified person who is barred from autonomous choice and action. To uphold the value of humanity by championing human rights within the framework of these paradigms is, perversely, to imply the super-humanity of some victims and the evacuated humanity of others. While pathetic victims may stir up people's deepest anxieties about their own vulnerability, heroic victims represent such a high moral standard that most of us can only dream of living up to it.

The heroic victim paradigm's conception of innocence as honorable dissidence idealizes these victims. *For a Song and a Hundred Songs*, Liao Yiwu's memoir of his years in detention as a political prisoner in China (1990–1994), provides an edifying corrective to typical media depictions of heroic victims. Liao is a poet, now living in exile in Germany, who was inspired by the 1989 Tiananmen Square slaughter of pro-democracy activists to make a voice recording of his poem "Massacre" and to join with friends to create a film *Requiem* based on his poem of the same name. The first sixty pages of *For a Song and a Hundred Songs* telescope Liao's louche existence as an avant-garde poet—his exploitation of his wife, his promiscuity and drunkenness, his political alienation and cynicism—culminating with his uncharacteristic rage at the state's repression of peaceful protest and his arrest while attempting to spirit the tape of *Requiem* into clandestine channels in Beijing. More than three hundred pages follow, chronicling his imprisonment—from his humiliating initiation by strip search to his release into a friendless world four years later.

Liao was extra-judicially incarcerated for his literary and cinematic expression of dissident political beliefs and for attempting to disseminate them. Yet personally he ill fits the heroic victim mold. Reproducing a conversation with a committed activist and fellow inmate, Liao faults himself:

> Even now, I don't have a set of mature political views. I'm an individualist, with many incorrigible habits . . . I was compelled to protest and put myself on a self-destructive path because the state ideology conflicted violently with the poet's right of free expression.
>
> (2013, 363–364)

Unlike the heroic victims heralded in the international press who are represented as being moved by deeply held principles and acting for the common good, Liao professes self-interested motives and undisciplined resistance. But Liao is not given to false modesty. He fairly delights in describing his clever repartee during interrogation sessions, his defiance of prison guards' absurd commands, and his tangles with the inmate hierarchy (e.g., 2013, 91–93, 132–134, 178–179). Still, he doesn't heroize himself. He candidly recounts the gamut of his responses to prison conditions, including behavior he regards as utterly disgraceful (e.g., 68, 137–138, 248, 272–276). And after enduring years of physical abuse and doggedly refusing to admit any wrongdoing, he relents: "In the end, I confessed all my crimes and pleaded guilty" (309).

For all I know, many heroic victims are cut from nobler cloth. My purpose here isn't to sully anyone's reputation. But I do find it hard to believe that they act on purely altruistic motives and never succumb to fear or despair. Moreover, it seems wrong to exclude Liao from the category because he is no paragon of super-humanity. After all, the Chinese state violated at least three of Liao's human rights—his right to freedom of opinion and expression, his right not to be subjected to arbitrary arrest and detention, and his right to a fair and public trial (*UDHR*, Articles 19, 9, and 10). He was persecuted for expressing oppositional political beliefs. His characterological shortcomings do not impugn the judgment that he was a victim of human rights abuse, though not an especially heroic one.

It becomes clearer why Liao counts as a heroic victim when we reflect on the interpretation of force and coercion that underwrites it. The heroic victim paradigm is premised on a universalist, absolutist stance regarding illegitimate applications of state power. As Appiah's Nobel Peace Prize nomination letter puts it, Articles 18, 19, and 20 of the *Universal Declaration of Human Rights* are "non-negotiable entitlements of every man and woman" (see section 1B of this chapter). The rights to freedom of conscience, free speech, and peaceful assembly entail that self-censorship of dissent and refraining from oppositional political organizing are not mandatory forms of self-protection against state-sponsored force or coercion. If not, an individual who opposes injustice using nonviolent means is innocent of wrongdoing that could justify any punishment. Her greatness of spirit or lack thereof is irrelevant. Consequently, any critic of the state is a victim of wrongful force when she is imprisoned for expressing her beliefs and a victim of wrongful coercion when she is required to recant her beliefs as a condition of release.

Retaining the pathetic victim paradigm's innocence-as-passivity criterion comes at too high a price. So stigmatized is the identity of a passive victim that many who have suffered violations of their rights repudiate it, choosing instead to identify as survivors (Dunn 2005, 1). Survivors are fully agentic, responsible individuals who are bearers of recognized rights. This shift in vocabulary signifies individuals' full humanity despite what they have been through. Yet, survivors must once have been victims if their rights-based claims are to gain traction. Since it is a mark of self-respect to stand up for your rights, and standing up for your rights sometimes requires affirming your victimization, the concept of a victim should not denigrate those whose rights have been violated. Nor should it rule out the possibility that a perpetrator could become a victim, but the innocence-as-passivity criterion has just this exclusionary consequence. Because they aren't believed to satisfy this innocence criterion, non-heroic prisoners occupy a "degrading and dehumanizing zone of no-rights" (Schaffer and Smith 2004, 179).[40] Because "smuggled" sex workers aren't believed to satisfy this criterion, immigration officers scorn and deport them, thereby condemning shocking numbers of them to re-trafficking.

Applying the ideas about force, fraud, and coercion that I've set out to pathetic victims is complicated, for a universalist, absolutist view of force, fraud, and coercion is even more obviously untenable in this arena. Because different conceptions of force, fraud, and coercion can be more or less reasonable depending in part on the social contexts they regulate, and because the evolving culture of human rights requires reinterpreting the concepts of force, fraud, and coercion to keep pace, demarcating these concepts with respect to various species of aggression and malfeasance is among the principal tasks of moral reflection and jurisprudence.

In international law as in federal law, the grounds for recognizing pathetic victims are manifold. Moreover, uncontroversial types of pathetic victim are diverse. For example, ever since the 1951 Geneva Convention on Refugees, targets of genocidal state policies have been recognized virtually worldwide as pathetic victims who are entitled to asylum. However, only since the Board of Immigration Appeals handed down its decision in the case of Aminta Cifuentes on August 26, 2014, has being subjected to domestic violence in a "culture of machismo and family violence" in a state that refuses to enforce women's rights officially counted as grounds for classifying a woman as a pathetic victim of human rights abuse and as a reason to grant asylum in the United States.[41] In view of this changing landscape, whether claimants who are coming forward for the first time have meritorious or specious cases for admittance into the class of pathetic victims—whether they ought to be considered innocent victims of force, fraud, or coercion in violation of human rights—must be judged on a case-by-case basis.

As a rough guideline that's in line with human psychology, with the importance of the goods protected by human rights, and with legal practices bearing on human rights, explications of force, fraud, and coercion should err on the side of recognizing the innocence of targets and blaming individual and institutional rights deniers and violators. In going to the absolutist extreme of mandating passivity as a criterion of innocence, the pathetic victim paradigm blatantly flouts this guideline. Troubling as well, though perhaps less regressive, is the heroic victim paradigm's idealizing conception of innocence as honorable dissidence. In my view, the poor fit between these criteria and the guideline I suggest signals an urgent need to rethink these paradigms given that realizing human rights is a work in progress and dismissing genuine victims is an injustice of the first magnitude. The source of much mischief and, I argue, superfluous at that, these conceptions of innocence should be abandoned.

C. Reconceiving the Innocence of Victims

All persons, as the familiar phrase goes, have human rights simply in virtue of their humanity. As bearers of human rights, all persons are potentially victims of human rights abuse. Consequently, it is suspicious that ordinary people are so different from paradigmatic victims. In one sense, this is as it should be, for victimhood isn't supposed to be the ordinary condition of right-holders, and violations of human rights can change the individuals they target, destroying some and bringing out the best in others. To this extent, the pathetic and heroic paradigms make sense. However, the innocence criteria embedded in these paradigms are at odds with normal human impurity of motivation, not to mention the plethora of strengths and weaknesses that combine to form diverse human personalities.[42] As preconditions for cognizability as victims, not the effects of being victimized, these innocence criteria open an indefensible gulf between our concept of a victim and our concept of a right-holder.

Determinations of innocence presuppose moral judgments about the acceptability of various types of agentic initiative in situations that are fraught with multifarious dangers. For purposes of human rights, innocence entails neither the absence of all initiative nor the enactment of transcendent virtue. As we have seen, Liao missed the transcendent virtue mark by a long shot. Likewise, many inmates of the Nazi death camps did not come close to the passivity mark— some because they helped one another, some because they revolted. Yet there is no doubt that they were victims of human rights abuse. In view of these conflicts between indisputable examples of victims and the victim paradigms, it is necessary to jettison the paradigms' respective innocence criteria. I'll now argue that a burdened agency criterion would better represent our considered beliefs and actual practices regarding the innocence of victims.

Although I believe that philosophers can contribute a great deal to a theory of human rights, I won't provide a general philosophical account of human rights here.[43] Because I want to keep the focus on victims and in subsequent chapters their stories, I'll sidestep philosophical disputes about which rights should count as human rights and why. Instead, I'll assume that human rights treaties, though in some respects controversial, indicate the rough contours of the benefits that human rights confer. A quick glance at the titles of major human rights documents reveals that their normative substance spans a wide spectrum. They encode civil and political rights, economic, social, and cultural rights, the rights of women, the rights of the child, and many more.[44] Yet the framers and States Parties to these covenants intend the human rights enumerated therein to collectively define respect for humanity. To the extent, then, that realizing these rights remains an aspiration, respect for humanity remains an aspiration.

Although there is considerable, but by no means universal, agreement that human rights are interdependent and indivisible, it is necessary to bear in mind that human rights priorities and understandings of what constitutes adequate respect for human rights are matters of ongoing debate, negotiation, legislation, and litigation. In section 3B of this chapter I noted a recent expansion of the concept of a victim of persecution. Here's another case in point. For most of human history, sexually assaulting an enemy woman during armed conflict was not regarded as immoral, let alone an abuse of human rights. The raped womenfolk in captured territory were considered spoils of war, not victims. Albeit belatedly, the 1998 Rome Statute of the International Criminal Court codified rape in war as a crime against humanity, and mass rape has been prosecuted and convictions have been gained both at the International Criminal Tribunal for the Former Yugoslavia and at the International Criminal Tribunal for Rwanda. In light of the political dimension of human rights, it is imperative to rule out relying on preexisting international accords or current statutory law to demarcate the class of victims. To acknowledge the fluidity of the culture of human rights while according right-holders the respect they deserve, it is necessary to attend to the quality of different kinds of humanly inflicted suffering—including its severity, its intensity, and its long-term detrimental effects—in recognizing victims or withholding recognition from claimants.

Failure to respect human rights burdens the agency of right-holders in many and varied ways. Because agency is a key feature of humanity, analyzing the impact of abrogating a human right on right-holders' agency provides a vital qualitative gauge of their resulting suffering. What I have in mind when I ascribe burdened agency to victims is the thought that human rights abuse locks right-holders in action spaces that are warped by wrongful force, fraud, or coercion. That is, humanly imposed, morally unacceptable constraints engineer action spaces that prevent right-holders from pursuing activities and goals that ought to be open to them and that oblige them to cope with predicaments that should never have come about.

Norms governing how persons stuck in warped action spaces may act to extricate themselves, coupled with norms governing how they may submit in order to avoid worse harm, define innocence in the context of victimization. Provided that right-holders conduct themselves within these parameters, they are innocent of complicity in incurring the harms they suffer. Inasmuch as our understanding of what constitutes wrongful force, fraud, and coercion is not static, the burdened agency approach to innocence invites critical reflection on which types of force, fraud, and coercion are wrongful and what it is permissible for targets to do by way of contending with them. The notion of burdened agency acknowledges that victims cannot easily escape from powers that inflict or threaten to inflict needless and terrible suffering on them, but it doesn't strip them of the agentic complexity and resilience that are characteristic of humanity.[45]

In accenting how human rights abuse imposes morally impermissible constraints on agency, this view underscores the way in which all human rights abuse disrespects the humanity of all victims, for it unites pathetic and heroic victims under a common liability. Both kinds of victims are wronged in the encumbrances that are imposed on their ability to choose and act. The paradigmatic pathetic victim's rights to security of persons are at stake. The paradigmatic heroic victim's rights to political participation are at stake. Still, they share the suffering of illegitimately constrained agency.

Unlike the stark contrast between innocence-conferring passivity or honorable dissidence, on the one hand, and culpability-conferring striving or other-directed violence, on the other, the contrast between burdened and full agency spreads out along a spectrum. Burdened agency is defined in part by qualitatively different kinds of agentic incapacitation. Compare, for example, the reluctance of many Jews to leave Nazi Germany before it was too late, submission to a manipulative and violent sex trafficker, and incarceration in a maximum-security prison. Moreover, because there are degrees of agentic incapacitation, agency can be more or less burdened. How diminished or distorted a person's agentic capacities become depends on the force, fraud, or coercion applied and also on the particular victim's agentic resources. Because the burdened agency criterion doesn't entail abject disempowerment, it spares pathetic victims that humiliating stigma. Contrariwise, because this criterion spotlights the contraction of political prisoners' agency, it places heroic victims on a continuum with pathetic victims. In keeping all victims within the orbit of humanity, this criterion comports with the values that ground human rights.

Now, it might be thought that the paradigms' clear-cut, stringent innocence criteria are necessary to defeat conniving claimants—people who pose as victims without being entitled to. Or it might be thought that such criteria are necessary to halt the proliferation of victims and a flood of rights-based claims. But merely pragmatic concerns such as these plainly do not justify retaining the innocence criteria in their present form. Nor does a misleadingly simplistic conception of innocence. Insofar as innocence is imagined as a straightforward, yes-or-no matter, it might not seem preposterous to expect there to be unassailable, unidimensional imprimaturs of innocence. Yet, honorable dissidence and helpless passivity are merely analytical shortcuts that belie real-world moral complexity.

There is no way to avoid judging the moral merit of anyone's claim to be a victim. Not only must the truthfulness of the claimant's testimony be evaluated, but also whether the claim is congruent with a credible interpretation of human rights must be settled. These are epistemological and normative questions that cannot be circumvented in good conscience by setting up pseudo-absolute sorting mechanisms.

My proposal to abandon the innocence-as-passivity and the innocence-as-honorable dissidence criteria and to recognize the burdened agency criterion offers important benefits to the project of advancing human rights. With respect to the pathetic victim paradigm, substituting the burdened agency criterion denies that pathetic victims must be so helpless and naïve that they seem like "losers." As well, the burdened agency criterion supplies an appropriately nuanced understanding of heroic victimization. It allows heroes to be human—that is, to suffer and despair, even as they lead and triumph. In addition, the burdened agency criterion makes room for heroes who engage in violent resistance but who are incarcerated as much for their beliefs as for their actions—I have Nelson Mandela in mind.[46] All of these implications are salutary departures from the paradigms' dichotomous moral categories, which flatten and freeze moral judgment by concealing subtle morally significant distinctions.

4. RECLAIMING VICTIM DISCOURSE

Our political and legal discourse makes it all but impossible to speak of violations of human rights without labeling some people victims and others perpetrators. But warnings about these polarized categories abound. Kay Schaffer and Sidonie Smith maintain that a cost of the gains made through the international human rights regime is that it "reifies the identities of 'victim' and 'perpetrator'" (2004, 232, also 151, 156, 160; also see McShane and Williams 1992, 262). According to Wendy Brown, this reification perverts rights claims into "sites of the production and regulation of identity as injury" when what is needed is "vehicles of emancipation" (1995, 134; also see Minow 1993).[47] Richard Rorty laments the morally paralyzing dialectic of contempt and disgust that the victim/perpetrator polarity generates (1993). Roger Fjellstrom adds another layer to Rorty's diagnosis of the moral perils of assigning people to these dichotomized identities. Perpetrators of evil and their victims are "frightening" because they represent "what we constantly strive to ensure our wellbeing against" (Fjellstrom 2002, 103). Fear of being victimized obstructs empathy with victims while also casting a shadow on the humanity of perpetrators. For these critics, the vocabulary of victims and perpetrators embedded in human rights discourse is morally deleterious, perhaps irremediably so.

To rebut these critiques, I have argued that the connotations of the term *victim* aren't univocal. The differences between the pathetic and heroic victim paradigms could not be more stark—passivity and degradation, on the one hand, leadership and veneration, on the other. Thus, it is clearly a mistake to generalize about the moral meanings and social consequences of being deemed a victim. It would be a mistake, as well, to regard these paradigms as they are presently constructed as definitive. Not only does each paradigm render victims as "other"—either as less than fully human or as superlatively human—but also both are invidious fictions, for historically recognized victims of human rights abuse often contravene their tenets. Plainly, the concept of a victim must accommodate these paradigm-bursting cases. Finally, a commitment to human rights implies at a minimum that the innocence of victims must be compatible with their humanity—their dignity and their agency. I have argued that the burdened agency criterion satisfies this fundamental requirement.

The culture of human rights is a work in progress. In the second half of the twentieth century, we witnessed the consolidation of the pathetic victim paradigm and the heroic victim paradigm. We should expect more permutations of the concept of a victim of human rights abuse in future. In addition to affirming the humanity of victims, the burdened agency conception of innocence that I endorse makes room for them.

Chapter 2

Narrative Structures, Narratives of Abuse, and Human Rights

Our memory changes with time. We forget details, we confuse dates, we mix up attacks, we make mistakes with names, we even disagree about how this or that man or woman and other acquaintances died. But we remember all the fearsome moments we personally lived through as if they had happened just last year. Time passes, but we keep our lists of specific memories and speak of them together when things are going badly; these memories become ever more truthful, yet we hardly know how to arrange them in the right order anymore.

Jeannette Ayinkamiye, quoted in *Life Laid Bare:*
The Survivors in Rwanda Speak (2006), p. 27

Victims of human rights abuse differ greatly with regard to their access to the media. Government officials fear some political prisoners because of their outsized voices and their vast audiences, whereas victims of other forms of human rights abuse, together with untold, unsung political prisoners, are easily stripped of any voice at all. Cognizant of this disparity, a number of late twentieth- and early twenty-first century political, legal, and theoretical movements put a spotlight on the value of listening to the silenced voices of victims. In consciousness-raising sessions, second wave feminists exchanged stories of their everyday lives and used these stories both to construct theories of gender and to formulate political agendas (e.g., MacKinnon 1989). Soon women of color and lesbians in Western as well as developing nations objected that middle-class white feminists had silenced them and consequently had misrepresented womanhood and the needs of women as a group (e.g., Calhoun 1994; hooks 1997; King 1997; Narayan 1997). In law schools, critical race theorists made the case that white supremacy could not be eradicated unless personal stories of racial oppression were injected into US legal proceedings (e.g., Delgado 1989). Truth commissions convened around the world—in South Africa (1995–2002), Morocco (2004–2005), and Peru (1986–1988)—and war crimes tribunals in The Hague (established 1993), Rwanda (established 1994), and Cambodia (established 2003) have reaffirmed victims' right to a voice of their own.

Picking up on these trends, philosophers have addressed two principal topics:

1. Respect—recognizing the equal status of victims by establishing contexts in which they can safely tell their stories and restore their sense of self and agency (e.g., Brison 2002; Walker 2003, 2006);
2. Credibility—the epistemic grounds for believing or doubting victims' stories and the problem of epistemic injustice (Code 1991; Dotson 2012; Fricker 2007; Govier 1993a, 1993b, 2005).

Less thoroughly explored is the relation between victims' stories and normativity. As a contribution to understanding how the stories of those who have endured the torments of human rights violations or who have endured the privations of unfulfilled human rights can advance moral understanding, catalyze moral innovation, and guide social change toward a culture of human rights, this chapter examines various forms of narrative representation and asks whether personal narratives of victimization bring a distinctive form of normative representation to human rights discourse.

In view of the fact that a number of prominent students of narrative build normativity into their accounts, it might seem obvious that there is a connection between victims' stories and moral insight (Amsterdam and Bruner 2000; Bruner 1990, 2003; Cover 1983; White 1987).[1] However, the category of victims' stories spans an enormous variety of texts—private diaries, memoirs written for publication, interviews with journalists or social scientists, depositions prepared by human rights workers, stories shared with like-minded activists or with support groups, stories told to medical professionals, and testimony in courts, truth commissions, and asylum hearings, to mention just some of the possibilities.

Another complication is that some victims' stories tell of witnessing, rather than being targeted directly for a particular human rights violation. Often women—grandmothers, wives, mothers—are compelled to witness unspeakable killings and mutilations in the midst of massacres of their menfolk, and they are the only ones left to testify to the monstrosity of what took place. The different types of abuse recounted, the different contexts of elicitation, the different rules governing expression in these varied sites, and the different vehicles for communicating victims' stories should make us wary of ready generalizations about the nature of these narratives.

Moreover, I doubt that existing explications of the way in which values figure in narratives yield satisfactory theories of the contribution that victims' stories can make to discovering and defending policies and practices that advance human rights. Here I consider two of the most prominent accounts of the relation between narrative and normativity. It is clear that victims' stories sometimes coincide with the narrative template Anthony Amsterdam and Jerome Bruner present in their work on narrative and law (2000) or the narrative template Hayden White presents in his work on narrative and history (1987). However, their accounts exclude a salient type of victim's story and thus fail to fully appreciate the capacity of victims' stories of human rights abuse to advance understanding of and increase respect for human rights. To address this oversight, I propose an account of the relation between normativity and what I'll call "hybrid" victims' stories that shows how these narratives can be integrated into a progressive human rights discourse.

1. THE AMSTERDAM/BRUNER ACCOUNT OF NARRATIVE

Anthony Amsterdam and Jerome Bruner adopt an Aristotelian traditionalist conception of narrative:

> [A narrative] needs a *cast of human-like characters*, beings capable of *willing their own actions, forming intentions, holding beliefs, having feelings*. It also needs a *plot* with a beginning, a middle, and an end in which particular characters are involved in particular events. The unfolding of the plot requires (implicitly or explicitly):
> 1. an initial *steady state* grounded in the legitimate ordinariness of things
> 2. that gets disrupted by a *Trouble* consisting of circumstances attributable to human agency or susceptible to change by human intervention,
> 3. in turn evoking *efforts* at redress or transformation, which succeed or fail,
> 4. so that the old steady state is *restored* or a new (*transformed*) steady state is created,

5. and the story concludes by drawing the then-and-there of the tale that has been told into the here-and-now of the telling through some *coda*.

(2000, 113–114)

Despite Amsterdam and Bruner's talk of redress and transformation, their account is structurally conservative because they conceive of norms as culture-dependent conventions, and narratives that conform to their account are riddled with localized norms. As a result, I argue, their view is inhospitable to many victims' stories.

Each of Amsterdam and Bruner's key conceptions—the steady state, trouble, and emplotment—is normatively tinctured and, in my view, perniciously so. The steady state that constitutes the beginning of a narrative is whatever people at that place and time regard as "legitimate ordinariness" or as "normatively valued states of affairs" (2000, 121; also see Bruner 2003). But if a narrative can't get started without positing a condition of acceptable normality, many victims have no social history from which to speak. The very conditions that others regard as legitimate and ordinary are the cause of their victimization.

Consider US slaves in 1700. No description of legitimate ordinariness in their ancestral homelands would have struck a chord with a sizable audience of powerful listeners (Mills 1998, chapter 6). Women's subordination is even less amenable to being cast in the Amsterdam/Bruner framework. There never has been a society in which gender equality was institutionalized and deemed to be legitimate. To assume, then, that people live in a world of legitimate ordinariness until "Trouble" crops up wrenches the tool of narrative out of the hands of many victims of human rights abuse.

Equally worrisome is the pressure that the orthodoxy of the Amsterdam/Bruner model exerts on activists and sympathetic scholars to envisage an original state of legitimate ordinariness. Some Afrocentric thought presents an unduly rosy picture of pre-colonial African tribal life that the slave trade and other colonial violence wrongly despoiled. Some feminist thought makes poorly supported claims about the existence of an ancient, forgotten matriarchy that was balefully supplanted by patriarchy. To plug African Americans' story of racial oppression or women's story of gendered oppression into the Amsterdam/Bruner model, it is necessary to posit prior, legitimate steady states, whether or not they can be substantiated. Later, I'll argue that the strategy of invoking a legitimate past state of affairs is liable to have unintended, unjust consequences. For now, I conclude only that meeting the demands of the Amsterdam/Bruner model can override truth by prompting narrators to manufacture beginnings for their stories that are too good to be true.

Within the confines of this model, the only alternative is to appeal to an imaginary state of peace and justice—say, the international human rights community's conception of what should be ordinary— and to project it onto the pre-Trouble circumstances of the victims. But I doubt that such a maneuver is necessary, and I suspect that it might prove counterproductive. Consider the genocide that commenced in Darfur in 2003. Virtually any conditions of life would be better than the attacks and deprivations the victims endured. Indeed, the predominant rhetoric of moral outrage during this violence did not point to a pre-genocidal state of affairs that the victims took to be legitimate. Journalists and activists simply told stories of what happened from day to day, stories that added up to an unrelenting campaign of murder, rape, and arson against a defenseless people. Later I'll argue for the moral power of non-classical forms of storytelling. For now, I merely suggest that incorporating human rights issues into a story does not necessitate conformity to Amsterdam and Bruner's account.[2]

Amsterdam and Bruner's conception of trouble is also prejudicial. That they capitalize *trouble* throughout their text is more than a typographical flourish. In their usage, "Trouble" is the name of the set of sanctioned wrongs in a particular society or in a determinate international community. As they put it,

> Trouble takes off from what is canonical or moral or taken as the accepted and orderly set of things. And it is precisely this canonicity . . . that gives Trouble its orderliness and systematicity.
>
> (2002, 131; also see 121)

But if a society's canonical and presumed-to-be-moral state of affairs includes systematic human rights abuse against certain people, the victims will be barred from articulating their troubles. Their plans haven't "gone off the track," nor have their expectations "gone awry" (2002, 31, 135). They understand perfectly well how things work. They expect abuse and suffering, and they get it. Their troubles haven't made it into the lexicon.

Miranda Fricker (2007, 149–152) invokes Susan Brownmiller's work to illustrate this sort of conceptual vacuum. In 1974, Carmita Wood did not have language in which to characterize what her boss was doing to her at her job in Cornell University's nuclear physics lab. His lewd gestures, his accidental-on-purpose touching of her breasts, the kisses he imposed on her in out-of-the-way places gradually brought on a variety of painful and disturbing physical symptoms. Despite her attempts to avoid these encounters, and after her request for a transfer to another department was denied, she finally quit her job, and her subsequent application for unemployment benefits was denied. The women who came to Wood's defense coined the now-familiar expression "sexual harassment" to reference wrongful sexual provocations in workplaces and educational settings. Eventually, the expression "constructive discharge," which applies to situations in which an employee is forced to quit her job in order to escape from an abusive work environment, also gained legal acceptance. From a historicized human rights point of view, conceiving rights abuse as "Troubles" is at best naive, for this conception of narrative complication denies abuses that do not yet have colloquial, let alone official, designations.

Once set in motion, the plot unfolds according to a "stock script" or a "charter narrative" (Amsterdam and Bruner, 2000, 121, 127). Stock scripts supply models of normality, wrongful disruptions, and fitting remedies, and they identify the kinds of obstacles that thwart different human purposes (2000, 121, 127). All of this is encoded in a culture's repertoire of genres—its *mental models representing possible ways in which events in the human world can go*" (2000, 133, italics in original). Well-known literary genres include tragedy, comedy, and romance. Amsterdam and Bruner regard the conceptions of actionable causes that are inscribed in common law writs as "legal genres" (2000, 133; also see Bruner 2003, 20, 58). As "tools of narrative problem solving," genres dictate how the story should proceed and how it should end—that is, what the protagonist should do in response to the trouble and whether the protagonist's complaints should be credited or dismissed (2000, 133).

Presupposing, as it does, authoritative precepts about who can be injured, this conception of emplotment instates a traditional paradigm of who has standing to protest wrongdoing by making legitimate claims—who is entitled to speak. Presupposing, as well, authoritative precepts that define how people can be harmed, it endorses a set of resolutions that may overlook the needs and life trajectories of unrecognized victims—those whose speech is preempted.

In this connection, it is worth recalling that it took a transnational feminist organizing effort and a different approach to storytelling to get traction for the women's rights as human rights movement (Bunch and Reilly 1994; Reilly 1994; Rogers 1994). The 1993 Global Tribunal on Violations of Women's Human Rights took place out of the hearing of all but a few of the official delegates in the basement below the chambers of the 1993 UN World Conference of Human Rights. The stories women told there did not start by describing a state of legitimate ordinariness, for these women had never experienced a system of social relations that they could accept as legitimate. Instead, their stories launched directly into descriptions of everyday horrors—non-canonical troubles that the speakers sought to have recognized as "Troubles." Nor could the women who testified recount "efforts at redress or transformation" or conclude by depicting a "new (*transformed*) steady state," for such efforts had been piddling, and the claim that women's rights are human rights met with outright derision in many quarters. Jettisoning the narrative template that Amsterdam and Bruner delineate, their testimony asserted the persistence of violence against women and girls around the world and demanded an end to this abuse. Offering little solace to voiceless victims of human rights abuse, Amsterdam and Bruner's view of narrative plot diagnoses a problem for human rights advocates, rather than proffering a solution.

2. NARRATIVE REGIMENTATION, SOCIAL EXCLUSION, AND TRUTH FORFEITURE

I have isolated the principal barriers to bringing victims' stories into human rights discourse that are erected by Amsterdam and Bruner's account of narrative. The picture is bleak, but not quite as bleak as one might surmise from my comments so far. In telling their stories, some victims can truthfully describe an initial state of affairs that they regard as normatively valued, and they can point to the "Trouble" that disrupts it. In Chapter 3, section 3, we'll see that Ishmael Beah starts his story this way. But we'll also see in section 6 that his story does not end with the resumption of a normatively valued state of affairs, and in this respect it diverges from Amsterdam and Bruner's prescription. I don't mean to suggest that victims never get satisfaction or that their stories can't conclude with a normatively valued resolution. My point is only that many victims' stories do not end that way because their human rights have yet to be realized.

Nevertheless, it is clear that human rights advocates see the benefits of conforming to the Amsterdam/Bruner model. Canny human rights workers realize that people who are in a position to aid victims of human rights abuse are comfortable with and responsive to this type of story. Consequently, they help victims craft their stories in conformity with this model whenever it's feasible to do so. Still, I'll point out that this discursive tactic, though often effective, can have significant drawbacks.

In stories collected by NGOs to solicit donations from Westerners, former male child soldiers in Sierra Leone tell a three-part tale of youthful innocence, abduction and forced killing, and hoped-for rehabilitation (Shepler 2006). The boys invoke a legitimately ordinary childhood cut short by the horrific trouble of kidnapping and coerced participation in atrocities. No longer under the control of their captors, they now express a single-minded desire to return to their families. Moved by the dissemination of these stories, affluent Western audiences have poured funds into aid agencies to educate and provide medical care for these boys.

As much as this narrative strategy has alleviated the suffering of these children and has helped them resume nonviolent lives, it also incurs substantial costs. One is an invidious gender disparity. Former female child soldiers are not telling this story, and they have no other story to tell. Because the abducted girls were raped as well as forced to commit atrocities, they are not candidates for rehabilitation in their communities if they tell the truth. In order to comply with cultural norms that mandate female purity as a precondition of marriage and marriage as a female imperative, they are obliged to adopt a strategy of secrecy concerning their lives as child soldiers and sex slaves (Shepler 2002, 11). Consequently, their stories are suppressed, and the model of reintegration that structures humanitarian publicity and aid projects for boys excludes them (Shepler 2002, 7, 9).[3]

The stories the boys tell, aided and abetted by human rights workers, together with the funds these stories attract, perpetuate the girls' silence, for arguably it is better that some of the child victims should get needed help than that all should lose out in the name of truth. Still, Shepler calls on international aid organizations to reflect critically on the meaning of "successful reintegration" into societies that are so unjust to women and girls (Shepler 2002, 16). Yet, short of uprooting the girls from their families and communities and turning them into refugees seeking asylum in countries where their sexual molestation would prompt a more sympathetic response, it is not clear how human rights workers could help the girls to construct stories that would "work" for them.

In this regard, Amsterdam and Bruner have some advice for NGOs that uphold standards of gender equity in their human rights work. They note that there are ambiguous scripting situations— situations where it isn't obvious which script applies—and that these situations prompt reflection about how to finesse the constraints of time-honored plots and arrive at suitable endings (2000, 112). These situations implicitly call the *status quo ante* into question and oblige decision-makers to entertain the possibility that nothing less than creating a "new (*transformed*) steady state" will suffice. If such a story does not constitute an altogether new "legal genre," it at least constitutes a significant reinterpretation of an existing genre—that is, an enlarged class of wrongs and potential victims and an enlarged basis for litigation. As Amsterdam and Bruner remark, "Perhaps it is because they have the power to expand the boundaries of possibility that the invention of new literary or political or legal genres is so important" (2000, 133).

Following the advice implicit in this line of thought, aid workers might encourage girl victims to tell stories that ambiguate the script of the sullied, irredeemable woman that currently applies to girl soldiers who reveal their sexual subjugation. In other words, the girl soldiers would need to insert a culturally accepted script that plausibly applies to them into their stories so as to compete with the sullied, irredeemable woman script. By creating a clash of scripts, the girls' stories would raise the question of how best to interpret their past, and perhaps their bravery would be rewarded. Perhaps their communities would see the unfairness of labeling them as outcasts and would modify their norms of female marriageability. But they might not. They might cling to the traditional norms and ostracize the girls.

Although I believe that victims' stories can drive cultural transformation, there is no guarantee that a liberatory ending rather than a tradition-bound ending will strike auditors as befitting an ambiguously scripted narrative (Amsterdam and Bruner 2000, 120). Moreover, it is undeniable that cultures don't transform overnight. As admirable as many of us might find the courage of girls who "out" themselves and tell ambiguously scripted stories of their time in captivity, it seems incumbent on human rights workers who encourage girl soldiers to pursue this strategy to have a backup plan for the girls if their communities repudiate them. No narrative template can protect victims who speak out from recriminations, but the Amsterdam/Bruner approach treats victims whose troubles vie with cultural norms as canaries in the mineshaft.

It is troubling as well that the boys' stories omit a great deal, and what they omit is not unimportant. The premise of childhood innocence from which these stories proceed invites audience distortion.

For ignorant Westerners, this story conjures up an image of a care-free childhood protected from harsh conditions. But many of these boys never experienced anything like this idyllic youth. Not coincidentally, the boys' stories leave out the unjust conditions that shape their own lives and that also fuel Africa's devastating wars.[4] Their stories mask grave, endemic human rights abuse—the non-fulfillment of social and economic rights, coupled with sham constitutions and governments that pay lip service to civil and political rights—for the sake of scoring short-term benefits. More shocking to their Western benefactors, no doubt, is the omission of the children's complicity in murderous warfare. Some boys report, for example, that they "enjoyed" firing their weapons, but facts of this sort don't find their way into the stories that human rights NGOs use in their funding appeals (Shepler 2006). Accuracy in testimonial records and audience comprehension of Africa's problems are casualties of the bowdlerized texts that Westerners are receptive to hearing and that local cultures find tolerable.

For many victims, adapting the Amsterdam/Bruner model to avoid the sorts of social exclusions and factual suppressions I've sketched is not possible. Yet this model is all but irresistible in emergency human rights campaigns and in legal proceedings following grievous human rights abuse. In these situations, producing a compelling case for aid or indisputable evidence of wrongdoing dictates tailoring victims' stories to fit into standardized formats and scripts that capitalize on moneyed or official listeners' preconceptions and do not jar their sensibilities. It appears, then, that the principal mechanisms of relief for victims and the narrative template that victims' stories are expected to fit in these contexts ill serve truth and justice. In contrast to funding campaigns and criminal trials, truth commissions give victims leeway to make more complete statements, to frame them in their own terms, and to utter them in their own style. However, the powers and purposes of truth commissions are limited. They do not mete out traditional forms of justice—they neither compensate victims nor punish perpetrators of abuse—and their official records may privilege the evidentiary tidbits gleaned from victims' stories over the testimony of the victims as such.[5]

Because many victims of the worst abuses are not able or not willing to cast their experiences in the narrative template that Amsterdam and Bruner specify, I take up an alternative approach to narrative. In what follows, I sketch Hayden White's theory of narrative, and then I consider whether White's account provides a satisfactory discursive home for mold-breaking victims' stories.

3. HAYDEN WHITE'S ACCOUNT OF NARRATIVE AND CLOSURE

In "The Value of Narrativity in the Representation of Reality," Hayden White distinguishes three types of historical representation: annals, chronicles, and proper histories (1987, 4–5). An annalist furnishes nothing more than a list of dated events, arranged in the order in which they occurred (1987, 5). No reason for the selection of events is given, nor are the listed events causally related to one another. Chronological sequencing is the sole organizing principle of the annals form. Chronicles, as the name implies, share this rudimentary organizing principle. But unlike an annalist, a chronicler focuses on a central subject, such as a personage, a town, or an institution, and includes only those events that pertain to this subject (1987, 16). In addition to chronology, a discernible principle of selection organizes a chronicle. Moreover, chronicles furnish a greater quantity of information than annals (1987, 16). Like an annalist, however, a chronicler draws no conclusion about the meaning of the series of depicted events (1987, 16). In White's words, a chronicle "aspires to narrativity" but falls short because of its "failure to achieve narrative closure"—the selected series of events stops without ending (1987, 5). In contrast, "history proper" attains "full narrativity" in virtue of revealing events "as possessing a structure, an order of meaning, that they do not possess as mere sequence" (1987, 5). The central question of White's essay is what kind of meaning a full-fledged narrative confers on events—that is, how narrative closure is accomplished.

Missing from the world of the chronicler but present in that of the historian is law or morality. According to White, every historical narrative aims to "moralize the events of which it treats" and stems from a "desire to moralize reality, that is, to identify it with the social system that is the source of any morality we can imagine" (1987, 14). Citing Hegel, White suggests that the reality that "lends itself to narrative representation is the conflict between desire and the law" (1987, 12–13). The subject of a full-fledged narrative is a struggle pitting a dissident agent against moral/legal authority. Unlike Amsterdam and Bruner, then, White does not maintain that a narrative must begin with a "normatively valued" or "legitimate" state of affairs. Quite the contrary, in White's view, narratives start from morally contestable states of affairs, and they end with a "passage from one moral order to another" (1987, 23). Only the determination that the last event in the chronological sequence is just or unjust can convert a termination into an ending and thereby secure closure, according to White.

One of my doubts about White's account concerns the claim that moral judgment is necessary for narrative closure. Assuming that closure is a necessary feature of full-fledged narrative, which is debatable, it nevertheless seems possible to produce a full-fledged narrative of a set of natural events and processes.[6] Consider a story of the Precambrian ice age. It could invoke geological and climatic forces to explain what precipitated the prolonged plunge in temperature and why warmer conditions eventually developed. It could conclude by describing an altered but stable balance of natural forces. The advent of a new environmental equilibrium could provide closure for this narrative of a geochronological period.[7]

My point holds for stories about human affairs, as well as for stories about nonhuman nature. Consider, for example, relatives of a victim of state terrorism whose only demand is that they receive a payment commensurate with their sense of their loss in order to put the incident behind them. They are motivated by pragmatic considerations, and the story of the measures they take to obtain compensation sufficient to enable them to regain their psychological equilibrium makes sense as a full-fledged narrative. Now consider relatives of a victim of state terrorism whose only demand is that the body of the victim be located and returned to family members for burial. They seek emotional closure, and the story of the rupture of their familial bonds, their search for the remains, and their graveside mourning makes sense as a full-fledged narrative.[8] Through the funeral ritual, they restore their ties to the victim and come to terms with their loss. Sometimes the relatives of a victim of state terrorism demand only to know what happened to the victim—for example, that she was flown out over the ocean and thrown from the helicopter in shackles. They seek epistemic closure, and the story of the mysterious disappearance of a family member, the survivors' quest for information, and the revelation of the truth makes sense as a full-fledged narrative. None of these stories breaks off at some arbitrary point. By receiving monies that restore their psychological balance, by recuperating and completing an emotional relationship, or by gaining crucial knowledge, they attain closure. I acknowledge that in many stories of the aftermath of state terrorism, equilibrium, emotional, and epistemic closure are apt to blend into one another. Still, I stress that they are analytically distinguishable, for they call for different resolutions.

In White's defense, it might be argued that he is concerned exclusively with historical narratives and that my counterexamples cite scientific and personal narratives. However, this rejoinder isn't convincing. Equilibrium, emotional, and epistemic closure are all options for histories. A historical narrative could achieve equilibrium closure by explaining how causal forces brought about an altered distribution of power and/or the establishment of novel social, political, or economic structures. A historical narrative could achieve emotional closure by tracing the aftermath of the assassination of a beloved national leader and the nation's subsequent tributes to her. A historical narrative of a political scandal could achieve epistemic closure by revealing the heretofore-undisclosed machinations of a politician who had not previously been implicated.

Moreover, White's text strongly suggests that his views do not apply solely to historical narratives. In his discussion of the moralization of reality and the state's role as the source of norms, he observes, "And this raises the suspicion that narrative in general, from the folktale to the novel, from the annals to the fully realized 'history,' has to do with the topics of law, legality, legitimacy, or more generally, authority" (1987, 13). Later, he maintains, "Where, in any account of reality, narrativity is present, we can be sure that morality or a moralizing impulse is present too" (1987, 24). It's safe to say that history is not the only discourse in which narrativity is present.

Moral closure is not the only kind of narrative closure. Still, White is on to something important, for moralization seems to be an ever-present temptation in storytelling. Many people succumb to an impulse to moralize natural phenomena by importing divine purpose and agency into their worldviews or by anthropomorphizing and sentimentalizing nature. The temptation to moralize stories is redoubled in stories of epistemic, emotional, or equilibrium closure, for they commonly depict events that have morally significant dimensions. It is natural, for instance, to say that the family of a terror victim whose persistence finally sparks an investigation and disclosure of the victim's fate has won a moral victory over official obfuscation or indifference (see Walker 2006). Likewise, it is natural to see completing family members' emotional relationship to the victim or securing family members' psychological equilibrium through a payment as moral advances, for they contribute to family members' well-being. Nevertheless, it would be misleading to conflate every form of human resolution with moral resolution. Equilibrium, emotional, and epistemic closure are not equivalent to moral closure.

4. SPELMAN'S ACCOUNT OF NORMATIVITY IN A VICTIM'S STORY

Although moral closure is not a necessary feature of full-fledged narratives, it nonetheless seems important to ask whether this type of normative content can be implicated in victims' stories. My discussion of White points to two problematic possibilities.

On the one hand, a victim's story of suffering and surcease might reach equilibrium, emotional, or epistemic closure. A victim's story that ends in one of these ways can be complete without moral resolution. Because the story achieves at least one of these kinds of closure, the audience may find nothing missing and may experience it as finished and done with. As a result, audience members may not register the story as making any moral demand on them apart from the respect due to any speaker.

On the other hand, the temptation to moralize emotional, epistemic, and equilibrium closure explains why telling victims' stories can be so useful and also so risky. Audiences can read the need to punish abusers or to augment legal protections into the story, but they can also read negligence or fault on the part of the victim into the story and assign blame to that individual. In Chapter 1, we saw how fragile victims' claims to innocence are under the reign of the two victim paradigms, and in Chapter 5, we will see that audiences for victims' stories are often prone to victim derogation and blaming. It is imperative, therefore, that victims' stories not be read as cunning tales of opportunistic greed, piteous tales of emotional instability, or disguised tales of power grabs.

If ensuring that victims are empowered to tell their own stories in their own voices is to function as an effective human rights tool, storytellers must avoid these snags. In this section, I'll explore Elizabeth Spelman's account of how that is accomplished in a well-known slave narrative.

Spelman's book, *Fruits of Sorrow: Framing Our Attention to Suffering*, could very well have been subtitled *Mis-framing Our Attention to Suffering* or *The Impossibility of Framing Attention to Suffering Well*. Her book is a veritable cavalcade of warnings, for every frame—every way to talk about and respond to atrocity—turns out to have alarming drawbacks. Accordingly, the main thrust of *Fruits of Sorrow* is to alert us to all the ways in which seemingly progressive concepts and templates for representing victimization can fail. Nevertheless, Spelman devotes a full chapter to a detailed and approving reading of *Incidents in the Life of a Slave Girl, Written by Herself*—the autobiographical story that Harriet Jacobs published under the pseudonym Linda Brent in 1861. Spelman's examination of the rhetorical devices Jacobs employs is instructive.

Slave narratives were written and published to elicit the compassion of white Americans and to further the abolitionist cause. Yet, a former slave's self-presentation as a victim was risky, for it could reinforce the master-slave relation by positioning the pitying, kindly whites as superior to the pitiable, needy blacks (1997, 59–60). To avoid reinstating the very system of domination she means to denounce, Jacobs must refuse to assume the guise of a helpless, passive pathetic victim. While attesting to the wrongs her owners did to her, she must also assert her standing as an equal—an active agent who is entitled to a voice in the debate over the meaning of slavery. How does she manage these seemingly opposed tasks?

According to Spelman, Jacobs both depicts and comments on her experiences, thereby guiding her readers toward appropriate responses. In describing encounters with abolitionists who took care not to "wound her feelings" and who judged people by their character, not the color of their skin, she conveys to readers what attitudes she expects them to adopt (1997, 72). Although she sometimes appropriates stock sentimental imagery of wretchedness, she also breaks out of those frames and reveals terrible truths about herself—truths that might lead readers to despise her.

For example, she recounts her owner's persistent sexual overtures, her elaborate evasive tactics, and her eventual decision to deflect her owner by entering into an affair with the unmarried master of a neighboring household. But she does not offer up these humiliating episodes devoid of moral commentary. Sexual abuse, she tells us, is a structural feature of the institution of slavery, not an episodic outbreak of passion that could be successfully defied (1997, 73). Victim though she is, she speaks of her shame, thereby insisting on being the keeper of her own conscience and repelling others' opinions (1997, 73). But she also offers an indirect tutorial on how to interpret her experience by describing how an empathetic abolitionist replied upon hearing her story:

> Your straight-forward answers do you credit; but don't answer everyone so openly. It might give some heartless people a pretext for treating you with contempt.
>
> (Jacobs quoted in Spelman 1997, 75)

In this passage, she weaves instruction as to what she takes to be the morally fitting response to her sexual misdeeds into her life narrative.

All things considered, to withhold compassionate understanding of the actions she took to cope with the coercive circumstances she confronted would be morally obtuse.[9]

Elsewhere in Jacobs's story, indirect moral tutoring gives way to direct moral condemnation:

> Could you have seen that mother clinging to her child, when they fastened the irons upon his wrists; could you have heard her heart-rending groans, and seen her bloodshot eyes wander wildly from face to face, vainly pleading for mercy; could you have witnessed that scene as I saw it, you would exclaim, *Slavery is damnable!*
>
> (Jacobs quoted in Spelman 1997, 79)

In this compelling passage, Jacobs boldly and unequivocally declares her moral position and demands that her readers embrace it, too.

Compassion for the victims of slavery, though clearly necessary, is ultimately too tepid an emotion in the face of the abuses of slavery that Jacobs depicts (1997, 78). Spelman urges that Jacobs aims to spark outrage by cataloguing the "unspeakable horrors" that were routinely inflicted on slaves (1997, 80). As much as Jacobs suffered under slavery, she reports that many slaves were worse off:

> I was never cruelly overworked; I was never lacerated with the whip from head to foot; I was never so beaten and bruised that I could not turn from one side to the other; I never had my heel-strings cut to prevent my running away; I was never chained to a log and forced to drag it about, while I toiled in the fields from morning till night; I was never branded with hot iron, or torn by bloodhounds.
>
> (Jacobs quoted in Spelman 1997, 80)

But others were. So nothing short of fiery outrage and ardent opposition to the institution of slavery suffices as a moral response (1997, 85).

Remarkably, Jacobs does not limit herself to objecting to the moral degradation, emotional damage, and physical violence perpetrated against slaves. She also bluntly denounces the corruption of the slave-owning class:

> It makes the white fathers cruel and sensual; the sons violent and licentious; it contaminates the daughters, and makes the wives wretched.
>
> (1997, 77)

Her forthrightness in pronouncing moral judgment affirms her status as a member of the moral community and thus her right to criticize social institutions and even to judge the individuals caught up in them (1997, 78). In so doing, she lays claim to her equality—her standing as a moral agent and a right-holder among others—despite her victimization.

Incidents in the Life of a Slave Girl is a full-fledged narrative in White's sense. Jacobs's story is moralized through and through, and it unabashedly seeks to recruit converts to the abolitionist cause.[10] Moreover, it concludes, though somewhat incongruously, when Jacobs's Northern white employer and friend purchases Jacobs from her erstwhile master and gives Jacobs her freedom. So ends the story of Harriet Jacobs's victimization and delivery from victimization—her entrance into a "new moral order." But, as Jacobs points out, it's by no means the end of the story of chattel slavery in the United States. In 1861, when Jacobs's story was published, the Civil War was just getting underway, and Lincoln had not yet issued the Emancipation Proclamation (1863). Worse, the ramifications of US slavery and racism persist to this day and continue to supply grim and sobering material for contemporary victims' stories.

5. STREJILEVICH'S SKEPTICISM ABOUT NORMATIVITY IN VICTIMS' STORIES

White's demarcation of three levels of narrativity provides another viewpoint from which to grasp both the dangers and the benefits of storytelling as a strategy for advancing human rights. Although some victims' stories fit the model of a full-fledged narrative—Harriet Jacobs's does, and so would the story of a vindicated heroic victim—many, probably most, don't. Indeed, many victims' stories fail to satisfy White's criteria for annals, chronicles, or full-fledged narratives, which in my view helps to clarify what is at stake in the relationship between victims' stories and moral closure.

For the most part, I'll illustrate my line of thought in this section with passages from victims' stories of the 1994 Rwanda genocide that journalist Jean Hatzfeld recorded in the late 1990s. Hatzfeld centered his work on the rural, agricultural district of Nyamata. As many readers may not be familiar with details of the survival strategies Tutsi villagers were forced to adopt in order to hide from their machete-wielding Hutu neighbors, I begin by offering one survivor's description of her existence during the killings:

> Mama and my little sisters and I managed to flee into the marshes. We lasted a month beneath the papyrus fronds, almost without seeing or hearing anything of the world outside.
>
> During the day, we lay stretched in the mud with the snakes and mosquitoes to hide from the attacks of the *interahamwe* [Hutu

extremist militias]. At night [while the genocidists returned to town to eat and drink beer] we wandered among the abandoned houses to find something to eat in the farming plots. Because we lived only on what we found, there were many bouts of diarrhea. . . .

One day the *interahamwe* unearthed Mama beneath the papyrus. She stood up; she offered them money to kill her with a single machete blow. They stripped her to take the money knotted up in her pagne. They chopped both of her arms off first, then her legs. . . .

My two little sisters saw everything because they were lying beside her. They were struck too. . . . I myself only heard the noises and screams, because I was concealed in a hole nearby. When the *interahamwe* had gone, I came out and gave Mama a taste of water. . . . I did not dare spend the night with her. I first had to take care of my little sisters, who were badly hurt but not dying. The next day, it was not possible to stay with her either, since we had to hide. That was the rule in the marshes: anyone who was seriously cut has to be abandoned, for safety's sake. . . .

Mama lay in agony for three days before dying at last.

(Jeannette Ayinkamiye, quoted in Hatzfeld 2006, 23–24; bracketed material added)

Other victims who spoke with Hatzfeld tell similar stories of days covered in wet mud surrounded by wounded people and corpses, followed by nights desperately foraging for anything edible and potable and trying to get a little sleep in a dry place (2006, 37, 51–53, 82–84, 101). Another victim sums up the terror of the genocide this way: "That's why, even when the situation seemed peaceful, both our eyes never slept at the same time" (Jean-Baptiste Munyakanore quoted in Hatzfeld 2006, 69).

Nora Strejilevich sketches a familiar picture of the stories many victims of human rights violations tell: They contain "discontinuities, blanks, silences, and ambiguities" (2006, 704). Several of Hatzfeld's subjects are aware of the tricks their memories play on them. For example, Janvier Munyaneza comments:

> Still, over time, I do feel that my mind sorts through my memories as it pleases, and I can do nothing about that. Same thing for us all. Certain episodes are much retold, so they swell with all the additions from one or the other of us. Such episodes remain transparent, so to speak, as though they had happened last year. Other scenes are neglected, and they darken as in a dream. I would say that certain memories are perfected, and others are abandoned.
>
> (quoted in Hatzfeld 2006, 55)

Again and again, victims tell their stories while also stating that their recollections may be distorted in one way or another (Hatzfeld 2006, 27, 86–87; 115–116).

Whether because Hatzfeld sought to protect his subjects' dignity by eliminating their emotional outbursts from his transcripts, or because his subjects were able to maintain their composure while recounting unforgiveable atrocities, the tone of the stories in *Life Laid Bare* is consistently matter-of-fact. But scholars who have studied other testimonies to human rights abuse describe discontinuities in victims' stories that are dramatic and heartrending. For example, Shoshana Felman describes K-Zetnik's collapse on the witness stand at the 1961 Eichmann trial in Jerusalem (Felman 2002, 135–137).

Such ruptured stories resemble annals in their genesis. Annals enumerate events but leave whatever connections there may be among them unspecified. The barely endurable conditions that White says give rise to annals bring acute neediness and imminent death to the forefront of their authors' consciousness and deprive them of the cognitive space needed to interconnect the events they report (1987, 10–11). The excruciating suffering that gives rise to Strejilevich-style victims' stories coincides with White's analysis of the psychosocial source of the annals form.

But the victims' stories that interest Strejilevich and Hatzfeld also resemble chronicles, for although they are by no means comprehensive, a central subject unifies them—a suffering person, family, or community.[11] Although varying peripheral details may be mentioned in different tellings of the story, the invariable core events are major harms the narrator has experienced at the hands of others.[12] Even victims' stories that are marked by sporadic recall and disjointed presentation exhibit this determinate principle of selection.

In my view, this common type of victim's narrative is a hybrid form. Because these stories are organized around a topic, they report a less random selection of incidents than annals. Yet because they do not reliably sequence events, they don't qualify as chronicles.

Neither annals nor chronicles reach moral closure. Presumably, they do not reach equilibrium, emotional, or epistemic closure either. Yet, those victims' stories that fit Strejilevich's profile *strive* for emotional closure. The elusiveness of this aim is a frequent theme in the testimonies Hatzfeld took:

> We felt like strangers in our own skins, if I may put it that way; we had been brought low, and were disturbed by what we had become. I think we didn't believe we would ever be truly safe again.
>
> (Angélique Mukamanzi quoted in Hatzfeld 2006, 84)

> I believe that in the survivor, during the genocide, something mysterious in the heart's core has become blocked. Survivors know they will never learn what this is. So they want to talk about it constantly.
>
> (Innocent Rwililiza quoted in Hatzfeld 2006, 117)

No, I don't feel guilty. I am not at fault, because there was nothing I could do for them. Still, I don't feel glad that I was lucky. I don't know how to explain this feeling, since it concerns a most intimate relation between me and people who are no longer alive. I'm upset and quite distressed when I think of them. I'm not simply sad, as with the ordinary dead.

(Claudine Kayitesi quoted in Hatzfeld 2006, 204)

When I think about the genocide, in a moment of calm, I mull over where to put it properly away in life, but I find no place. I simply mean that it is no longer anything human.

(Sylvie Umubyeyi quoted in Hatzfeld 2006, 235)

These individuals identify different kinds of emotional obstructions that trap them in disquietude. Jeannette Ayinkamiye gives the past's emotional grip on them an apt name: "thought-aches" (Hatzfeld 2006, 27).

However, telling the stories of the genocide is not necessarily emotionally futile. For some, it is therapeutic:

When we children talk, someone may mention the genocide, so then each starts to tell what he saw. That can take a long time. Now and then someone wants to change a detail, but usually we repeat the same memories to one another. Talking together clears away pain and sadness.

(Cassius Niyonsaba quoted in Hatzfeld 2006, 15)

For these child survivors, sharing their stories is a means of "working through traumatic loss"—putting the suffering in the past and regaining a present that is not overwhelmed by the past (Strejilevich 2006, 701, 706–707, 708; also see Brison 2002, 103). When successful in this endeavor, these stories, like many full-fledged narratives, bring about emotional closure.

Strejilevich adds that these stories are a means for "social and cultural resistance" and thus for the "ethical recovery of a community" (2006, 707). This has the ring of moral closure. But what Strejilevich describes is not the closure of acknowledgment, restitution, or protection from future wrongs. Rather, she holds that "the truth told in testimony, even if it cannot stop the reiteration of such crimes, is one of the reservoirs of dignity left for humanity" (2006, 706). Rather than achieving moral closure, these stories contribute to a practice of maintaining awareness of the meaning of human rights abuse and the need for vigilance if renewed brutality is ever to be averted. Telling these stories signifies an existential repudiation of bad faith, which keeps sticking thorns into the tough hide of complacency and indifference. Here, a continuity comes into view between the moral import of hybrid victims' stories and the normative task that heroic victims take on. Both bear witness to grave abrogations of human rights.

It seems, though, that Strejilevich has given up hope of moral closure. Borrowing from Shoshana Felman, she calls victims who tell their stories "post-narrators" (2006, 713). Yet, their post-narratives share features of annals, chronicles, and full-fledged narratives (if you agree with me that emotional closure suffices for narrative closure). In my judgment, there is much to be gained by thinking of these stories as hybrid narratives and exploring whether some form of moral closure is possible and desirable for them.

6. VARIETIES OF MORAL CLOSURE

Empirically, Strejilevich's wariness of moral closure and her circumspection about the power of victims' stories to advance human rights stem from post-Holocaust, post-Nuremberg history. As we have seen, international human rights declarations and treaties have promulgated reforms. But as is evident from casual acquaintance with a respectable news source on any day whatsoever, this new moral order is honored as much in the breach as in observance. Genocide, mass rape, extra-judicial detention and execution, torture, and trafficking in persons continue all but unabated and seldom punished. All of this despite the steady stream of victims' stories in the media and in national and international tribunals.

If moral closure for victims' stories means putting human rights abuses in the past by putting an end to them, no victim's story has ever achieved moral closure. But this conception of moral closure idealizes and mystifies moral closure by giving it a utopian, absolutist twist.[13] If the concept of moral closure is to be of any use in interpreting human affairs and setting human goals, it cannot require achieving perfect subjective, interpersonal, juridical, or social harmony. Moments of moral closure are just that—moments in a life, moments in a relationship, moments in a legal system or social history. Any instance of moral closure is an incomplete, non-definitive rapport that arises from a particular history and reflects the needs of a particular present.[14] Whatever their merits, the understandings and arrangements that constitute moral closure eventually crack open, revealing flaws in perception, understanding, or moral imagination. Thus I stressed in Chapter 1 that the culture of human rights is and will remain a work in progress. Think of moral closure, therefore, as a respite that temporarily allows a person or a society to attend to other matters. In this respect, there is no difference between moral closure and equilibrium, emotional, and epistemic closure. All are liable to dissolution.

Hayden White is responsible for another misconception. As a legalistic moral conventionalist, White is suspicious of the moral closure of full-fledged narrative. In his view, moralizing reality is necessary to achieve moral closure, but to moralize reality is to indulge in a kind of fabulism that is in thrall to hegemonic norms. Full-fledged narratives suffuse reality with norms that are generated and sustained under the aegis of political power and that determine how outcomes are evaluated. In one respect, White's distrust of moral closure is warranted. If presumed to follow from indubitable norms, moral closure underwrites moral stagnation and quashes destabilizing voices.[15] But this assumption is baseless, and I doubt that White endorses it, for he maintains that a passage from one moral order to another is the only intelligible form that narrative closure can take (1987, 23).[16] If so, the state cannot be the only source of moral norms—there's room for Harriet Jacobs and other dissidents to intervene. Nor can moral closure be permanent—novel social critiques are sure to come along.

Amsterdam and Bruner propose an explicitly elastic conception of moral closure. What they call the "dialectic of culture"—a process of ongoing contestation and negotiation among members of society and within society's institutions that is fueled by ambiguous scripting situations—is forever disrupting and replacing extant moral and legal understandings (2000, 112, 231; also see Bruner 2003, 13–14). There is moral closure, in their view, but there is no finality.

Building on this line of thought, Bruner argues that narrative genres are not only "tools of narrative problem solving" but also tools of "problem finding" (2003, 20). Thus, he countenances two types of moral closure. A problem-solving narrative concludes with a coda that delivers a lesson. It decrees a norm or practice. In contrast, a problem-finding narrative concludes with a coda that enunciates a plight. It reveals a previously hidden type of moral perplexity. For Bruner, then, one form of moral closure is achieved through the representation of a moral problem.

This brings us closer to grasping a relationship between hybrid victims' stories and moral closure. But there is another source of confusion that needs to be addressed. It is important to keep personal, legal, and social closure separate from narrative closure. But it is easy to conflate them because narratives can recount a process through which personal, legal, or social closure has been reached and because telling stories often functions as a means to reaching personal, legal, or social closure. People tell themselves stories in order to satisfy themselves that they did no wrong, and they also tell stories about how they developed the narrative that enabled them to accomplish this aim. But unless you subscribe to an ontology in which discourse is the only reality, the psychological sense of moral resolution is not identical to the story you tell yourself, and the moral resolution is not identical to the story of producing that story.

There are several ways in which victims of human rights violations can attain personal moral closure (see Walker 2006). First, they can obtain moral vindication by getting a fair judgment from a court or by negotiating a fair disposition of their claims. Here moral closure is expressed by "I'm satisfied that my persecutors have been appropriately punished or that I've received the restitution I deserve." Second, they can seek moral rapprochement. This form of moral closure is expressed by "I've purged myself of anger and hatred, and I forgive my tormenters." Third, they can discharge moral obligations they believe they have incurred as a result of their ordeal—such as, helping to bring wrongdoers to justice or bearing witness to what has happened and speaking for those who perished. "I've done what I can, and I've done enough" expresses this form of moral closure.

Telling a story of reaching personal moral closure is a direct route to narrative moral closure. *Incidents in the Life of a Slave Girl* is a case in point. Such a story may fit comfortably into the Amsterdam/Bruner template or White's model of full-fledged narrative, and I don't think Strejilevich would deny this possibility. More elusive is the potential for moral closure in victims' narratives that don't have satisfying moral endings—where no recompense can be adequate, where forgiveness is impossible, or where the responsibility to the dead is so enormous that it can never be discharged. At this point, it's tempting to appropriate Bruner's literary conception of moral closure as the articulation of a plight. And doing so would be justified to some extent, for the hybrid victims' stories that Strejilevich characterizes have indeed revealed the immensity of human savagery and the depths of human depravity, and they have brought to light the agonies of post-traumatic stress disorder. However, Bruner's view seems to sidestep the issue, for it is an odd sort of narrative closure that leaves its audience in suspense.

7. MORAL CLOSURE WITHOUT MORAL RESOLUTION

Here it is useful to revisit White's account of the annalist and the central subject of a chronicle as they apply to hybrid victims' stories. The annalist, recall, is a person in the grip of consuming fear and abject wretchedness. The central subject of a hybrid victim's story is also a suffering person. However, unlike annalists who are so overwhelmed by suffering that White claims their lives lack agency and meaning, the narrators of hybrid victims' stories do not encounter or represent a normatively neutral world. Just as third-person chroniclers choose to include events based on their relevance and importance to their topics, so too a first-person narrator of victimization selects events that caused the author/speaker to suffer and that woefully constricted her agency.

Like works of full-fledged narrative, moreover, hybrid victims' narratives imbue the events they represent with normative significance. People who have suffered human rights abuse experience what they have endured as bad—often as terrifying and debasing. The staggering harm they have experienced is no mere conflict between desire (what someone happens to want) and law (enforced social conventions), as White would have it. In their stories, though, victims may refrain from overtly moralizing—pointing fingers at villains or denouncing others' misdeeds.

Although Spelman exhibits the power of Harriett Jacobs's explicit moral pronouncements, assuming an accusatory mien can draw attention to the accuser and distract attention from the moral significance of the abuse she depicts. For this reason, victims may opt to rely on other rhetorical strategies to convey the normative inflection of their experience.[17] I think this is what Strejilevich has in mind when she affirms both the "poetic voice" and the narrative structure of hybrid victims' stories (2006, 704, 708). In delineating character, in the pacing and punctuation of episodes, in silences and gaps, in figurative language, and in tone, victims convey the normative significance of the events they portray. Narrative time—the cadence of the story—may slow to linger on particularly painful or important incidents. Scattered shards of detail may signal insupportable pain—suffering so excruciating that it defeats unbroken awareness. Recourse to figures of speech may signal brutality so vile that it defies ordinary descriptive categories. The performative dimension of oral storytelling—including the emotional tenor of a speaker's demeanor, whether phrasing is smooth or spasmodic, and how the timbre of voice is pitched—extends the capacity of victims' stories to dramatize normative significance.

Susan Slyomovics's discussion of Nomonde Calata's 1996 testimony at the South African Truth and Reconciliation Commission poignantly illustrates the impact of the nonverbal features of a victim's telling of her story. At one point, the transcript of Calata's testimony reports an interval of sobbing in brackets and the announcement of a recess. What happened is that she "broke down, wailing in anguish," and radio listeners found her screams so piercing that they rushed to switch off their radios (2005, 73). Although the transcript is a technically accurate record, it nullifies the normative significance of this part of her testimony. Worse, it gives the misleading impression that her testimony stopped at this point and continued later—as if her sobs were extraneous to her story.

Even when consigned to written texts, hybrid victims' stories seem unlikely to reach a recognizable state of completion. Yet narrative closure—regardless of whether the narrative is a conventional Amsterdam/Bruner-style narrative or a hybrid Strejilevich-style narrative and regardless of whether the closure is equilibrium, emotional, epistemic, or moral—is never solely a function of the text. It presupposes extensive background information and shared cultural norms that give rise to discursive expectations. Readers mobilize their interpretative skills together with these expectations to generate a sense that the story is complete or has loose ends (Bennett 1997). Since every form of narrative closure depends on know-how and systems of beliefs and values that audience members must bring to the text if anyone is to comprehend it, the question of how moral closure is possible for hybrid victims' narratives poses a pair of problems. First, what kind of moral completion is appropriate to their subject matter and their structure? Second, what frameworks render such exposition cogent and underwrite judgments about completeness?

These stories recount inflicted harm so horrendous that their narrators have not been, arguably cannot be, adequately compensated, nor can their perpetrators be proportionately punished. Since any individualized remedy would be too paltry in comparison with a mass atrocity such as genocide, none could secure personal moral closure. Likewise, no description of such a remedy could secure narrative moral closure. If moral closure is possible for hybrid narratives, it must be a different species of closure from mundane legal provisions for conflict resolution. Inspired in part by White's (1987, 4) rather cryptic claim that narrative mediates between the real and the imaginary and Robert Cover's (1983, 9–10) similar claim that narrative mediates between the actual and the possible or utopian, I propose that a victim's story that successfully represents a moral void, together with an implicit moral imperative that has been systematically ignored, achieves this alternative kind of moral closure. Such a victim's narrative fully expresses a moral demand.

Such an appeal to conscience consists in nothing more than a compelling articulation of what the narrator has endured.[18] Now, it might seem that the moral demand is a consequence of a formal defect in the victim's story—namely, the absence of a morally gratifying ending. On this view, narrative moral closure depends on real-world moral closure to supply an ending and complete the story. To adopt this approach, however, is just to insist that White's full-fledged narratives and Amsterdam and Bruner's problem-solving narratives exhaust the category of morally complete narratives. But confining the concept of moral closure to these formats does an injustice to many storytellers and arbitrarily excludes some orthodox narrative forms. Consider parables and allegories—narratives that are complete in themselves and that express moral meaning without explicitly stating it. That these literary forms require interpretation to discern their normative significance is no reason to deny that they can achieve moral closure, and, in my view, the same goes for hybrid victims' stories.

Further justification for admitting the form of moral closure I'm ascribing to hybrid narratives comes from the fact that we can specify the background frameworks that make it possible to interpret them in a morally insightful way and that thus make moral closure possible for them. Chief among them are everyday interpersonal psychology, basic literary competence, and human rights discourse. Knowledge of human psychology is necessary to grasp the horror of the experiences that victims depict—that is, to comprehend the torment of merciless pain, the anguish of frustrated agency, and the terror of unpredictable peril. Literary competence is necessary to appreciate individualized as opposed to formulaic expression and to decode the lyric, allusive, or metaphoric language in which the victim may couch a normative claim. Familiarity with human rights is necessary to provide a vocabulary in which a moral practice that answers to the storyteller's suffering can be envisaged and advocated. These frameworks supply criteria that enable listeners/readers as well as the narrators themselves to judge whether hybrid victims' stories are morally complete or not. When people—whether storytellers or audience members—fail to discern moral closure in hybrid victims' stories, it is an open question whether the problem stems from flaws in the narrator's text, deficient human rights literacy, or, most challenging of all, the need to expand the scope of human rights protections.[19] Explaining the perceived failure of a hybrid victim's story to express a moral demand sets conscientious audience members on an arduous path of moral self-examination.

What I am suggesting is that a full account of moral closure for the hybrid stories that traumatized victims of dehumanizing abuse often tell depends on developing an aesthetics of morally valuable representations of extreme moral disvalue. Although there is nothing arcane about the frameworks that render the moral import of these stories intelligible, it is by no means obvious how to theorize the capacity of these stories to contribute to debates over the meaning of human rights.[20] Nor is it obvious how a case can be made for regarding them as legitimate forms of advocacy discourse. I'll take up these issues in later chapters.

Here, I conclude only that moral closure is both possible and desirable for hybrid victims' stories. Aristotle claims that a well constructed story "must represent, one action, a complete whole" and that moral considerations are intrinsic to representations of human action (*Poetics*, 1151a 30, 1450b 5–10). My view parallels his point, for I am suggesting that one way in which a victims' story can be morally complete is to represent a complete experience and that a sequence of assaultive or privative incidents stripped of any moral dimension is inconceivable. Whether because she models moral closure on the theories of Amsterdam and Bruner or White, or for some other reason, Strejilevich underestimates the potential of victims' stories to advance human rights discourse. Telling these stories is not merely a matter of gaining emotional closure, confronting grisly truths, or eschewing bad faith. It is the fulfillment of a vital task in critical moral reflection—namely, issuing a clarion moral appeal.

Chapter 3

Emotional Understanding
and Victims' Stories

I would dream that a facelesss gunman had tied me up and begun
to slit my throat with the zigzag edge of his bayonet. I would feel
the pain that the knife inflicted as the man sawed my neck. I'd wake
up sweating and throwing punches in the air. I would run outside
to the middle of the soccer field and rock back and forth, my arms
wrapped around my legs. I would try desperately to think about my
childhood, but I couldn't.

Ishmael Beah, *A Long Way Gone* (p. 149)

Contrasting the power of photographs of human suffering with that
of stories of human suffering, Susan Sontag comments that photographs "haunt us" whereas "narratives can make us understand"
(2003, 89). Among students of narrative, however, there is much
debate about just what kind of understanding, if any, narrative conveys. Some claim that narrative can impart moral insight; others
accuse narrative of purveying normative disinformation or of tempting people to mistake feelings for truth. In this chapter, I critically
examine these disparate views, defend one that takes an affective/
normative position on narrative understanding, and draw out some
implications of this account for understanding a victim's story of
human rights abuse.

Noël Carroll, Hayden White, and J. David Velleman differentiate narrative discourse from other discursive forms in order to analyze what binds the incidents that comprise the plot into a whole and gives stories their characteristic structure and epistemic status. For Carroll, the narrative glue is a causal network, and to understand a story is to comprehend the causal connections that hold the depicted events together (2001, 118–133). For White, the narrative glue is an ideological viewpoint, and to understand a story is to grasp the moral lesson the author embeds in the story (1987). For Velleman, the narrative glue is an emotional arc, and to understand a story is to find out how you feel about the depicted events (2003, 2009).

There are several reasons that militate against adopting Carroll's, White's, or Velleman's position for purposes of theorizing victims' stories. First, all three of them endorse Aristotle's requirement that a story be a complete whole with a beginning, middle, and end. But as we saw in Chapter 2, victims' stories don't necessarily satisfy this requirement. Traumatized victims often tell disjointed stories that start in medias res, jumble remembered incidents, and stop for no readily apparent reason. Others opt for a diary form that does not observe the Aristotelian canons. Many break off before any resolution has been reached.

Second, a victim's story may, but need not, represent causal connections internal to her experience and may, but need not, attend to the causes of her suffering. Many Tutsi survivors of the Rwanda genocide causally link different components of their experience. For example, Jeannette Ayinkamiye speaks of the diarrhea caused by the victims' diet of foraged food, and Francine Niyitega explains her difficulties organizing her experiences and trusting her perceptions by citing having "lived through a waking nightmare for real" (both quoted in Hatzfeld 2006, 23, 43). But some victims' stories articulate the incomprehensibility of their experience. Sylvie Umubyeyi describes an eerie state of apathy in the face of violence:

> So we sat down on the ground and waited for death. I had thrown off my fear. I was growing numb to the uproar of shrieking; I was waiting for the blade. Sometimes you are afraid when a situation arises, but as it develops you proceed under a kind of anesthesia. I had become patient.

(quoted in Hatzfeld 2006, 225)

Umubyeyi tells us about the state of mind that comes over her, but her words don't convey a causal network connecting her loss of fear, her imperviousness to noise, and her patience. In a similar vein, some of the survivors speculate about the motives of the Hutu genocidists (Hatzfeld 2006, 28, 41, 106, 110, 113). But many confine their narratives to describing episodes of acute affliction during and after the killings without attempting to make sense of the motives of their tormenters or the larger social forces at play in their persecution (for additional discussion of these stories, see Chapter 2, section 5). Because I believe that the power of these stories and others like them to advance human rights depends on their depictions of grievous abuse, rather than on the causal cogency of the experiences they recount or their interpretations of the psychological roots of Hutu hatred or other causes, I won't examine Carroll's causal position any further.

Third, I am concerned that Velleman underestimates or underplays the cognitive significance of emotional understanding and that White fictionalizes moral values and disvalues. As a result, I argue, their views trivialize what victims' stories have to offer for purposes of moral reflection about human rights. Section 1 fleshes out this line of criticism.

In contrast, Jenefer Robinson (2005) limits her purview to great novels and explores how they can be morally instructive. Like Velleman, Robinson regards emotional responsiveness as key in understanding narrative fiction, but unlike Velleman, she does not regard the deliveries of emotion as merely subjective or as hindrances to reason. Like White, Robinson contends that narrative fiction encodes moral values, but unlike White, she denies that the moral significance of these texts falsifies reality.

In relation to victims' stories, I find Robinson's affective/normative approach more helpful than the accounts that Carroll, Velleman, and White put forward. Arguably the greater promise of Robinson's view with respect to victims' stories stems from a difference between the framing of her project and the framing of Carroll's, White's, and Velleman's. Whereas they ask what unifies a story and thereby gives it a special type of narrative meaning, she asks what sort of moral insight people can glean from stories that they can't obtain from philosophy or anywhere else. In this respect, Robinson's work seconds Martha Nussbaum's claims that literature can represent and exhibit the merits of philosophical positions that could not be adequately articulated and defended in theoretical discourse and that literature "squeeze[es] out the value" to be found in life (1990, 132–143, 157, 160–164).[1] Although it is necessary to be mindful of the differences between experiencing the kind of fiction that Robinson's and Nussbaum's work explicates and experiencing victims' autobiographical stories, section 2 of this chapter argues that the view Robinson espouses is in important respects transferrable to victims' stories of human rights abuse.

To make my case for the value of emotionally understanding victims' stories, I examine Ishmael Beah's *A Long Way Gone: Memoirs of a Boy Soldier*. There are pitfalls associated with emotionally understanding his story, for, as with many victims' stories, some of the incidents he recounts are emotionally stupefying, and these intense responses tend to overpower other feelings aroused by other parts of his story. Section 3 presents two passages from Beah's book that exemplify this concern. Sections 4 and 5 aim to allay it. Plainly, antidotes are needed to prevent readers' interpretations from going awry. Section 4 examines the phenomenon of imaginative resistance and explains how Beah's writing both elicits this response and employs it for moral ends. Section 5 offers an interpretation of the inflammatory passages presented in section 3 in light of the events that precede it in Beah's story. By showing how emotional excess can be curbed by a victim's story, I support Robinson's contention that affective engagement with literature can yield substantial benefits to moral understanding.

Yet it is not obvious how victims' stories connect with human rights doctrine. Section 6 contrasts victims' stories that explicitly invoke the concept of a right and victims' stories that leave the concept of a right implicit. I acknowledge the usefulness of the former type of story. However, in the spirit of Robinson's thought, I urge that structuring victims' stories to mirror human rights theory is less productive overall from a moral point of view. If I am right about the downside of authorial moralizing and superintendence over interpretation, it follows that the victims' stories that have the greatest potential for moral generativity are also stories that are vulnerable to readings that are hostile to human rights. Open as they are to individual readers' interpretations, they may or may not prompt readers to draw on human rights norms to conceptualize their affective responses. Although this indeterminacy exposes victims' stories to misinterpretation, it awakens readers' affective capacities and their powers of imagination to better grasp the meanings of human rights in human lives and perhaps to identify shortcomings in current conceptions of human rights.

This chapter concludes, as does Beah's memoir, by briefly contemplating the relations between human rights and peace (section 7). A story of the miseries and shocks of war, *A Long Way Gone* fittingly ends with an allegorical representation of the dilemmas that mass violence creates and the wages of peace.

1. NARRATIVE ARTIFICE: ARBITRARY AND NON-RATIONAL?

Hayden White and David Velleman have so little in common philosophically that it is of interest that they agree about the artificiality of narrative:

> When it is a matter of recounting the concourse of real events, . . . we cannot say, surely, that any sequence of real events comes to an end, that reality itself disappears, that events of that order have ceased to happen.
>
> (White 1987, 23)

> There are no beginnings or endings in the flow of events.
>
> (Velleman 2003, 14)

Historians select material to include in their narratives from a superfluity of information. They harness rhetoric to their purposes by couching their stories in evocative language and structuring them so as to sustain readers' interest. This artifice, in conjunction with what White and Velleman take to be the undifferentiated flow of events, induces each of them to question the connection between nonfiction stories and what has actually happened. White maintains that stories necessarily inject alien material into reality. Velleman holds that stories traffic in emotional connections rather than tracking the causes that shape reality. Hence each of them undertakes to explain what stories do—why they are so seductive and why we should be wary of their wiles.

To recapitulate some points made in Chapter 2, recall that White holds that narrative embellishes reality with values:

> [W]hat other "ending" could a given sequence of such events have than a "moralizing" ending? I confess I cannot think of any other way of "concluding" an account of real events.
>
> (White 1987, 23)

In historical writing, the ending is a "passage from one moral order to another" (1987, 23). But morality, for White, is nothing more than a byproduct of raw social power and the political authority that accrues from it (1987, 11–13). Given his deflationary view of morality, narrative closure reduces to a shift from one system of institutionalized power to another overlaid with a complementary ideological reconfiguration. Unlike annals and chronicles, which confine themselves to recording facts, narrative history soaks mere actualities in moral meaning (1987, 24). In representing sequences of events as if they themselves carried these meanings, the historian satisfies the infantile human yearning for "coherence, integrity, fullness, and closure" at the cost of fictionalizing reality (1987, 24–25).[2]

Velleman takes White to task for this illusionist position (2003, 19–20). Yet he hardly throws his weight behind narrative history:

> Insofar as historical discourse conveys understanding by organizing the past into stories, what it conveys is not an objective understanding of how historical events came about but a subjective understanding of how to feel about them.
>
> (Velleman 2003, 20)

Rejecting Carroll's causal account of narrative unity, Velleman argues that narrative's principal cognitive defect is precisely its failing to supply an accurate causal account of how the depicted events came about (2003, 5, 20–22). Because a text provides objective under-standing only if it truthfully explains what caused the events it depicts, and because stories need not make these connections, stories *qua* stories provide only affective apprehension of depicted events.[3] They secure emotional closure, rather than intellectual closure.

Velleman is suspicious of narrative discourse because he thinks emotional resolution is likely to be mistaken for causal intelligibility (2003, 20). Although he denies that stories are impenetrably mis-leading, he asserts that people are prone to conflate the feelings a story elicits with the course of events it describes. As a result, audi-ence members tend to regard an emotionally gratifying tale as a true causal explanation and, I presume, an emotionally frustrating or disorienting tale as a false report (Velleman 2003, 21). With this in mind, Velleman opines that the recent vogue in narrative philoso-phy of law—championed, for example, by Ronald Dworkin (1986) as well as Anthony Amsterdam in collaboration with Jerome Bruner (2000)—substitutes the easy persuasive power of storytelling for rational argument: "Telling a story is often a means to being believed for no good reason" (2003, 22).[4]

As if giving an argument were not. Many arguments are valid but misleading because of their faulty premises. Even sound argu-ments can rest on emotionally charged premises—premises that are believed because of the affect they arouse rather than because of the evidence for their truth. Moreover, arguments can rely on true premises and seem convincing but make invalid inferences. If this weren't enough, studies by Amos Tversky, Daniel Kahneman, and many other psychologists point up reason's reliance on heuristics and biases and its liability to inferential errors—strategies that com-pound its waywardness (Kahneman, Slovic, and Tversky 1982). Why does narrative stir up Velleman's epistemological ire?

Velleman relies on a homology between emotion and narrative to ground his account of understanding stories and his concerns about the reliability of claims communicated in story form. The idea is that narrative beginnings, middles, and ends mirror the corporeal cycle of affect—"provocation, complication, and resolution" (Velleman 2003, 12). Stories move from instigating emotional excitation to culminating in emotional dissipation and rest (Velleman 2003, 13). Any story-like text that does not elicit this sequenced response is a "bad story," though Velleman concedes that it might be a "great novel" (2003, 10).

Although Velleman's model of a story is familiar, even beloved, it is stipulative to exclude every plotted representation that doesn't conform to it from the category of stories or to disparage all such representations as flawed storytelling.[5] Many aesthetically satisfying and intellectually rewarding stories don't fit this pattern. As Jerome Bruner remarks, "great narrative is an invitation to problem finding, not a lesson in problem solving" (2003, 20). If so, an excellent story can leave you emotionally troubled. Moreover, Velleman's own thesis, which is shared by many others, that people's self-conceptions are encoded in ongoing stories that shape their conduct would make little sense if his story template were accepted as definitive (e.g., 2006, chapters 9 and 10).[6] Either that, or we're all fated to live out defective stories.

Nothing is to be gained by adopting the highly restrictive conception of stories that Velleman espouses. Still, his skepticism about the intellectual content of narrative is worth examining. He is surely right that emotional understanding is integral to narrative understanding,[7] yet his argument betrays an unresolved conflict with respect to what you gain through emotional understanding.

Whereas Velleman's analysis of narrative understanding strips emotion of any cognitive content and decries its gullibility, his critique of White's view depends on emotion's cognitive function.

According to White, narrative necessarily misrepresents history. But Velleman replies:

> The storytelling historian thus brings his audience to some emotional closure about a course of events viewed in retrospect. This effect of narrative history is not in itself an illusion or projection—not, at least, unless all emotion involves an illusion or projection of significance that events do not really have.
>
> (2003, 20)

Velleman's rebuttal plainly presupposes that emotion does not always project illusory significance onto otherwise neutral events. If emotion never registered any genuine meaning and if narrative understanding is an emotional process, White would be right. Thus, Velleman's critique depends on the assumption that emotional responses can disclose moral values and disvalues.

Nevertheless, his account of understanding stories insists that all you learn from narrative is how it feels to have the experiences that are depicted and how you feel about the plot taken as a whole (2003, 19; 2009, 198–200). But in what way does a historical narrative "render events intelligible" if what Velleman calls the "conclusory emotion" that colors the emplotted events reveals nothing of significance about the events, other than the fact that they spark this emotion when told in a particular way?

Despite acknowledging that emotions alert you to what's going on in your environment and prepare you to act appropriately, Velleman downplays emotional intentionality and intelligence by repeatedly pointing to the biologically regulated, corporeal nature of emotions (2003, 13–14). In seeming tension with this aspect of his thinking, Velleman tones down his criticism of narrative understanding in his more recent work on affect and narrative. Although he continues to insist on the primacy of causal explanation, he concedes that narrative helps us to "clarify how we feel about [our actions] or what they mean to us" (2009, 186, 201; bracketed material added). If this is his considered view, and if the meaning of our conduct is not an altogether subjective matter, it would seem that Velleman needs a better-developed account of the cognitive dimension of emotion. Otherwise his affirmation of the role of narrative in practical reasoning—with the caveat that narrative understanding in an optional extra—seems arbitrary (2009, 203–204).

Like sense perceptions, emotions can be misleading, but, for the most part, they aren't. Moreover, they are remarkably sensitive to the complex twists and turns of human relations, and they make subtle discriminations—for example, between conduct that warrants outrage rather than indignation, or conduct that warrants shame rather than embarrassment. Nor are they governed entirely by physiological programs or inculcated cultural scripts. People's emotional economies are individualized, responsive to novelty, and receptive to fine-tuning.

The root of Velleman's oddly dismissive treatment of emotional understanding may be his assumption that causal chains constitute an undifferentiated flow. Perhaps from the standpoint of eternity there's no segmentation and punctuation in passing time, and nothing ultimately matters. But from a human standpoint this is hardly the case. Lives begin and end. Plans are made, acted on, and succeed or fail. The incidents that fill a human life are classified as good, bad, and countless variants thereof. As long as people are around—with their needs and interests and their emotional and intellectual complexity— what exists and what happens are discriminable both quantitatively and qualitatively. Many nonfiction stories latch onto discrete, value-laden features of human life, and in this respect they are not arbitrary.

As Joel Kupperman (1999, chapters 2–3) and Mark Johnston (2001) argue, affect is an indispensable means of apprehending what's valuable and what's not and, I would add, of comprehending stories about such things. In section 2, I consider a theory of narrative understanding that takes this view of emotion as its point of departure.

2. AFFECTIVE INTELLIGENCE AND MORAL UNDERSTANDING

Like Velleman, Jenefer Robinson treats emotion as a corporeal phenomenon, but unlike Velleman, she underscores the cognitive dimension of emotional experience. In Robinson's view, preconscious, corporeal evaluations—she calls them "affective appraisals"—constitute the core of emotional experience (2005, 45).[8] These rudimentary assessments of features of your environment as good or bad, concordant with or opposed to your interests, strange or familiar, and so forth, automatically bring about physiological arousal, which in turn reinforces the appraisal, fixes your attention on the object of concern, and prepares you to act appropriately (2005, 46, 89).[9] Brought to conscious awareness, these affective appraisals correspond to basic emotions, such as fear, disgust, anger, and surprise (2005, 68–69). However, in case affective appraisals misjudge your surroundings, more sophisticated forms of cognitive monitoring stand ready to override wayward affective appraisals and inhibit your action tendency (2005, 75). Still, affective appraisals generally provide indispensable information about the agentic significance of the situations you find yourself in (2005, 73).

Because these appraisals are crude, in and of themselves they do not give rise to cognitively complex emotions. Although cognitively complex emotions, such as compassion, elation, indignation, and jealousy, are rooted in the same affective appraisals as basic emotions, Robinson argues that it is in virtue of subsequent cognitive processing and naming that people experience affective shading (2005, 89–90). In this connection, she cites Ronald de Sousa's influential view that culturally inherited "paradigm scenarios" specify the kinds of circumstances in which different complex emotions are appropriate and thus provide the cognitive resources that individuals need to refine their understandings of the ebb and flow of their emotional lives (2005, 90; also see Velleman 2009, 194).

A specialist in aesthetics, Robinson applies her account of emotion to the problem of enjoying and understanding works of literature, music, and art. Her discussion of affective engagement with nineteenth-century European and American "great realistic novels" is particularly germane to the problems posed by victims' autobiographical stories of human rights abuse (2005, 106, 159). Here in outline is her view.

Relying on empirical studies, Robinson urges that readers follow stories both emotionally and intellectually. Because there are gaps in narratives, people cannot understand stories unless they fill them in using factual background knowledge, including knowledge of causal connections (2005, 119–120). As well, their emotional responses synthesize information that a text furnishes about a character or a situation, and these affective syntheses enable them to infer meanings that the author does not explicitly state (2005, 122, 126). For Robinson, interpreting a literary text requires figuring out what emotional responses you had as you read, what in the story elicited them, and whether they were justified in light of the text (2005, 123, 158). "To discover," for example, "the source of my compassion for Anna Karenina . . . is to discover the pitiable nature of her situation in all its details" (2005, 123). Accordingly, interpretation involves reconciling affective responses with features of the text and discerning meanings that are implicit in the emotions stirred by the text.

Robinson's integration of feeling and thinking in her account of emotion and emotional understanding is invaluable.[10] But because she focuses on the psychological and physiological evidence for her claims about affective appraisals, I want to pause to examine the phenomenology of affective appraisals. As well, I think it is necessary to address a possible objection to her views about the epistemology of literary interpretation before going further.

People's affective systems maintain running commentaries on their surroundings and their behavior, corporeally apprehending sundry values and disvalues and readying them to act (Meyers 2013, 7). No doubt, much of this commentary takes place at the preconscious level and never rises to consciousness. For example, the bodily relaxation of comfort and security need not grab your attention, for it does not suggest any modification in what you're doing. But affective appraisals need not remain outside awareness. Preconscious affective appraisals enter consciousness as basic emotions, and in some situations your attentiveness to them increases. Especially when you are trying to cope with some difficulty or trying to master a new skill, you are likely to make a point of noticing positive as well as negative affective corporeal feedback that might go unremarked in a less challenging context. Moreover, some affective appraisals force their way into consciousness. The fearful knot in the pit of your stomach, the triumphal thrill running through your sinew, the abashed blush— these insistently self-assertive affective appraisals are hard to ignore. And no wonder, for they signal matters that are crucial for choice and action, including danger, accomplishment, and unworthiness. Yet, they can pose stubborn problems for agency, for they are notoriously intractable—that is, difficult to reorient, modulate, or extirpate if on reflection they are found to be routinely misdirected or excessive. Phobias are an obvious case in point.

Presumably the subset of affective appraisals that press into consciousness plays an analogous role in the emotional understanding of narratives, alerting readers to critically important material and concentrating their attention on it. If so, these affective appraisals exert a high degree of influence on interpretations of stories, and astute authors undoubtedly capitalize on their cognitive clout. However, if a reader's vividly conscious emotions fasten on inappropriate parts of a story or exaggerate the importance of certain story elements, they can distract attention from the overall plotline and subvert the reader's interpretation of the story. Sections 3–5 below consider how poorly modulated emotional responses to episodes in a victim's story can distort interpretation and suggest remedies for this problem.

Robinson points out that the differences among people's emotional dispositions and hence among their emotional responses to narratives account in part for their interpretative disagreements (2005, 122, 183). Moreover, she argues that a rich realistic novel, such as Edith Wharton's *The Reef*, elicits "a hundred different shades of emotion, one continually shifting and sliding into another, and it is only the broad outlines of my emotions that I can 'catalogue in recollection'" (2005, 182).[11] Thus, divergent interpretations also reflect differences among people's repertoires of emotion concepts and differences in the salience of different emotion concepts within these repertoires. I would add that the very indefiniteness of ongoing preconscious affective appraising creates a desirable sort of latitude that allows new understandings of a story to surface as attentive readers contemplate texts and as new conceptual resources become culturally available to readers. Reducing the dependency of interpretation on what a reader already presumes to know is a salubrious consequence of this latitude.

Whereas Robinson pictures emotional understanding of narrative as limber and agile, Velleman's (2003, 19) characterization of emotionally understanding stories as *déjà senti*—already felt—presumes that emotion is regimented and routinized. The advantages of Robinson's fluid view of emotion notwithstanding, it is worrisome that the indefiniteness of much ongoing preconscious affective appraising increases the indeterminacy of interpretation.

More specifically, this indeterminacy raises questions about the role Robinson ascribes to emotional understanding and literary interpretation with respect to educating the moral sentiments (2005, 158). Is it really possible for reading to refine moral sensitivity and to generate moral insight if emotional understanding is so murky? Here Robinson's subjectivism appears to be at odds with her moral agenda. On reflection, however, I think this concern is overblown.

Suppose that, as Robinson argues, some emotions are basic and others are cognitively complex. Basic emotions are recognizable on the basis of the intentional content of bodily affective appraisals together with the syndromes of physiological arousal these appraisals trigger (2005, 68–69, 87, 89–90). This set of "basic emotion systems" also undergirds cognitively complex emotions (2005, 68–69, 87, 89–90). However, cognitively complex emotions require additional "cognitive monitoring" to assess the context in which the basic emotion system has been activated and to apply a suitable, culturally available emotion label to the affective state. As a result of this cognitive input, individuals come to experience permutations of basic emotions—for example, indignation and resentment as well as basic anger (2005, 89–90).

Returning to the epistemological issue, if the basic human stock of affective appraisals is reliably attuned to major types of value and disvalue, it seems that the cognitive overlay that interprets embodied affectivity can't go too far wrong. It's more likely to overlook or muddle subtle moral distinctions than it is to confuse disvalues with values or vice versa. As long as our disagreements are about whether a state of affairs calls for outrage or indignation, and not about whether it calls for outrage or delight, our disagreements are relatively innocuous. Even so, Robinson's theory of interpretation includes a corrective for affect gone astray, whether in large or small ways. She prescribes returning to the text to confirm that your emotional responses are indeed congruent with it. By retrospectively scrutinizing your inchoate emotional responses to a story, connecting them to specific features of the text, and on that basis formulating an understanding of what you have felt and what the story means, conscientious readers minimize the chance of settling on insidiously misguided interpretations.

Summing up, I agree with Robinson that emotionally following a story is an important part of understanding it. Understanding plot and characters isn't exclusively propositional, for emotional response constitutes "a kind of bodily understanding" (Robinson 2005, 127; also see Velleman 2003, 13; 2009, 195). Moreover, I agree with Robinson that the cognitive dimension of emotional responsiveness is well documented in the empirical literature and that emotional responses make you aware of a vast spectrum of values and disvalues that call for your attention, if not for immediate action. Finally, I agree with her that tracing the springs of your emotional responses to the textual features that elicit them provides a necessary check on "getting carried away" and missing the story's nuances, as well as a check on the tendency to project your inveterate feelings and attitudes onto situations and characters whether or not the way they are depicted warrants it. This last pair of points is especially important in reading victims' narratives, for these stories prompt extremes of feeling that tend to linger, crowding out other plot elements and motivating facile moral judgments.

3. SCENES FROM A CHILD SOLDIER'S STORY

Preliminary to exploring the rewards and perils of emotionally understanding the normative content of victims' stories, I present a pair of provocative excerpts from Ishmael Beah's *A Long Way Gone*.[12] But a bit of background is needed for the passages I'll quote to make sense.

In some respects, Beah's story fits the model of narrative that Amsterdam and Bruner propose (Chapter 2, section 1). It begins by sketching a pleasant youth of swimming, watching TV, and forming a rap and hip-hop dance group—a state of legitimate ordinariness, as Amsterdam and Bruner would say. But within a few pages, those diversions are gone forever. "Trouble," in Amsterdam and Bruner's sense of the term, swiftly descends upon him. When Beah was roughly twelve years old, rebels attacked his village in Sierra Leone, and he was lucky to escape into the dense surrounding rain forest.[13] Almost half of his book tells the story of his fleeing the fighting and eluding capture by one of the rebel forces. Beah and several other boys who had met in the forest traveled together, seeking safety and rest while also hunting for their missing families.

Sometime before the age of fifteen, when he was picked up by UNICEF workers and taken to a rehabilitation center for child soldiers, more "Trouble" erupted. National army troops took the band of boys to a village where the army had established a camp and where they briefly believed they would be protected. Soon, though, the commander of the post gave them an ultimatum—they could join the army and fight alongside the government forces, or they could leave the village and face all but certain death at the hands of rebel combatants in the forest. Under duress, they chose to stay in the village and join the army. After minimal training, they were sent into battle, their nerve and energy fortified by cocaine and marijuana.

Here is one episode from Beah's soldiering period:

> We had been in the village for only a few minutes when the rebels attacked again. They didn't want to give up the village easily. We looked at each other around the fire and angrily changed our magazines and went out to get rid of the attackers for good. We fought them throughout the night and the following day. None of us wanted to give up the village to the other, but in the end we killed most of the rebels and captured a few more.

The others ran away into the cold and rainy forest. We were so angry with the prisoners that we didn't shoot them but, rather, decided to punish them severely. "It will be a waste of bullets to shoot them," the lieutenant said. So we gave them shovels and demanded, at gunpoint, that they dig their own graves. We sat under the huts smoking marijuana and watched them dig in the rain. Each time they would slow down, we would shoot around them and they would resume digging faster. When they were done digging, we tied them and stabbed their legs with bayonets. Some of them screamed, and we laughed and kicked them to shut them up. We then rolled each man into his hole and covered him with the wet mud. All of them were frightened, and they tried to get up and out of the hole as we pushed the dirt back on them, but when they saw the tips of our guns pointed into the hole, they lay back and watched us with their pale sad eyes. They fought under the soil with all their might. I heard them groan underneath as they fought for air. Gradually, they gave up, and we walked away. "At least they are buried," one of the soldiers said, and we laughed. I smiled a bit again as we walked back to the fire to warm ourselves.

(Beah 2007, 150–151)

Can anyone read this without feeling revolted? Admittedly, I have taken it out of context, which may magnify its stomach-turning effect. However, reading it in context didn't lessen its impact on me. All of the sympathy for the young narrator that I had built up as he recounted his travails—his terror in the face of natural and human dangers, his rage at much of what he witnessed, and the hardship that strangers gratuitously inflicted on him—was shaken by this single paragraph. Although I knew very well that this was a war in which neither side took prisoners—captured opponents were always killed, sometimes by brutal means—nothing in the events that preceded this scene quite prepared me for it. Nor had anything in my experience of anger and recreational drugs readied me to comprehend it emotionally.

A few lines below, on the very same page of the book, Beah is in the care of professionals at a rehabilitation center, Benin Home. His story continues as follows:

> In the morning I would feel one of the staff members wrap a blanket around me saying, "This isn't your fault, you know. It really isn't. You'll get through this."
>
> (Beah 2007, 151)

Not his fault? Callously murdering at least eight people? Laughing at their death throes? Schooled in American middle-class patterns of feeling and thought, I'm quick to notice and admire intelligence, self-reliance, and responsible agency. Thus, my affective and intellectual toolkit combined with my revulsion at the galvanizing scene Beah had just described to spotlight and reinforce my memory of those parts of his story that demonstrated his maturity.

My feelings about Beah couldn't settle—war criminal or victimized child?

4. IMAGINATIVE RESISTANCE TO A CHILD SOLDIER'S STORY

Although Robinson has little to say about imagination, it's clear that her account of emotionally understanding narrative assumes that readers are imagining the events depicted in the text that they are affectively following.[14] For this reason, I'll preface my considered interpretation of these two passages with discussion of some questions about imagination that Beah's book raises.

Recent work on imaginative resistance provides an illuminating way to frame my affective dissonance in response to the passages I quoted in section 3. For Hume, imaginative resistance sets in when moral scruples obstruct a reader's ability to take up an author's invitation to imagine and appreciate a depiction of morally abominable conduct. Tamar Gendler expands the scope of the phenomenon: "any sort of case where subjects find it unexpectedly difficult to (bring themselves to) imagine what an author describes, or to accept such a claim as true in the story" (2009, 351). Many recent discussions of imaginative resistance center on works of fiction that ask readers to imagine that norms that are morally abhorrent to them in real life nevertheless hold true in the story. However, Hume does not confine his view to fiction, and some of the most promising current accounts of imaginative resistance apply to nonfiction stories and fiction stories alike. It seems clear to me, moreover, that nonfiction victims' stories, perhaps because they diverge so markedly from the worlds their audience members typically inhabit, can give rise to imaginative resistance.

A consensus has emerged that the problem of imaginative resistance is a cluster of four problems. One of them is clearly irrelevant to victims' autobiographical stories, and another is tangential to the role victims' stories can play in the politics of human rights. The fictionality puzzle, which asks why authorial authority in fiction prevails in positing outlandish factual matters but not in positing outrageous moral beliefs, is irrelevant to nonfiction victims' stories (Gendler 2009, 352). The aesthetic value puzzle, which asks whether morally deviant contents are detrimental to the aesthetic value of texts, would be relevant only to victims' stories that (improbably) advocated for human rights abuse or other odious practices (Gendler 2009, 352). In contrast, the imaginability puzzle, which asks "why, in certain cases, readers display a reluctance or inability to engage in some mandated act of imagining," and the phenomenology puzzle, which asks why certain passages "pop out" and prompt overt reader skepticism, raise questions about how victims' stories of human rights abuse enter into human rights discourse (Gendler 2009, 352).

My brief comments on the two passages from Beah's memoir in section 3 anticipate points of potential imaginative resistance. Gendler maintains that imaginative resistance can arise with respect to the introduction of aberrant normative concepts, attributions of mental states, or representations of incidents (2009, 351). So a reader might resist replicating as vile an episode as Beah's "burying alive" incident in the vivid theater of her imagination. Likewise a reader might have trouble giving imaginative life to Beah's casual brutality and amusement at others' agony in the same scene. As well, incorporating the counselor's affirmation of Beah's non-responsibility into the imagined plotline might be problematic, for this soothing credo clashes with widely shared beliefs about the bounds of excusable behavior.

Gendler's account of "pop-out" passages can be plausibly extended to explain the alarms that went off when I first read the rehab counselor's morally reassuring statement upon finding Beah asleep outside the dormitory. Although Gendler grants that imaginative resistance occurs in nonfiction as well as fiction, she nests her discussion of "pop-out" passages in the problem of authorial authority and thus binds her analysis of "pop-out" to works of fiction. I believe, however, that her view of "pop-out" passages can be extricated from the problem of authorial authority and applied to nonfiction.

Gendler characterizes "pop-out" as follows:

> Pop-out passages are passages where, instead of taking the author to be asking her to *imagine* some proposition p that concerns the fictional world, the reader takes the author to be asking her to *believe* a corresponding proposition p^* that concerns the actual world.
>
> (2006, 159)

Typical "pop-out" passages are editorializing statements—such as "so-and-so did the right thing"—that are ascribed to the narrator of, as opposed to a character in, the story. When such appraisals are superfluous because they are implicit in the plot or proscribed because they conflict with the plot, they provoke imaginative resistance (2006, 161–162). This resistance does not go unnoticed, for encountering imaginative resistance to a "pop-out" passage is associated with a distinctive phenomenology. When readers decline the seeming invitation to believe p^*, Gendler says that they "respond . . . with something like 'That's what you think!'" (2009, 352).

In the same vein, my initial response to "This isn't your fault, you know. It really isn't" was something like "Are you kidding?" Although Beah doesn't put these words in the mouth of the narrator, he attributes them to an authority figure. Insofar as readers are disposed to trust the judgment of a trained, experienced counselor, they may well feel that they are implicitly being urged to agree with his pronouncement. Yet, in close proximity to Beah's confession to committing a gruesome atrocity, the counselor's affirmation of his innocence sparks resistance.

Both Julia Driver and Karsten Stueber argue that imaginative resistance arises when a story lacks textual material sufficient to enable the imaginative exercise to go forward. According to Driver, readers assume that "the world described by the author is complete *for the purposes of understanding the story*" (2008, 305). So, given that people take their moral beliefs especially seriously, readers will refuse to imagine endorsement of incompatible norms unless the story supplies good reasons to accept those norms (2008, 304, 306). Yet, as Driver notes, reading stories could not be morally edifying unless it were possible for writers to provide readers with good reasons to adopt moral views antagonistic to their own (2008, 306; for an example, see Chapter 2, section 4). Is the counselor's reassurance a case in point?

Driver's view complements Gendler's explanation of why the counselor's dismissal of Beah's responsibility pops out. To be sure, the counselor's reassurance comes across as editorializing—and ethically dubious editorializing at that.[15] But in addition, at that point in Beah's story, readers don't yet have anything like sufficient reason to absolve him of fault, nor do they have anything like sufficient reason to view such a consoling utterance as a wise treatment intervention. So suspicion takes hold, along with imaginative resistance. As we'll see in section 5, this noncompliant reader response foreshadows the assessment that Beah himself eventually reaches of his entanglement in the war crimes of the army that conscripted him.

Stueber situates the thesis that narrative deficiencies account for imaginative resistance in a simulationist framework. Briefly, he holds that understanding another person involves imaginatively taking on board the other's beliefs, desires, and moral commitments while quarantining those of your beliefs, desires, and moral commitments that don't match those of the other (2011, 169). Having adopted the other's perspective in this way, you're now in a position to imaginatively consider how the other is thinking about a situation (2011, 170). When a story fails to supply sufficient information to enable readers to quarantine their psychological attributes and moral beliefs and input those of the protagonist, they experience imaginative resistance to claims about the protagonist's state of mind or moral convictions that conflict with their own beliefs (2011, 172–173).

Stueber's approach helps make sense of the obstacles to imagining the post-battle actions of the soldiers, as well as Beah's cavalier attitude toward what they had done. How could people be so angry that they would force their adversaries to dig their own graves and then bury them alive? How could anyone be so high that he would have no qualms whatsoever about torturing people this way—in fact, just the opposite, would take pleasure, even find humor in the suffering he had helped inflict?

In thinking about this scene, I am struck by how easily imaginable it is in one respect and how unimaginable it is in another. What is all but impossible not to imagine is the torment of the condemned prisoners. And that is because Beah portrays it so compellingly. Lying in their graves-cum-execution chambers, the condemned men gaze up at Beah and his fellow soldiers "with their pale sad eyes." Undeterred, the soldiers shovel heavy, viscous, airless "wet mud" on them. Tied up and buried deep in the mud, the men "fought under the soil with all their might" as they suffocated. Whether or not their struggling heaved or even rippled the surface soil, their effortful, dying groans reached Beah's ears. Readers might prefer not to imagine this nightmarish scenario, but Beah's evocative writing blocks escape. I defy any reader not to imaginatively register how utterly terrified, desolate, and wretched these men were.

In contrast, Beah does almost nothing to render the soldiers' motives and attitudes intelligible. They were angry. They were high. Readers might add, "War is hell." Still, the soldiers' actions and their sick humor at the expense of their victims are mystifying. As Stueber would say, Beah doesn't give readers enough information about the soldiers' personalities or their reasons for fighting this war for readers to be able to simulate their perspective(s). Instead of being quarantined, readers' traits of character and moral beliefs flood the scene, and produce imaginative resistance.

Rather than criticizing this absence of detail as a narrative deficiency, however, I commend it. For it functions to mobilize readers' capacity for imaginative resistance, thus ensuring that the memoir makes no excuse for the squad's conduct. Beah doesn't say so outright, but his sparse portrayal of his and the other soldiers' point of view—conjoined as it is to his rich portrayal of their victims' suffering—leaves little doubt that he is recounting a war crime. In other words, the omissions in Beah's text that might otherwise be considered narrative defects actually redound to his credit, both as a highly sophisticated writer and as a morally sensitive human being.

Although Beah confronts his readers with the possibility that he bears no responsibility for his participation in the burying alive episode, he does not in any way imply approval of what he and the others did. Still, his book asks readers to understand that a decent, thoughtful youth enthusiastically joined in that atrocity. In my judgment, *A Long Way Gone* achieves that aim. The preceding discussion of imaginative resistance makes a start in the direction of understanding the power of narratively elicited affective dissonance to raise questions about the moral status of individuals who are both perpetrators and victims. I now turn to showing how affectively interpreting the two passages I quoted against the background of the narrative as a whole can guide a productive process of moral reflection and resolution.

5. EMOTIONALLY UNDERSTANDING A CHILD SOLDIER'S STORY

There is no question that my revulsion at the burying alive scene—and, note, it was definitely conscious and decidedly bodily—was justified by the text. Although Beah matter-of-factly recounts what happened after that fierce, hard-won firefight, his description compels readers to empathetically imagine the suffering of the prisoners, and his measured tone doesn't diminish the emotional impact of the episode. Indeed, this passage stirs such potent and unequivocally condemnatory affect that I found it difficult to resist experiencing it as climactic—difficult to suppress my inclination to let my revulsion suffuse everything else that I had read before and to reconfigure my responses to it. Exactly how old, I wondered, was this boy when this incident took place? Hadn't he proven himself extraordinarily resourceful during an extended period of surviving, sometimes alone, in the rain forest foraging for food and eluding savage beasts? Just how badly can marijuana and the addictive drugs he was taking warp an individual's personality?

Beah's self-inculpating revelations in this single unforgettable paragraph temporarily superseded the panoply of feelings and understandings about him that my earlier reading had prompted. In Velleman's terms, I was tempted to take my revulsion to be a "conclusory emotion," even though I was nowhere near the end of Beah's book. Furthermore, that my revulsion had the power to raise doubts in my mind about what it means to classify Beah (or anyone) as a "child soldier" lends support to my earlier observation that vibrantly conscious affective appraisals can have a disproportionate influence on your interpretation of a text and on your judgments about the real or fictional personages who populate the story (see section 2 of this chapter). It doesn't seem strange, therefore, that the exculpatory sentiment expressed by the rehab counselor in a passage immediately following the burying alive passage would aggravate my affective disorientation.

Stuck in this affective impasse, I reread earlier parts of Beah's book, seeking to reconcile Beah's fine sensibility with the merciless depravity of the burying alive scene. Robinson would characterize my project as an effort to juxtapose my emotional abhorrence of the atrocity and my emotional disquiet at the thought of Beah's blamelessness in order to "regestalt" my understanding of Beah's life prior to his recollection of this horrific incident.

To reprise Beah's story in light of my responses to the two quoted passages is to witness the dissolution of his personality as a result of severe trauma. Beah and his pals are just kids who play marbles, wrestle in fun, and so forth (2007, 59). Yet, for years, once the war reaches their village, they are never out of danger. Beah expresses fear very convincingly—"Even the air seemed to want to attack me and break my neck" (2007, 49). The boys' emotions are labile, as if an affect switch were flipping—causing surges of feeling to alternate with numbness. One moment, they're all crying and grieving for a frail, elderly man who has helped them, who is dying, and whom they have just left behind; the next moment they are playfully horsing around and joyously singing; then suddenly they go silent (2007, 89–90). When triggered, Beah's anger is combustible, capable of igniting frenzied aggression (2007, 95, 96, 112, 133).

Eventually, he and the other boys reach a village where they expect to be reunited with their families. But instead they come upon a massacre that is still playing out as the last living people dash from burning buildings in flames (2007, 93–95). When Beah learns that his parents and brothers are among the dead, his responses bolt from paralyzed shock to crazed pugnacity to paroxysmal rage (2007, 95). Afterward, Beah begins to suffer from migraines and flashbacks, symptoms that let up once he starts consuming a steady army diet of pot, cocaine, and narcotics, but that worsen dramatically once he has been separated from the army (2007, 101–103, 121, 160, 184–185).

In biomedical terms, Beah had succumbed to post-traumatic stress disorder (PTSD). After recalling the burying alive incident, he remembers that his skin had been repeatedly grazed and bruised by bullets during the engagement that preceded it, but that he was "too drugged and traumatized" to notice how close to being killed he had been (2007, 151). Most of the second half of Beah's memoir is devoted to tracing the course of his recovery from PTSD. Throughout his stay at the UNICEF rehab facility and to this day, he is plagued by horrifying flashback memories of what the war did to his family and what he did as a warrior. The burying alive incident is but one of his shattering war memories.

To the best of my recollection, Beah never states that he was diagnosed with PTSD. Yet, my realization that Beah must have been suffering from PTSD after reviewing the history he describes revived my sympathy for him, for it recentered his vulnerability and his youth, accented what he had endured as opposed to how well he had coped, and recontextualized my moral revulsion. In other words, the diagnostic category counterbalanced my revulsion and pressed me to reconsider my initial skeptical response to the counselor's assertion of his blamelessness.

As it turns out, though, Beah doesn't welcome absolution. The rehab staff's catchphrase, "it's not your fault," infuriates him (2007, 140, 148, 151, 160, 165). Because he had taken care of himself for years in the face of desperation and deprivation, Beah experiences being told that he wasn't in control as an affront to his character and competence. Moreover, he resents being removed from his army unit. His squad had become his surrogate family (2007, 126). By mastering military techniques, he gained the respect of his superiors and was awarded the rank of junior lieutenant (2007, 125). Killing members of the rebel force that had murdered his family gave him the satisfaction of avenging their deaths (2007, 199). So naturally, the patronizing, infantilizing therapeutic refrain angered and alienated him.

Insipid and simplistic as the counselor's pronouncement was, Beah ultimately conceives a more complex, modulated understanding of the moral significance of his actions. Although Beah gradually comes to believe that he really was a child and was not responsible for what he had done, he nevertheless feels guilty (2007, 165–166). By refusing the solace of guiltlessness and owning the stain of guilt, Beah finds a way to acknowledge his own victimization without sacrificing his dignity as a moral agent. He was forced to commit the crimes he did, but commit them he did. So he doesn't allow himself to wipe his conscience clean. He takes a measure of responsibility for his complicity, though he couldn't have avoided it and no one would be justified in punishing him for it.

Alas, Beah did not gain release from the anguish of flashback memories and the sting of guilt as readily as his memoir augmented my emotional repertoire, set my affective responses at rest, and dispelled my moral misgivings. In this and the previous section, I've sketched some prospective benefits of affectively engaging with victims' stories. In the next section, I'll sort through some hazards of emotionally understanding victims' stories with respect to building a culture of human rights.

6. HUMANITARIANISM, HUMAN RIGHTS, AND AFFECTIVE UNDERSTANDING

Benin Home, the rehabilitation center where Beah was taken, is a therapeutic institution. It is charged with healing the physical damage and psychic wounds incurred by former child soldiers. The staff there shepherded Beah through withdrawal, sheltered and supported him emotionally, and facilitated his confrontation with and partial reconciliation to his past. After years of mayhem, his emotions slowly stabilized—so much so that after eight months he was "repatriated" to his uncle's family in Freetown (2007, 179 ff). Shortly after, though, rebel forces invaded the capitol, and Beah became terrified that he would again be recruited to fight or be killed if he refused (2007, 205, 209). Still a teenager, he again fled the war—this time bribing and conniving his way into neighboring Guinea and then to New York City. There Laura Simms, a woman he had befriended not long before while he was participating in a UN conference on the problems of children, took him into her home and eventually adopted him (2007, 196, 197, 209).

Beah's memoir imparts an indelible affective understanding of the collapse of human rights in the midst of armed conflict, as well as the urgent need for and the utter puniness of humanitarian interventions. Grateful as he is for his own good fortune, Beah denies readers the false comfort of clinging to the story of his halting emotional recovery and harrowing escape from his war-torn homeland. By stressing that one of his friends had already returned to the army and presumably a life of war crimes palliated by morally anesthetizing pharmaceuticals, Beah ensures that readers will finish his memoir with mixed feelings—gratified, to be sure, that one boy has been spared, yet distraught that many, if not all, of the other boys will cycle back into combat, drug addiction, and human rights abuse. Invaluable as aid workers' humanitarian efforts are, their achievements fall far short of a solution to the conflagration that engulfed Sierra Leone. In this respect, A Long Way Gone departs from Amsterdam and Bruner's formula and instead resembles the hybrid victims' stories I discussed in Chapter 2, for it perspicuously represents a moral void and issues a resounding moral demand.

Still, it is necessary to ask whether A Long Way Gone contributes in any direct way to readers' understanding of human rights norms—say, the rights of the child. Jean-Jacques Rousseau is among the very few philosophers who try to articulate the concept of a right in narrative form. So I'll preface my reflections on A Long Way Gone's engagement with human rights discourse by reviewing Rousseau's treatment of this topic.

In Emile, Rousseau endeavors to capture the concept of a right narratively and affectively in his proposal for teaching his young pupil about property rights ([1762]1979, 97–99). Rousseau presents a scenario in which Emile decides he wants to garden, turns the soil in the gardener's plot, and plants beans there. Rousseau and Emile tend the seedlings and take pleasure in the growth of the plants. All the while, Rousseau is telling Emile that the beans belong to him because he has worked to cultivate them and imbued them with "his very self." But one day they visit the garden and find the soil tilled and their bean plants turned under. Emile is chagrined, and he feels the "sorrow and bitterness" of injustice. All of his work has come to naught. When the gardener arrives, Emile protests. But the gardener replies emphatically that it is Emile who has wronged him by destroying the precious melon seedlings he had previously planted. Rousseau intervenes, asking the gardener to forgive them and suggesting a compromise that would allow Emile to use a corner of the garden in exchange for half the crop. The kindly gardener replies that Emile may use a designated area free of charge provided that he agrees not to wreck the gardener's crops.

Robinson's theory of emotion explains why subjecting Emile to this experiential pedagogy, accompanied as it is by Rousseau's rights-saturated interpretation of what's going on, might effectively engrave the rights of property and exchange on the boy's (and perhaps a reader's) heart. Inasmuch as there is no introspectively distinctive constellation of sorrow and bitterness that only injustice prompts, her theory classifies the sorrow and bitterness of being wronged as a cognitively complex emotion that can only be recognized for what it is in virtue of cognitive processing and naming. Rousseau's text supports Robinson's view, for in this passage Rousseau is rather ham-fistedly teaching Emile to connect the concept of injustice to his emotional response and the pattern of events that brought it about. If Emile learns to identify sorrow and bitterness stirred by certain sorts of behaviors with injustice, he will gain the ability to affectively recognize violations of property rights, whether in everyday life or in stories.

However successful Rousseau's educational methods might be with Emile, I'm inclined to think that Rousseau's story may leave many readers cold. His doctrinaire commentary and negotiation to strike a fair bargain with the gardener are irritatingly didactic. His writing doesn't entice readers to care about or viscerally imagine the fortunes of Emile or the gardener. For what it's worth, this passage makes me feel sorry for Emile and the gardener for falling into Rousseau's clutches and contempt for Rousseau for engineering Emile's distress and missing out on the gardener's delicious melons.

A Long Way Gone does not betray a comparable didactic impulse. Quite the contrary, it sets up a dialectic between the text and readers' affect that might initiate or substantiate, depending on where you start from, a case for the rights of the child. It gestures toward a right to nurturance and a right not to be conscripted into military service, but it stops well short of formulating and defending these rights. The limitations of narrative in general and victims' stories in particular raise questions about how Beah's story compares to those of other victims and whether consigning important moral questions to readers' affective interpretations is advisable.

Because Beah's memoir is the story of a single boy, readers might wonder whether his experience is typical. Extensive journalistic coverage confirms that countless children are orphaned and witness atrocities during wars, and many are drafted into militias, plied with mind-altering substances, and compelled to commit atrocities. As in Beah's case, PTSD is woefully common among these children.[16] It seems reasonable to infer, then, that my emotional responses to salient elements of Beah's story would transfer to the stories of many other children caught in war zones, and my responses suggest that there are hardly any circumstances that could justify putting children at risk of the deracination of PTSD.

If so, someone who is open to the idea that children have rights to nurturance and to be kept out of harm's way is likely to find independent support for those norms in her emotional understanding of Beah's memoir. But there is much more to the concept of human rights and to the more specialized concept of children's rights than these affective responses signal. Consequently, extensive conceptual mediation is needed to access human rights norms from a study of Beah's story.

Affective understanding can at best intimate and may be a poor gauge of one belief that is necessary to conceptualize rights that children possess *qua* children—namely, the belief that juveniles are incapable of rational consent, never mind rational consent to dangerous activities. It might seem that this idea hinges on affective understanding. But two prevalent Western affective deformations are apt to mislead thinking about children's rights. Culturally normative sentimentality about children is one obstacle to undistorted affective understanding. Another is nostalgia for the idyllic childhoods that many middle-class Americans profess to have had. Because these widespread affective biases are liable to hijack affective attention and skew affective understanding, explicit cognitive monitoring is necessary in order to avoid misplaced or exaggerated responses to children's misfortunes.[17]

In addition, neither the concept of rational consent nor the boundary line between childhood and adulthood is derivable from emotional understanding, although both are affectively valenced. Feelings of approbation are associated with free choice, and tender feelings are associated with children. However, the emotions that instances of free choice or childhood arouse presuppose conceptual sophistication. Like Emile's bitter and sorrowful feelings before he has been convinced that he hasn't been treated unjustly, they are cognitively complex emotions.

Here, another layer of disjuncture between affectively understanding victims' stories and the concept of human rights abuse comes into view. Beah describes an explosion of human misery, but respect for human rights is not equivalent to the obverse of humanitarian cataclysm. Because rights are claimable entitlements, a human rights regime requires more than the adventitious absence of avoidable, unjustifiable human suffering (Feinberg 1979, 91). But it is doubtful that the concept of an entitlement that ought to be politically secured can be articulated narratively and grasped emotionally.

Taking the question of emotional understanding first, I agree with Charles Taylor that moral revulsion—say, upon reading Beah's burying alive episode—doesn't feel the same as nauseated revulsion—say, in the presence of putrid food (Taylor 1989, 6). By itself, however, my affective response doesn't tell me whether I am apprehending a violation of a right or some other type of moral debacle. In section 4, I urged that Beah's withholding of sufficient detail about the mindsets of the soldiers combines with the plethora of detail he provides about the suffering of their prisoners to strongly suggest that he is describing a war crime—a violation of the rights of enemy combatants. Yet, absent a familiarity with human rights and the laws of war, no textual detail in Beah's depiction and nothing intrinsic to my affective response to it obliges me to understand this moral infraction as human rights abuse.

To represent a right as such, it seems, a narrative must implicitly or explicitly invoke the concept of a right. As Rousseau shows us, it is perfectly possible to devise a story modeled on the concept of a right—that is, a story in which a character feels entitled to certain forms of respect and makes corresponding claims on others, in which other characters regard these claims as probative or reject them, and so forth. Victims of human rights abuse could follow Rousseau's tendentious example and structure their stories to represent key constituents of the concept of a right. These stories might have compelling plots, gripping suspense, and stylistic refinement. Yet, they would merely illustrate human rights precepts and serve as object lessons.

No doubt there is a place for illustrative victims' stories in moral education.[18] However, a drawback of such victims' stories is that they interfere with the kind of free-form processes of bodily affective appraisal that, according to Robinson, conduce to moral exploration and discovery. Thus, I lean toward the view that when victims' stories are addressed to audiences receptive to safeguarding human rights, authors can heighten their impact by resisting the temptation to decree which moral categories befit their experience. Victims' stories that encourage the flow of inchoate affective responses release readers' imaginative capacities from rigid preconceptions and afford readers an opportunity to apply culturally available concepts in novel ways and to reach for fresh moral insight. Through affectively charged processes of conceptual appropriation and recombination, readers may be moved to revamp standing norms, to give serious consideration to alternative norms, or to conceive innovative norms.

Because there is no corporeal affective equivalent of injustice—that is, no type of affective appraisal that uniquely corresponds to violations of rights—victims of human rights abuse face constraints on what they can expect to achieve by telling their stories unless they resort to preempting the indeterminacy of affectively guided interpretation and deliver a determinate human rights message. Beah opts not to adopt this strategy. He lets his story speak for itself. His memoir makes readers privy to his outpouring of grief over the loss of his family, the zombie-like nonchalance with which he kills, and the acute pangs of guilt that grip him because of the murders he committed as a conscript. Beyond that, he lets human rights concepts and norms that are culturally available to his audience do the work of linking his story to the rights of the child, the rights of civilians in combat zones, and the rights of enemy combatants. By steering clear of casting his story in a human rights mold, he entrusts readers with the responsibility to take up the difficult issues his story raises.[19] Thus, his memoir catalyzes moral reflection by drawing attention to moral concerns that may be unfamiliar and raising questions about the adequacy of existing rights protocols to address them. But, as we'll see in the concluding section, Beah also hints at a solution to the quandaries he poses.

7. A HUMAN RIGHT TO PEACE?

From the beginning of the human rights regime in the mid-twentieth century, major human rights documents, including the *Universal*

Declaration, the *Covenant on Economic, Social, and Cultural Rights,* and the *Covenant on Civil and Political Rights,* spotlight world peace as one of three core values underpinning human rights. In these documents, realizing human rights is seen as necessary to ensuring peace. Conversely, Beah's story shows that war all but guarantees a maelstrom of human rights abuse.

At the end of *A Long Way Gone,* no one's human rights have been vindicated except perhaps Beah's rights as a refugee—the sad, auxiliary rights that come into play when all your other rights have been trounced. Fittingly, then, Beah's memoir ends on a note of paralyzing despair admixed with tenuous hope. He retells a story he heard more than once as a boy:

> There was a hunter who went into the bush to kill a monkey. He had looked for only a few minutes when he saw a monkey sitting comfortably in a tree. The monkey didn't pay him any attention, not even when his footsteps on the dried leaves rose and fell as he neared. When he was close enough and behind a tree where he could clearly see the monkey, he raised his rifle and aimed. Just when he was about to pull the trigger, the monkey spoke: "If you shoot me, your mother will die, and if you don't, your father will die." The monkey resumed its position, chewing its food, and every so often scratched its head or the side of its belly.
>
> (Beah 2007, 217)

At this point, the storyteller always asked the listening children what they would do, and no child ever answered (Beah 2007, 217–218). Still, Beah thought hard about the dilemma. Here is the last line of his book:

I concluded to myself that if I were the hunter, I would shoot the monkey so that it would no longer have the chance to put other hunters in the same predicament.

(Beah 2007, 218)

This folktale of tragic choice allegorizes the vortex of implacable violence in Sierra Leone from which Beah had just narrowly escaped, and Beah's "solution" at the tender age of seven is his fervent wish for peace—a wish that stopped coming true five years later. Then he learned all too well why he was right to put such a high value on peace: Human rights are an ignes fatuus without it.

Chapter 4

Empathy and the Meanings
of Human Rights in Human Lives

I began to scream; I shrieked. He pushed me in that room onto the bed. He raped me. Because I was shrieking, he stuffed a piece of paper in my mouth. Later I didn't have the strength to scream or do anything. He took his weapon and aimed it at my forehead. He told me he would murder me if I yelled. I didn't have any strength left. I tried to wiggle loose as best I could. He kept going until deep into the night. I don't know exactly. I lost any sense of time. When he wanted to sleep, he stayed on top of me. He was always there. He didn't want to sleep. There was a table with handcuffs; he cuffed me to it so I couldn't escape while he slept. He was on top of me; he had a gun he hid under the pillow.

Edina, quoted in *Surviving the Bosnian Genocide*,
by Selma Leydesdorff, p. 61

One of them came and hit me in the face. Really hard. I think he hit me from the left. When he hit me, it felt like something broke. Then my nose began to bleed. I saw blood coming out of my nose, and after that I know and remember nothing. . . . I do remember things as in a dream, and in that dream I was fighting. I shoved something in front of me away, I don't know, but in the dream, I was in pain here [she points to her lower abdomen]. Here. I opened my eyes and it was day. It was morning. I tried to turn over, but I couldn't move my head at all. I didn't know what was wrong with me. I couldn't see where my children were. I couldn't move my hands, legs, nothing moved, and I heard my little boy crying. . . . I saw him and then lost consciousness again. . . . When I came to the second time, I saw that I was bloody and covered with bruises. My legs . . . blood everywhere.

> Hamra, quoted in *Surviving the Bosnian Genocide,*
> by Selma Leydesdorff, pp. 172–173

Victims' stories of human rights abuse ask us not only to take in what happened but also to care about it. Since gleaning nothing more than a bunch of facts from a victim's story, perhaps getting very upset about it, or abstractly connecting it to human rights norms misses at least half the point, it is necessary to consider what capacity might move addressees beyond curiosity about what transpired and enable them to take a moral interest in those events. Empathy stands out as a candidate for this role.

Yet, empathy's reputation as a moral power has come under attack in a number of recent discussions. Simulation theorists find that people empathize only with others who are similar to themselves (Goldman 1992, 35). Neuroscientists find that mirror neurons, which some consider to be the subpersonal basis of empathy, won't fire unless the other's movements resemble motor experience that you yourself have had (Rizzolatti and Craighero 2004, 179; also see Pineda 2009). Jesse Prinz mounts a concerted attack on the claim that empathy is a precondition for moral judgment and discredits empathy's role in moral motivation (2011a, 2011b). J. D. Trout declares that empathy makes us "feel bad for others" but doesn't tell us what to do about it (2009, 42). Catriona Mackenzie and Jackie Leach Scully point to the profound influence of embodiment on cognition and imagination before concluding that able-bodied people usually fail to empathize with severely disabled people (2007, 338).

Undeniably, the simplistic advice to "put yourself in the other's shoes" invites people to project their own experiences and values onto others and thus to do violence to others' distinctive points of view. Worse still, psychologists maintain that people's need to believe in a just world can thwart empathy by inducing them to derogate victims of injustice or blame them for their suffering (Furnham 2003; for discussion of these phenomena, see Chapter 5, section 1). All of these criticisms must be taken seriously. Nevertheless, I argue that empathetic engagement with stories told by victims of human rights abuse plays a vital part in promoting understanding of and commitment to human rights norms and that no other moral power can replace empathy in this role.

It has become a truism that the philosophical and social scientific literatures are awash in variant definitions of empathy (e.g., Aaltola 2013, 76–77; Coplan and Goldie 2011; Debes 2015; Gruen 2009, 26; Nussbaum 2001, 301–302, 331; Stueber 2010, 27). So I'll preface my inquiry with a brief review of empathy's roles in various contexts.

Coined for purposes of aesthetic theory, the term *empathy* subsequently found homes in psychology and philosophy, where it took up residence in disparate research programs and practical endeavors. Early in the twentieth century, Robert Vischer invented the term we translate as *empathy* to characterize our experience of artworks as a process of "feeling into" (Debes 2015, 296). Soon thereafter, theorists invoked empathy to explicate our recognition of and access to other minded beings. To this day, philosophers of mind regard empathy as a candidate answer to the problem of other minds (e.g., Goldman 2011; Stueber 2010).[1] How do we know that other minds exist? How do we know what anyone else is thinking or feeling? Or as current philosophical lingo would have it, how is accurate mentalizing or mind-reading possible? Assuming that empathy enables knowledge of other minds, clinical psychologists are trained to use empathy as a therapeutic technique—a means of fathoming clients' psyches.

In contrast, moral philosophers ask about empathy's role in moral epistemology—its contribution to distinguishing right from wrong—as well as its role in moral psychology—its contribution to moral motivation. Some contemporary moral philosophers look to David Hume's and Adam Smith's eighteenth-century discussions of sympathy to anchor their accounts of empathy. Others look to more recent phenomenological approaches—for example, Max Scheler's account of fellow feeling or Edith Stein's account of empathy. Spanning work in the philosophy of mind and ethics, social philosophers invoke empathy to account for social cohesion and coordination. Complementing these philosophical views, experimental psychologists ask what conditions induce empathy and whether empathy motivates helping behavior.

By no means confined to scholarly discourse, *empathy* enters into everyday speech as a term of approbation. To say that a person is empathetic is to say that she is disposed to "resonate" emotionally with others—usually to "share their pain"—and to respond compassionately. Some philosophers call attention to this Anglo-American colloquial usage to guide their accounts of empathy. Likewise, one prong of neuroscientist James Blair's tripartite account of empathy coincides with this conventional understanding. Emotional empathy consists of responding appropriately to others' emotional displays or to descriptions of others' emotionally laden circumstances (2005, 699; 2008, 159–160).[2]

We have inherited a veritable empathy diaspora. Since each of these academic fields poses a different set of questions, and vernacular usage serves still other purposes, conceptions of empathy sited in those disparate projects proliferated. Thus, there is no consensus on whether empathy is a shared emotion or feeling, a type of cognition, or a type of imagination that amalgamates affective, cognitive, and/or conative elements. Rather, there is a welter of terminology and conceptualization that baffles generalizations about the role of empathy in moral life. In view of the chaotic cross-disciplinary and vernacular usages I've sketched, clarity demands a certain amount of stipulation. The account of empathy I'll set out blends key elements from ordinary speech with helpful distinctions that can be traced back to David Hume and Adam Smith.

I begin by presenting Peter Goldie's incisive work on empathy (section 1). Goldie maintains that the simulationist camp in philosophy of mind and moral philosophers who ascribe a motivational or epistemological role to empathy greatly exaggerate what empathy can achieve. Because I find Goldie's critique tremendously powerful, I develop and defend my conception of empathy in the context of his views. While I think that his extremely exacting conception of empathy may well befit the simulationist program he opposes, I doubt that his conception of empathy can be transplanted into ethics without extensive alteration. Thus, my conception of empathy is designed to furnish a view that is closer to colloquial usage and that is better aligned with the concerns of moral philosophy (section 2).

With an account of empathy in hand, it is necessary to consider how empathy enters into moral life (section 3). In contrast to Goldie, who denies that empathy is a moral response, Martha Nussbaum, Nancy Sherman, and Stephen Darwall find a place for empathy in moral relations (Goldie 2000, 215; Sherman 1998; Darwall 1998; Nussbaum 2001). Yet, all agree that empathy does not necessarily lead to virtuous behavior.[3] So it seems inadvisable to locate empathy's chief contribution to moral life in the moral psychology of altruism (section 3A). For this reason, I turn to questions of moral understanding. Catriona Mackenzie and Jackie Leach Scully, who follow Goldie's pre-2011 account of empathy, distrust empathy as moral power. After probing their critique of the claim that empathy enables you to mind-read well enough to grasp the life satisfaction enjoyed by someone whose embodiment differs significantly from your own, I urge that when properly understood, empathy enables you to viscerally comprehend values and disvalues as another person experiences them (section 3B).

My proposal gains support while also facing a powerful challenge from Sonia Kruks's claim that sexed and gendered embodiment facilitates visceral empathy between females and impedes visceral empathy between females and males. In my view, however, well-wrought victims' stories can mediate corporeal differences and enable differently embodied individuals to grasp alternative normative realities (section 4). By taking their cues from what the other communicates about herself and her experience and imagining what she is going through or has been through, people can extend their understanding of the scope of human rights norms as well as their understanding of the urgency of protecting people from human rights abuse. To show how this works, I analyze passages from a German woman's anonymously published diary of the Red Army's mass rape campaign at the end of World War II, *A Woman in Berlin: Eight Weeks in the Conquered City* (section 5).

My aims in the remainder of this chapter are modest, yet not, I think, morally inconsequential (section 6). I argue (1) that empathetic engagement with a victim's story can spotlight elements of common humanity in the midst of a highly individual life trajectory; (2) that empathetic engagement with a victim's story can heighten the empathizer's awareness of just how bad it is to be subjected to a certain form of abuse; and (3) that empathetic engagement with a victim's story can sensitize empathizers to the gravity of ruptures in the human rights regime. By dispelling ignorance of or confusion about victims' moral claims, empathy with victims' stories can erode indifference to them. Empathetically processed, moreover, the horror of the moral void that a victim's story depicts and the urgency of the demand that it issues for a moral response (see Chapter 2, section 7) are viscerally encoded. Consequently, empathy with victims' stories can transform your value system—enabling you to grasp values and disvalues that might previously have been opaque to you and consolidating your grasp of the necessity of respect for human rights.

1. PETER GOLDIE'S CRITIQUE OF EMPATHY

Goldie offers a single account of empathy to address issues in both philosophy of mind and ethics. Thus, his critique of empathy takes aim at two distinct claims. On the one hand, he denies that empathizing is a good way to grasp what others are thinking and feeling. On the other hand, he denies that empathizing is a good basis for moral relations. In order to clarify Goldie's conception of empathy, I need to briefly review the account of empathy that he ascribes to simulationist theories of mind-reading and the grounds for his bleak assessment of empathy's ostensible contribution to mind-reading. However, I leave the defense of simulation theory to others and turn my attention to empathy's prospective contributions to ethics. For purposes of moral philosophy, Goldie develops a series of contrasts between empathy and related concepts, such as sympathy and emotional contagion, and he maintains that sympathetic inquiry into others' needs provides both the information an agent requires to conceive a helpful response and the motivation an agent requires to take helpful action.

To flesh out and ultimately debunk the simulationist account of understanding other minds, Goldie contrasts empathy with other ways in which people imagine one another. For Goldie, the distinction between "in-her-shoes"[4] imagining and empathetic imagining is crucial (2000, 195–203; 2007, 79; 2011, 302–303). Although both are forms of central imagining or perspective-shifting—that is, the imaginer constructs her imagined scenario as if she occupied another person's position—they are fundamentally and importantly different. When you engage in in-her-shoes imagining, you centrally imagine how you would feel if you were in the other's situation. You shift your circumstances but keep your identity. When you empathize, you centrally imagine being another person in a situation different from your own. You shift both your circumstances and your identity. Although in-her-shoes imagining allows you to access another's feelings when the other's relevant traits match your own and the other's situation and options are clear-cut, it's unreliable when the other's psychological profile differs from yours and the other's situation and options are complex. In the latter types of cases, a different imaginative project is called for. And if that imaginative project must be a project of central imagination, it will have to be empathetic imagination.

Alas, Goldie argues, empathizing so understood is impossible.[5] To empathize, you must have a "substantial characterization" of the other—a subtle, detailed portrait of the other's desires, values, abilities, affective dispositions, and so forth—and you must imagine the other as if those attributes were your very own (2000, 195; 2011, 308). In other words, the characterization must remain in the background and must function "holistically," as it does when you're centrally imagining yourself as the protagonist in a scenario (2000, 198–199, 202; 2011, 308–309). Moreover, if empathy is to succeed in anticipating how someone will feel and act, it must take into account non-rational influences on her decisions, such as moods and temptations (2000, 206; 2011, 311–313). Until 2011, Goldie held that empathy is contingently impossible because managing these mushrooming demands exceeds human powers of imagination (2000, 205). In the end, though, he came to believe that empathy is conceptually impossible because an empathizer cannot "operate with the appropriately *full-blooded notion of first-person agency* that is involved in deliberation" (2011, 303). Only the agent can take this stance toward her own subjective states and values, for she alone is authorized to interpret or prioritize them (2011, 313–316). So empathy is necessarily impossible, and simulationist accounts of mind-reading are untenable.

In view of this unconditional repudiation of empathy, it's clear that empathy can have no place in Goldie's moral philosophy.[6] According to Goldie, sympathy or caring about someone's plight, as opposed to sharing her suffering, is ethically key, for it motivates ameliorative action (Goldie 2000, 213–215). In addition to sympathy, Goldie recommends taking what he calls the external perspective on others (2007, 70–72). In order to treat someone well, what you need to do is to assiduously think about her while attending to how her needs, beliefs, and feelings and her perspective on the world differ from yours (2000, 181; 2007, 70, 82, 83; 2011, 302).[7] You need to sympathetically dwell *on* the other's state of mind and circumstances in life, not empathetically *in* them. For Goldie (2007, 72, 81, 83), this discipline is an antidote for mistaking the other's feelings and troubles for ones you've experienced, as well as for agentic breakdown due to submersion in the others' feelings and troubles. He notes, though, that thinking about others from the external perspective does not suppress emotion or imagination (2007, 77). Indeed, he has no objection to acentrally "imagining-how-it-is" for someone else (2011, 305–306).

I agree with Goldie that sympathy is a moral response, but I think that his conception of sympathy is a bit narrow. I take the death of a friend's loved one to be a paradigmatic occasion for sympathy (Meyers 1994, 31–32). In this situation, "I'm sorry for your loss" standardly expresses sympathy. If sincere, these words betoken concern for the bereaved person, together with willingness to be of help.[8] As Goldie points out, this response need not be correlated with any sense of loss on your own part (2000, 214). Still, there is another familiar form of sympathy that does bring shared feelings into play – feeling along with another. This type of sympathy presupposes both caring about the other person's well-being and being attuned to her sensibility.[9] It may, but need not, be reinforced by sharing the person's reasons for feeling as she does. Sympathizing with a bereaved person in this way, you too would experience feelings of grief.

Like registering someone's suffering and being ready to help her, feeling along with another person is a moral response. That's because, faced with adversity, people often need to experience the community of affect that such sympathy creates. Neither of these modes of mutuality—neither relieving someone's workaday burdens nor joining her in mourning—more properly counts as sympathy, for both can be a great solace. I note, though, that neither form of sympathy comes free of moral liabilities. Goldie's conception of sympathy as an emotion that motivates alleviating others' suffering can go wrong if someone's suffering is deserved, and it can be futile if someone's suffering is unavoidable. The additional type of sympathy I propose can go wrong if you sympathize with overwrought or misplaced emotions that may in turn warp your perceptions and lead you to act unwisely.

Although sympathetic "feeling-along-with" someone resembles emotional contagion, neither type of sympathy is identical to emotional contagion. Emotional contagion occurs when you are merely caused to feel as someone else does (Goldie 2000, 189–191). Some philosophers treat emotional contagion as a rudimentary, automatic form of empathy (Darwall 2011, 8–9; Prinz 2011a, 212; Slote 2007, 13). However, I agree with Goldie that emotional contagion is a distinct phenomenon, for you need not care about others or share others' reasons for feeling as they do in order to "catch" their affective state. Continuing the bereavement case, you might detest the deceased and her family, yet you might become sad as a result of the somber tone of the funeral and the grim visages and the weeping of mourners. Unlike sympathy, emotional contagion isn't a moral response at all.

I also agree with Goldie about the moral limitations of in-her-shoes imagining. You imagine yourself just as you are—your strengths and weaknesses, your value system and desires, your commitments to others, and so forth—transposed into someone else's life situation.[10] Insofar as you are different from the person who actually occupies that position, in-her-shoes imagining reveals more about you and your subjectivity than it does about the other individual's identity and subjectivity.[11] Nevertheless, in-her-shoes imagining has its place. The ability to imaginatively project yourself into a different social position is indispensable to personal autonomy. Without this capacity, you'd have little basis for judging whether a contemplated change would be good for you to undertake. It can also enable you to furnish a certain type of advice. Sometimes, when a person asks for advice, she is asking for your distinctive perspective on the issue—that is, what you would do if the decision were yours to make. Here, what's being sought is your opinion based on in-her-shoes imagining. Other times, an advice-seeker wants to know what you think would be the best thing for her to do, given her particular needs, desires, values, and so forth. Providing this second type of advice requires empathy.[12]

Although admonishing someone to put herself in someone else's shoes is a colloquial way to exhort someone to be more empathetic, in-her-shoes imagining differs from empathy, for it has liabilities that empathy doesn't share. When mistaken for empathy, in-her-shoes imagining can be misleading if not harmful—misleading if you falsely believe that you understand someone else; harmful if you injure someone by acting on your mistaken beliefs. As Goldie points out, in-her-shoes imagining can satisfactorily substitute for empathy only when the relevant features of your motivational economy coincide with the other person's, but such a coincidence is unlikely when you are struggling with a difficult moral problem.

2. A CONCEPTION OF EMPATHY FOR MORAL PHILOSOPHY

As noted earlier, stipulation is necessary to disambiguate the term *empathy*. But arbitrary stipulation can be minimized, and I intend to do so as much as possible by motivating and formulating my view in light of past and contemporary philosophical discussions and current colloquial usage. Because Peter Goldie's work on empathy repeatedly accents how different the person you want to understand may be from you and how morally necessary it is to apprehend those differences, his thought holds promise for an account of the moral insights to be gained from victims' stories of human rights abuse. As we have seen, though, Goldie is an empathy skeptic who denies that empathy can serve as a route to moral understanding. To make my case for empathy, then, I'll need to argue that Goldie's alternative to empathy—sympathetic imagining from the external point of view— poses problems comparable to those posed by empathy, that a more capacious conception of empathy is defensible for purposes of moral philosophy, and that empathetic imagining augments moral insight in ways he overlooks. In this section, I aim to provide an account of empathy that recommends itself as a plausible human capacity and also in virtue of its fruitfulness with respect to learning from victims' stories.

Recall that Goldie holds that empathy requires developing a "substantial characterization" of the other person, casting yourself in the role of the other so characterized, grasping the other's life story or a significant narrative thread from the larger story, and "centrally imagining" the narrative, perhaps continuing the narrative, as if you were the other (2000, 195–198; 2011, 308). To empathize, then, is to imagine a real-life scenario from within someone else's viewpoint.[13]

Developing a substantial characterization of another person isn't easy unless you already know her well. Not only do you need to become familiar with the interplay of her beliefs, emotions, desires, and values, you also need to understand her circumstances and how she experiences them. For Goldie, this characterization must not only be "deep," it must function "holistically" while you're centrally imagining the other (2000, 202; 2011, 308–309). In other words, you must identify with this characterization so thoroughly that you can imaginatively experience the narrative as if you were the other person. A formidable challenge, to be sure, for Goldie contends that you must temporarily suspend your own cognitive, affective, conative, and normative viewpoint in order to think and feel as the other thinks and feels (Goldie 2000, 198–199). He takes this to mean that adducing propositional information about the other person during the imaginative process defeats empathy, for introducing such material interrupts the flow of the imagined narrative. In work preceding his conclusion that empathy is altogether impossible, Goldie likens empathizing to method acting that is confined to the arena of imagination (Goldie 2000, 178). I find much of value in Goldie's account, but I take exception to it in a number of respects.

First, I am at a loss to understand what is gained morally speaking by resolutely maintaining a third-person perspective on another's state of mind and "imagining-how-it- is" for her (acentrally imagining another person), rather than empathetically tracking her subjective experience (centrally imagining it). Moreover, I doubt that the line between acentrally imagining someone and centrally imagining her is as sharp as Goldie maintains because acentral imagination and central imagination of other individuals tend to blur phenomenologically.

Suppose you are imagining your friend receiving news of her promotion to a coveted new position. You certainly can acentrally imagine her behavior—her ear-to-ear grin, her characteristic exclamations, and so forth—and you can think that she's feeling gleeful. But to imagine *her* glee, you must centrally imagine her subjectivity—that is, you must empathize. What, after all, would it be like to acentrally imagine someone else's feelings of glee? Of course you could imagine feeling gleeful yourself, and you could infuse your picture of her happy face and joyous utterances with that feeling. However, her feeling gleeful isn't an affective tint coloring her behaviors. It's a gleeful feeling that she's experiencing. Whereas your infusion strategy misses her subjectivity, empathetically imagining her glee attends to her subjectivity as such. Consequently, your third-person perspective on your friend is likely to segue into her first-person perspective as you attempt to grasp her experience. That is, imagining-how-it-is for her is likely to segue into empathetically imagining her, and much is lost by limiting yourself to imagining-how-it-is for her—specifically, the poignancy of her interiority.

I suspect, moreover, that the only way to sustain a clear distinction between central and acentral imagination of another's point of view would require dropping the imaginative component of third-person apprehensions of the other and adopting a purely analytical approach to her. However, there is reason to question the feasibility of excluding imagination from interpersonal engagement except when the other is absent. Recent studies of the role of off-line motor emulation of others' movements and expressions in perception suggest that this visceral form of mimetic imagination operates automatically when the other is present (Wilson and Knoblich 2005).[14] Accordingly, the course of wisdom would seem to be to accept the challenge of constructing an account of imaginative engagement with others that better serves the aim of leading a morally worthy life.

Second, it troubles me that Goldie's pre-2011 account renders empathy virtually impossible, almost mystical, when it's not trivial.[15] In excluding propositional thinking from empathy, he turns empathizing into something like a waking dream in which you're possessed by someone else's identity and a story unfolds from within that perspective. I appreciate Goldie's insistence that empathizing is a demanding imaginative activity. But, outside debates in philosophy of mind, I fail to see what is gained by treating the process of developing a characterization of another person as a precondition for, but not a constituent of, empathy.

Whereas an actor playing a role must, so to speak, shed her identity and become her character for the duration of the performance, you do not fail to empathize by making use of the hermeneutic process of rallying various faculties and feeling your way that Goldie calls "*tâtonnement*" (2000, 189). Given that people aren't transparent to one another, accurate empathy requires gradually building up propositional and intuitive knowledge of the other that is then fed into an imagined scenario, which may in turn be corrected and reimagined after further observation and thought, and so on.[16] In other words, alternating between the first-person perspective of the individual you are empathizing with and your own third-person perspective on her is part and parcel of empathy.

Presumably, empathetic psychotherapists work back and forth between the third-person and the first-person perspectives—characterizing and reasoning about their clients, on the one hand, and imaginatively entering into their emotional lives and patterns of thought, on the other. More casually, because friends constantly accumulate propositional knowledge about one another and become attuned to one another's shifting states of mind, they can empathize with one another with relative ease. Although empathy always requires empathizers to obtain considerable background knowledge concerning the other, empathizing may be more or less difficult, depending on the nature of the relationship between the empathizer and the other. For purposes of engaging in moral relations and for moral theory, there is no reason that empathy must be a pure feat of central imagining.

Third, falling in line with some experimental psychologists (e.g., Hodges and Wegner 1997, 321), Goldie conflates empathy with what I call *sizing a person up*.[17] For Goldie, a key difference between empathy and sympathy is that the latter involves "*caring* about the other's suffering" but the former does not (2000, 214). According to this view, you could empathize with someone who is suffering out of detached curiosity as to what makes her tick and complete your empathetic endeavor indifferent to her weal or woe. I agree with

Goldie that empathy does not entail wanting to provide morally mandated aid to the other. However, ordinary usage suggests that the motivation behind empathy differentiates it from sizing someone up, and, to my way of thinking, experimental psychologists and philosophers would be well advised to follow this lead.

People size each other up for relatively benign as well as nefarious reasons. A shrewd real estate agent tries to figure out how high a price a prospective buyer would be willing to pay. An astute torturer tries to divine a prisoner's vulnerable points. In pursuit of their ends, both might "channel"—that is, centrally imagine—their targets.

But in ordinary speech it would be exceedingly odd to label what they're doing as *empathizing*. Because empathy is considered a morally desirable attribute, saying that someone is empathetic is normally taken to express a measure of moral approval. In many career niches, sharp sizing-up skills are prized, but for tactical rather than moral reasons. In contrast, practitioners of the helping professions are believed to rely on empathy to do their ameliorative work. That we ascribe empathy to good nurses and social workers but not to successful real estate agents and torturers, at least not in their professional capacities, argues for building a presupposition of concern for the other into the concept of empathy.[18]

Accordingly, I propose that empathetic concern is something like taking a humane interest in another person with a distinctive point of view—an interest that stops short of entailing a desire to help but that does not reduce to bare non-maleficence.[19] Unlike sizing others up, empathizing presupposes sufficient concern for the other to rule out an unabashedly instrumental attitude toward her. Still, I follow philosophical precedent, which distinguishes empathetic concern from sympathetic concern. Whereas empathetic concern for a person jump-starts and frames the task of imagining her experience from her point of view, sympathetic concern for a person prompts you to respond to her perceived needs by providing assistance.[20] If so, empathy is not what moves members of the helping professions to provide benefits to their clientele. Duty, sympathy, or solidarity must fuel the provision of aid.

Fourth, I follow Adrian Piper in holding that embodiment is central to empathetic imagination (1991, 735–737).[21] I'm not sure whether Goldie would object to viewing empathy as a kind of visceral imagination, for there are divergent strands in his work. On the one hand, he likens empathy to "acting in your head," which suggests a mentalist view (2000, 178). On the other hand, one of his (many) wonderful exercises invites readers to centrally imagine swimming among jellyfish and feeling something slippery tugging at their ankles, which injects corporeity into central imagining (2000, 195–196). Inasmuch as Goldie seems generally receptive to acknowledging the bodily dimensions of affective life, I'll assume that he and I are in accord on this point. The importance to moral epistemology of recognizing that visceral imagination is constitutive of empathy will become apparent in sections 3b and 4, where I consider the charge that accurately empathizing with someone whose embodiment is markedly different from your own isn't possible.

To sum up, I position empathy between sizing another person up and sympathizing with her. Motivated by proto-moral concern, empathetic engagement is an imaginative activity that seeks to understand another person "from the inside"—that is, to imaginatively replicate the other's subjective experience, including its cognitive, affective, corporeal, and desiderative dimensions. Without information about the other individual's past, her larger social context, and how she is positioned in it, empathy is likely to go astray. However, it is prudent to confine empathetic imagining to a defined set of circumstances—a persisting situation, a series of events, or a combination of the two—for whole-life empathy exceeds most people's capacities and hardly ever serves a useful purpose.

3. WHY EMPATHY IS (ISN'T) A MORAL POWER

There is no consensus among philosophers about how empathy fits into ethics. Nancy Sherman and Stephen Darwall pursue an approach to this topic that centers on moral psychology. They invoke social psychological research to argue that empathy can, but does not necessarily, inspire morally commendable action. In contrast, Catriona Mackenzie and Jackie Leach Scully inquire into the epistemological role of empathy in ethics and draw pessimistic conclusions. Inasmuch as they too write as empirically informed philosophers, their skepticism about the usefulness of empathy as a tool of moral understanding is worrisome. This section examines these assessments of empathy's potential contribution to leading a morally worthy life. After urging that there is reason to remain agnostic about whether empathy promotes altruistic action, I turn my attention to moral epistemology, and I argue against underestimating empathy's capacity to refine and extend moral insight.

A. Empathy and Altruistic Action

Sherman's reading of the developmental psychology literature together with accounts of simulation convinces her that "empathy predisposes us to active forms of respect [for human dignity] and to a responsiveness to violations of respect" (1998, 115; bracketed material added). Along similar lines and citing some of the same psychological studies, Darwall argues that what he calls "proto-sympathetic empathy" can give rise to sympathy and hence to altruistic behavior (1998, 271–272).

Sherman cites positive statistical correlations between empathy and helping behavior, and Darwall adds a psychological explanation of the bridge between empathizing with a person and the desire to assist her. Incorporating visceral imagination into his account, he maintains that you feel "some level" of distress when you empathize with someone who is suffering (1998, 271). If your own discomfort galvanizes your attention, you'll be moved to soothe yourself (1998, 271). However, if you reassign your distress to the other person, you'll become "distress[ed] at his distress" (1998, 272). In that case, empathy develops into sympathy, and you'll be motivated to help out (1998, 272). Both Sherman and Darwall emphasize, however, that there is nothing automatic about the conversion of empathy into sympathy and prosocial action.

Darwall notes that an emotion such as resentment or envy, a belief that the suffering is deserved, or an agonistic relationship blocks the transition from empathy to sympathy (1998, 272). In my view, though, the problem starts before the conversion of empathy to sympathy becomes an issue. Adopting a conception of empathy that better approximates ordinary usage implies that the emotions, beliefs, and desires Darwall mentions would prevent you from empathizing in the first place. If I am right that concern for the other is a precondition for empathy, the problem Darwall points up isn't about empathetic understanding languishing ineffectually because an antithetical emotion, belief, or desire blocks its conversion into sympathetic helpfulness. The problem is that you never empathized with the person you resent or envy in the first place. Believing she's in the wrong or wanting to vanquish her, you merely sized her up. If so, it's possible that empathy does promote altruistic behavior.

Sherman worries about the context of empathetic engagement and suggests that the way in which a narrative or image of suffering is framed can spark or crush prosocial responses (1998, 115–116). Ongoing work on the Belief in a Just World hypothesis pioneered by Melvin Lerner reinforces her concern (Furnham 2003; Lerner 1980; Ross and Miller 2002; for further discussion see Chapter 5, section 1). Confronted with wrongful suffering that they feel powerless to alleviate, people derogate the victims and blame them for their plight in order to preserve their belief that the world is basically just. There are ways to overcome this hostile tropism, but the Belief in a Just World research program raises doubts that laboratory correlations between empathy and altruism carry over into real world motivation and action when need is dire. Grievous, widespread neediness activates the blame-the-victim defense by making onlookers feel impotent.

This countervailing evidence is certainly troubling. Yet, absent an analysis of how researchers are defining and measuring empathy in their studies, it seems to me that the jury is still out on the question of whether empathy's most important role in moral life is catalyzing sympathetic respect for and kindness to others. While awaiting more conclusive evidence regarding the relation between empathy and altruism, I propose to explore how empathy might contribute to moral epistemology.

B. Empathy and Moral Understanding

In the context of biomedical quality-of-life assessments regarding disability, Mackenzie and Scully turn away from debates about moral psychology and altruistic motivation and consider an alternative account of how empathy might figure in moral life. They follow Goldie in assuming that empathy is a mind-reading faculty that is supposed to enable people to grasp what others are thinking, feeling, and wanting now and also to anticipate what others will think, feel, and do in future. Likewise, they follow Goldie in maintaining that empathy's failings as a mind-reading capacity imply that empathy also has shortcomings with respect to moral epistemology. But Mackenzie and Scully introduce a variable that Goldie neglects and that I agree is of the utmost importance—namely, diverse forms of embodiment. Connecting empathetic imagining to embodiment, they argue that when individuals who do not have disabilities undertake to empathize with individuals who do, their resulting judgments about the quality of life of individuals with disabilities are unreliable. Consequently, these judgments should not be used as a basis for decisions about treatment or social policy regarding people with disabilities.

Most non-disabled people believe that being born with a serious disability or becoming disabled later in life would result in an intolerably low quality of life, despite the fact that people who actually have disabilities report a good quality of life (2007, 344–345). Adducing Merleau-Ponty's account of the corporeal grounding of cognition, together with studies in cognitive science that support his views, Mackenzie and Scully diagnose the source of this imaginative interference as "being/having a specific form of embodiment" (2007, 342–343). In light of the empirical evidence for the impact of embodiment on cognition and the well-documented mismatch between imagined experience of disability and actual experience of disability, they take a dim view of the supposition that people can easily imagine what it's like to be in a corporeally different condition. Thus, they raise doubts that in-her-shoes imagining enables nondisabled people to comprehend what it would be like for them to be disabled and that empathetic imagining enables non-disabled people to comprehend the subjective experience of persons with disabilities. Merging the mind-reading problem with the moral epistemology problem, they add that there is little reason to believe that centrally imagining what it's like to have a body that greatly differs from your own can serve as a trustworthy guide to moral judgment (2007, 337–338). Because non-disabled people lack bodily experience comparable to that of disabled individuals, their prognostications about the impact of disability on life satisfaction seldom hit the mark.

Appropriating Goldie's pre-2011 account of empathy draws Mackenzie and Scully perilously close to mystifying people whose bodily condition and experience diverge from prevalent norms of able-embodiment. I take their cautionary points seriously. Still, it seems to me that, like Goldie, Mackenzie and Scully set such high standards for successful empathy that failure is all but inevitable. According to Goldie, "prediction of others' decisions and actions is rather like listening to a Bach fugue for the first time and trying to imagine what will come next" (2000, 207). Does it follow that because we usually can't make such predictions when novel, complicated, and momentous decisions must be made, empathy is a poor basis for moral understanding compared to imagination from the external point of view? I'll argue that it doesn't—that Mackenzie and Scully's deflationary conclusion about empathy is rebuttable. It seems to me that their argument for curtailing empathy's role in moral understanding is inconsistent with their contention that moral imagination fosters broadened moral sympathies. Specifically, I'll argue that their claim that the role of "imagination in moral engagement with others is to expand the scope of our sympathies" presupposes that we can do a better job of empathizing with differently embodied others than they acknowledge and entails that they should regard empathy as an epistemically valuable moral capacity (2007, 338). If so, they should be less averse to recognizing empathy's role in moral understanding.

Despite their conviction that centrally imagining yourself with a very different body (in-her-shoes imagining) and centrally imagining the inner life of a person with a body very different from your own (empathetic imagining) seldom succeed, Mackenzie and Scully urge that imagination has much to offer conscientious agents. They assign imagination the task of "making the other's perspective vivid" to you, and they contend that "imaginative engagement with the perspectives of others" can extend people's moral sympathies—their willingness to care about others' welfare and to help those in need (2007, 346–347; also see Mackenzie 2006, 308–309). In their view, failure to recognize the other's personhood and distinctive subjectivity is a major obstacle to sympathy, but by virtue of "making the other's perspective vivid to us" acentrally imagining-how-it-is for the other can surmount this obstacle (2007, 346; also see Mackenzie 2006, 321–322). They stress, however, that if imagination is to accomplish these tasks, it must be grounded in preliminary empirical work (2007, 347). You must first develop an empirically informed, imaginative representation of the other from the third-person perspective, and then you must respond emotionally to that representation (2007, 347; also see Mackenzie 2006, 322–324). You sympathetically feel for the other as you have imaginatively represented her, rather than imaginatively feeling with her.

At this point, it is necessary to recall that, far from magically transporting one person into another's consciousness, empathy, as I have urged we should understand it, requires navigating between imagining the other's first-person perspective and gathering relevant information about her from your own third-person perspective— that is, communicating with a different other or otherwise educating yourself about what it's like to be her, gradually augmenting your understanding, and hence improving your imaginative representation of her point of view. The aim of shifting back and forth between third-person inquiry and central imagining is to sort out how you differ from the other and to learn what she experiences that you don't in order to avoid imaginatively misrepresenting her. But if you can sufficiently suppress irrelevant features of your own bodily perspective while sufficiently mobilizing relevant ones to succeed in "making the other's perspective [third-personally] vivid" to you, you can also sufficiently suppress irrelevant features of your own bodily perspective while sufficiently mobilizing relevant ones to centrally imagine the other's perspective from her own point of view.[22] In other words, you can empathize with a differently embodied person. Adopting a realistic conception of empathy—a conception that departs from

Goldie's and is at odds with Mackenzie's and Scully's endorsement of his conception—implies that significantly different embodiment is no more formidable an obstacle to empathy than it is to acentral imagining.

Disputing the power of empathy to grasp differently embodied others' subjectivities, Mackenzie and Scully invoke Iris Young and Lorraine Code to affirm the "irreducible strangeness" of others (2007, 346; for related discussion, see Mackenzie 2006, 321–323). I agree that not even your closest intimates fully understand you, that non-congruent bodily experience can increase the likelihood of misunderstanding between people, and that empathizers must regard their imaginings as tentative and stand ready to modify them in the face of contrary information. However, I do not agree that imagining-how-it-is for someone is more likely to be accurate than empathizing with her, for it is no less possible to segregate irrelevant attributes of your own from empathetic imagination than it is to segregate them from imagining-how-it-is for someone. Moreover, working to avoid self-contamination of your empathetic imaginings is well worth the effort because empathy can afford you a substantial acquaintance with the subjectivity of another distinctive individual.

I would add that Mackenzie and Scully's characterization of moral imagination as increasing your understanding of "how others perceive and experience the world" misses something morally important about what that substantial acquaintance with another's subjectivity amounts to (2007, 347). In section 2, I said that imagining-how-it-is for someone misses the poignancy of her interiority. What that means is that, unlike imagining someone from the external perspective, empathetic imagination opens a window on values and disvalues as someone whose situation is profoundly different from your own is experiencing them. I suspect that it is this poignancy that Nussbaum (2001, 331) is getting at when she says that by empathizing with someone who is suffering you get a "sense of what it means for her to suffer that way" and what Darwall (2011, 13) is getting at when he says that empathizing with someone accesses what she is "going through."

One of the many extraordinarily moving passages in Jean-Dominique Bauby's chronicle of being "locked in" as a result of a massive stroke superbly illustrates the distinctive value of empathy. Bauby's disability is unusually severe, for his mouth, arms, and legs are all paralyzed. Unlike most people with more manageable disabilities, Bauby portrays his life as a relentless cavalcade of indignities and torments. In this passage, he describes a visit to the beach near the hospital where he is cared for, accompanied by his partner Sylvie de la Rochefoucauld and their two young children. Although he has learned to communicate using a complicated method that requires blinking on his part and guessing letters on his interlocutor's part, communicating is cumbersome and contracted. In the holiday setting of the beach, he longs to engage in playful repartee with his children as he once did. But the greatest loss of all is that he cannot touch his son:

> His face not two feet from mine, my son Théophile sits patiently waiting—and I, his father, have lost the simple right to ruffle his bristly hair, clasp his downy neck, hug his small, lithe, warm body tight against me. There are no words to express it. My condition is monstrous, iniquitous, revolting, horrible. Suddenly I can take no more. Tears well and my throat emits a hoarse rattle that startles Théophile.
>
> (*The Diving Bell and the Butterfly*, 1997, 71)

I find empathizing with Bauby's frustration irresistible. Reading this passage, I cannot help but viscerally imagine his impulse to caress, to hug his little boy, together with his wrenching grief at his impenetrable isolation despite the presence of his beloved and loving family. Bauby's first-person authorial position pulls readers into his subjectivity. I suppose, though, that a reader could self-consciously maintain an external perspective and imagine the scene from a distance. Noting that Bauby feels frustrated and isolated, this reader might feel sorry for Bauby and wish there was something she could do to help him or people like him. However, she would be missing the human meaning—that is, the subjective experience—of the disvalues Bauby so powerfully represents.

Empathetic encounters with values and disvalues are not to be confused with in-her-shoes imaginings, which for the most part replicate your value system as you project yourself into an alternative set of circumstances. Nor are they to be confused with grasping inventories or theoretical distillations of unfamiliar value systems, for in empathizing you are viscerally apprehending what the values and disvalues mean concretely in the life of another human being. If so, empathy imparts something more than third-person imaginative representations that you take in intellectually or respond to emotionally, and empathy should count as a valuable moral power for Mackenzie and Scully.

Mackenzie and Scully wonder why empathy fails so miserably when non-disabled individuals, including healthcare workers who interact regularly with people with disabilities, try to grasp the inner worlds of people with disabilities. They blame overconfidence about human empathetic powers for this disconnect. However, it is easy to think of other reasons why there is such a glaring disparity between the negative judgments made by non-disabled people about disabled people's quality of life and the acceptable quality of life that many persons with disabilities profess to have.

Perhaps disability is so stigmatized that many non-disabled people can't bring themselves to centrally imagine being disabled. Perhaps many people in countries where health care is unavailable or extremely expensive can't imagine a good quality of life with a disability because obtaining the specialized health care that many disabilities necessitate seems utterly far-fetched. Perhaps some studies oblige non-disabled respondents to estimate disabled people's quality of life in an information vacuum—that is, lacking anything but superficial knowledge of the practical consequences of different disabilities. Perhaps the non-disabled people who were interviewed have never heard of "adaptation level theory," which predicts that neither great good fortune nor very bad misfortune has an enormous impact on an individual's degree of happiness in the long run (Brickman, Coates, and Janoff-Bulman 1978).

Whatever the truth may be, I have argued that Mackenzie and Scully's explanation is not correct. Still, I agree with Mackenzie and Scully (and with Sherman) that people ought to cultivate the imaginative skills that conduce to understanding others whose life experience differs from their own (Mackenzie and Scully 2007, 347; Sherman 1998, 119). Only my reasoning for this conclusion is at odds with theirs.

4. EMPATHY, EMBODIMENT, AND SUFFERING

Sonia Kruks offers a promising suggestion about embodied empathy that complements the position that I've advocated. Moreover, because she shifts away from disability, which can result from a disease or an accident as well as from human aggression, and directs her attention to severe, unnecessary, humanly inflicted suffering, her discussion is especially pertinent to the question of how empathy bears on advancing human rights. However, because Kruks couples her proposal with a gendered caveat about the limits of its reach, I have reservations about her view.

Kruks holds that non-conceptual, intercorporeal communication between people is possible—that is, "we can 'speak' a certain lingua franca through our bodies" (2001, 164, 165). Interested chiefly in how somatic interpersonal understanding might contribute to feminist solidarity among women, she recalls encountering an abused woman when she arrived for work at a battered women's shelter in London (2001, 166). Seeing that the woman's "eye was bruised and closed, her cheek grazed, her lip gashed," Kruks felt physical pain (2001, 166). Following Sandra Bartky, she calls her response "feeling-with."[23] Although she was aware that she and the abused woman were not members of the same race, ethnicity, and class, Kruks affirms that the female body she shared with the abused woman broke through these differences to prompt an immediate "sentient and affective response" to the woman's palpable misery. Imagining "the blows raining down, on the woman's face, what they must have felt like as they landed, and how much her face must still ache," she felt nauseous, which is a common somatic concomitant of fear and pain (2001, 166). Kruks goes on, however, to deny that her empathetic response to the client of the shelter would have been as strong if the victim had been a man, and she attributes her diminished empathy to the difference between male bodies and her own female body image (2001, 167–168).

In the same vein, Kruks asserts that her visceral imagining of Nawal El Saadawi's clitoridectomy at the age of six is more vivid than her visceral imagining of Nelson Mandela's circumcision at the age of sixteen (2001, 168; also see El Saadawi 1980, 7–8, and Mandela 1994, 45–48).[24] She points up key contextual differences between the two cases. Culturally, female genital cutting condemned El Saadawi to male control over her sexuality and fertility, whereas male genital cutting ritually transformed the boy Mandela into a man and conferred customary male privileges on him.[25] Phenomenologically, a child's being yanked out of bed in the middle of the night to have excruciating and unexpected pain inflicted bears little resemblance to a teenager's preparing for and undergoing a painful public ritual surrounded by communal festivities (2001, 168). Still, Kruks maintains that because of the differences between their bodies, women and men "are condemned to a degree of sexual solipsism," though not, she stresses, to a complete intercorporeal blackout (2001, 168–169).

I think there is something to this claim, but there might be a temptation to overdo its ramifications. Thus, I offer some considerations that argue for contracting the sphere of this alleged female-male corporeal insularity. Moreover, I highlight the fact that, where direct embodied empathy breaks down, victims may turn to discursive invention to communicate their experience to uncomprehending others.

Returning to the matter of facial battering, I confess that I can't bear the sight of any human face being smashed.[26] I can't watch boxing, even when I know the blows are being faked for a movie scene. I can't watch the movie sequences because I can centrally and viscerally imagine what's being portrayed all too well.[27] I might be kidding myself, but I don't detect any gendered disparity in my ability to empathize with the stun and smart of a facial pummeling.[28] No doubt, the pre-fight opportunity for masculine swagger and the wished-for glory of triumph in the ring consort with financial rewards to draw men into the sport.[29] For the boxers, these perceived values presumably override the disvalues of pain and injury, yet the values don't cancel out the disvalues. If the disvalues of pain and injury could be eliminated, back-up teams would not be busy nursing boxers' bruises and wounds between rounds, and ringside physicians would not be on hand to diagnose fight-stopping injuries.

I have no basis for contesting Kruks's self-report that her embodied empathy with a male battered face would be less compelling than the embodied empathy a female battered face elicited from her. Speaking for myself, however, whether the target has a beard or not is immaterial. In my experience, then, the *human* face is what Kruks terms a "tactile-kinesthetic invariant," or what I would call an empathetically compelling element of common humanity.

Here Kruks alerts us to a dimension of empathy that neither Goldie nor Mackenzie brings out. In the case Kruks recounts, a substantial characterization of the other person is not necessary for empathy because the experience she is viscerally imagining is a particular attack on an element of common humanity. Such immediate, incident-specific, corporeal empathy is important because it viscerally transmits a moral problem. What happened? Is someone responsible? If the injured individual is in fact a victim of someone's violence, your corporeal empathy is then likely to arouse the sort of concern for the other that undergirds the longitudinal form of empathy I discussed in sections 2 and 3b. When seeking to empathize with a victim's whole experience of being wronged, it is necessary to bear in mind that non-accidentally accurate empathy with the person who has undergone such an experience must be based on a substantial characterization, for individuals' responses to and capacities to cope with such violence are highly variable. In the case of empathizing with a victim's story, the victim's perspicacity and summoning of evocative detail in her representation of her experience over time can supply a sufficiently substantial characterization to enable empathy and thus to enable the empathizer to appreciate the values and disvalues that are in play and to envisage the sort of response those values and disvalues call for.

Returning to Kruks's account of immediate, incident-specific, corporeal empathy: What about viscerally imagining the searing pain of having a body part that's packed with sensitive nerve-endings amputated without anesthesia? It seems to me that the main uncertainty about the adequacy of my (Kruks's?) visceral imagining of genital cutting stems from the fact that the qualitatively similar pain I have experienced is probably far from comparable to the suddenness of onset and off-the-charts intensity of El Saadawi's pain. If, like me, Kruks needs to extrapolate from experience of less severe pain to the excruciating agony of female genital cutting, she may not be accurately tracking El Saadawi's childhood torment despite the congruence of their genitalia.

Indeed, I am reluctant to accept that Kruks's differential response to El Saadawi's and Mandela's stories was facilitated or impeded by anatomical gender difference because, her protestations to the contrary notwithstanding, the two texts support a much less recondite explanation. Each text culturally contextualizes the author's experience of genital cutting, and both invite a more temporally extended form of empathy. El Saadawi's recollections make me wince in panicky terror and recoil at the explosion of pain that the blade of the *daya* (midwife) visited on her. Moreover, her story corporeally communicates the immense and irremediable disvalue that female genital cutting signifies for her. Mandela's chronicle of his initiation conveys nothing remotely like disvalue *simpliciter*. Because he presents the fiery pain of circumcision as a necessary and transitory moment on his path to the exalted status of manhood, I would venture that Kruks's feeling-with Mandela's pain is diminished, not because his genitals differ from hers, but rather because he plays it down. It really hurt, he says, but it doesn't matter.

Absent similar experience of your own, exposure to rich and evocative firsthand description is indispensable to empathetic insight into the values and disvalues embedded in another person's life experience. Attempting to empathize with a victim on the strength of a thin story is inadvisable unless you too have been subjected to the same kind of abuse, for a telescoped representation of a victim's experience invites incautious, non-victimized addressees to indulge in self-centered in-her-shoes imagining to supply missing information.[30] In principle, though, I see no insurmountable obstacle to empathizing with female or male genital cutting, especially not if someone who has been through either procedure unstintingly portrays it—what she or he endured in the context of its cultural meanings and norms, how she or he coped or couldn't cope with the inflicted suffering, and how this ordeal shaped her or his subsequent self-understanding. I have no doubt that people can be gendered, raced, or otherwise somatically marked in ways that are difficult to communicate to and render viscerally imaginable for people whose bodies don't share those markings. Nevertheless, I submit that these socio-corporeal divisions can be overcome, and I next present an analysis of a victim's story as further refutation of any presumption that humanity is partitioned into corporeally demarcated, empathetically walled-off compartments.[31]

5. *A WOMAN IN BERLIN: EIGHT WEEKS IN THE CONQUERED CITY*

The date is April 27, 1945. The city is Berlin. The scene is the basement of an apartment building. Soviet forces have taken the city. The anonymous author of *A Woman in Berlin* knows a bit of Russian, and she uses it to intercede with a Soviet officer to prevent two soldiers from sexually assaulting one of her neighbors, the wife of the local baker. Anonymous[32] records what ensued in her diary:

The baker's wife asks, hoarsely, "Are they gone?"

I nod, but just to make sure I step out into the dark corridor. Then they have me. Both men were lying in wait. . . .

I scream and scream . . . I hear the basement door shutting with a dull thud behind me. . . . I end up with my head on the bottom step of the basement stairs. One man stands there keeping watch, while the other tears my clothes, forcing his way—

I grope around the floor with my left hand until I find my key ring. I use my right hand to defend myself. It's no use. He's simply torn off my garter, ripping it in two. When I struggle to come up, the second one throws himself on me as well, forcing me back on

the ground with his fists and knees. Now the other keeps look-
out, whispering, "Hurry up, hurry."

(2005, 53)

This narrative excerpt includes some gender-specific and culture-
specific elements, and I have not edited them out because I want to
contrast them with other elements that, I argue, appeal to common
humanity—or in Kruks's phraseology, "tactile-kinesthetic invariants."
Basements are peculiar to certain kinds of architecture. Key rings are
peculiar to societies in which doors must be locked for safety. The
self-defense norm that Anonymous enacts is gender-specific and is
limited to cultures that presume that a woman is consenting to sex
unless she fights back. The significance of these details is self-evident
to anyone who shares Anonymous's cultural framework. The dark-
ness and dankness associated with basements and dungeons magnify
the foreboding atmosphere. That her key ring has fallen out of her
pocket and is up for grabs points up the precariousness of her link to
the security of home. Anonymous's struggle, however futile, demon-
strates her innocence and feminine respectability. For people who
readily grasp these meanings, these details help enlist empathy.

But the story doesn't need these culture-specific, gender-specific
details to convey the horror of Anonymous's experience. Three other
elements suffice: surprise attack, involuntary exposure, and physical
control. Norms of what is to be expected vary across cultures. But
a surprise attack shocks the system, and shock is by definition violent and traumatic. As a blow to bodily integrity, it is a blow to the
integrity of the self. Dress practices vary across cultures. But regardless of how states of dress and undress are defined in a given context,
people experience forced nakedness as threatening and humiliating.
That's because your body image and therefore your sense of self
extends beyond your skin to the covering that clothing provides.[33]
Technologies of coercion vary across cultures. But being pinned

down against your will is the most palpable form of domination. By neutralizing your enculturated, skillful body and reducing your body to afflicted, defeated flesh, physical control crushes agentic selfhood. In other words, shock, forcible nakedness, and de-agentification[34] are empathetically compelling attacks on common humanity. Just as you don't need to be familiar with the sport of boxing to empathize with a boxer whose head is taking a beating, you don't need advance knowledge of cultural norms of what is to be expected, what constitutes appropriate dress, or what constitutes an imposition of force to empathize with someone who suffers a shock, who is stripped bare, or who is physically overpowered.

I have said nothing of the singular horror of rape as a violation of bodily integrity because Anonymous never describes undergoing rape as such. She writes about the possibility of pregnancy and what is to be done should it occur, about the mutual support women give each other by exchanging their stories, and about an official euphemism for rape (2005, 72–73, 147, 215). Although she uses the word *rape*, she does not write about being raped. She confines herself to remarking ancillary violence—"my underclothes are ripped apart"—and invoking colloquial formulas—"they had their way with her" (2005, 63, 225).[35] What she does describe explicitly is another kind of bodily penetration:

> Suddenly his finger is in my mouth, stinking of horse and tobacco. I open my eyes. A stranger's hands expertly pulling apart my jaws. Eye to eye. Then with great deliberation he drops a gob of gathered spit into my mouth.
>
> (2005, 63)

I don't think it would be wrong to read this stunning passage both as a factual report of the particulars of an assault and as a metaphor for forced genital penetration. But what interests me here is Anonymous's success in picking out a ghastly detail of the sexual mortification she is enduring that casts her ordeal in universally comprehensible terms.[36] You needn't be a woman to feel the full force of this revolting act as you imaginatively enter into Anonymous's consciousness.

The behavior of Anonymous's neighbors, as well as that of her assailants, crystallizes the moral import of her story. Her neighbors are so panicked by the occupation of Berlin that they repeatedly abandon her. In the basement episode they literally slam the door on her. Plainly, they adopt this "every-man-for-himself" ethic and never hesitate to betray Anonymous because they are terrified that the foreign soldiers might abuse them as they are abusing her. Add to this the soldiers' telltale furtiveness—an unmistakable sign that they know they're engaged in ignominious behavior. The narrative that Anonymous bequeathed us leaves no doubt, then, that she is a victim caught up in a brutal, serial crime.

So far, I have focused exclusively on the "this is what they did to me" dimension of Anonymous's text. I have argued that Anonymous positions herself as a surrogate for common humanity in virtue of the way in which she represents the harms inflicted on her. The "this is how it affected me" dimension—how I felt about it and what I did because of it—is no less important with respect to grasping the disvalue of the onslaught of sexual abuse that took place in Berlin. However, it has a different rhetorical function. Rather than appealing to empathetically compelling aspects of common humanity, Anonymous's portrayal of how she was affected provides the substantial characterization needed to empathize with this particular victim.[37] Violations of human rights seek to despoil the target's self-image as a person worthy of respect and to destroy the target's capacity to choose and act. Psychological and ethnographic studies of victimization have detected typical patterns of subjective response to human rights abuse (for example, Herman

1992). Nevertheless, the subjectivity of victimization is ineluctably individual, and Anonymous humanizes her story by acquainting her readers with her personal viewpoint. The "this is how it affected me" component of a victim's story does not articulate what is true of everyone. Rather, it offers an intimate glimpse of what is true of a unique human being. Human rights enshrine the value of this uniqueness, along with the disvalue of attacking the humanity that people share.

Anonymous acknowledges the variability of responses to rape by telling us about a woman who leaps from a fourth floor window fleeing from rapists, and about a young victim of gang rape who stops eating and drinking (2005, 60, 110). She does not respond so self-destructively. Her rage sparks clearheaded calculation, and she launches a damage control program. At the same time, she is beset by sickening feelings of degradation.

After being raped several times and hearing of the rape of many other women, Anonymous reaches a decision:

> Damn this to hell! I say it out loud. Then I make up my mind.
>
> No question about it: I have to find a single wolf to keep away the pack. An officer, as high-ranking as possible, a commandant, a general, whatever I can manage. After all, what are my brains for, my little knowledge of the enemy's language?
>
> (2005, 64)

Carrying out her plan, Anonymous makes a devil's bargain with a Soviet officer. Becoming his "mistress" puts her off-limits to other sexual predators.[38] But shielding herself from random rape does not shield her from psychic wounds:

> I am constantly repulsed by my own skin. I don't want to touch myself, can barely look at my own body. I can't help but think

about the little child I was. . . . So much love . . . and all for the
filth I am now.

(2005, 75)

Despite her pluck and fortitude, Anonymous feels debased, and she
portrays her self-revulsion in aching exactitude. In a terrible moment
of anguish and despair, she contemplates the, for her, impossible possibility that she has surrendered to prostitution (2005, 117).

Anyone who is acquainted with discussions of post-traumatic
stress disorder in the aftermath of abuse knows that the disvalue of
attacks on human rights is not confined to the horror of a moment
(see Chapter 3, section 5). Thus, empathizing with a particular victim's story provides an affectively powerful understanding of how the
disvalue of human rights abuse persists beyond particular episodes
of aggression. Still, there is no one way in which such disvalue always
plays out. Thus, victims' various stories provide insight into the range
of harms consequent upon human rights abuse. It is important to be
mindful, as well, that not every reader will be empathetically engaged
by Anonymous's responses.[39] Some might find her feelings and
actions incredible. Some might find them abhorrent. Some might
empathize more fully if they could read the story of the woman who
was driven to suicide or the refugee girl who starves herself. There is
a risk, then, in portraying individual subjectivity. But to leave it out is
to produce a story of a stick figure—a cipher of humanity that is not
plausible as a human protagonist and that can neither rouse empathetic concern nor adequately represent the disvalue of human rights
abuse.[40]

Certain features of Anonymous, her circumstances, and the story
she tells facilitate empathy—at least for early twenty-first-century,
middle-class Euro-American readers and anyone who identifies with
the values they frequently espouse. Anonymous is a German female
noncombatant. Laced with sardonic humor at the expense of Hitler

and Nazism, Anonymous's diary distances her from the evils of the Third Reich. Without these wry remarks, would her status as an innocent civilian be undermined? What if she had consorted with upper-echelon Nazi officials? Her rapists are Soviet soldiers, and the Soviet Union became the cold war enemy of the United States and Western Europe after the war. What if the rapists had been US or British soldiers? Would her German nationality taint her credibility? Would her gender taint her credibility? What if she hadn't been a talented professional journalist? If her prose hadn't been fluent and lucid, how much would literary deficits interfere with empathy?[41] None of these counterfactuals can be addressed in the abstract. The effects of these alterations would vary depending on who is reading the account.

6. EMPATHY, VICTIMS' STORIES, AND HUMAN RIGHTS

One reason I've selected *A Woman in Berlin* for extended commentary is that Kruks claims that different embodiment "may be one factor . . . in accounting for the prevalence of rape perpetrated by men on women" (2001, 169). If men can't "directly feel-with the pain and humiliation of forced vaginal intercourse," they are likely to be less inhibited from sexually assaulting women (Kruks 2001, 169).[42] Regardless of whether men can "directly" empathize with victims of male-on-female rape, I have argued that Anonymous's image of forced, non-penile oral penetration detaches sexual assault from the genital dimorphism that, according to Kruks, may obscure from men the normative meaning for women of male-on-female rape. In so doing, this image casts her suffering as an affront to common humanity as well as to her particular personhood. Anonymous's reflections on the self-loathing born of her degradation compound the impact of this image and other incidents that she recounts, for the self-estrangement she documents affectively and viscerally conveys to readers how the torment of being subjected to daily sexual abuse reverberates throughout her subjectivity. Although I have acknowledged that no single victim's story is guaranteed to get through to any and every person, I believe that Anonymous's (to me) unforgettable story amply illustrates how it is possible to discursively traverse the rifts between one individual's embodied subjectivity caught up in a sociohistorical outbreak of unbridled violence, on the one hand, and people whose embodiment and/or circumstances are vastly different, on the other.

Iris Young's comment that stories "pull on thought through desire" provides a missing link between victims' stories and the passion that Kruks rightly holds is vital to moral and political commitment (Kruks 2001, 155; Young 1997, 71). Not only is emplotment a powerful tool of meaning generation, but also literary devices that may be more strongly associated with poetry than prose—such as cadence and figurative speech—suffuse and supplement narrative structure. Accenting, reframing, and elaborating on motifs, narrative discourse galvanizes attention and animates affective and visceral sensibilities. In virtue of these powers, well-crafted victims' stories can bypass corporeal barriers and span the experiential chasms that often separate people. The empathetic connectedness that a victim's story can bring about between people stops far short of homogenizing humanity or equating the victim's experience with that of the addressee. What attuned empathetic engagement with a victim's story can accomplish is to bring a reader or auditor close enough to a victim for the addressee to grasp the colossal disvalue of human rights abuse, irrespective of who is undergoing it. Implicitly, the imaginative identification with the plight of a different "other" that a victim's story can prompt exposes invidious distinctions between social groups as the trumped-up rationalizations for cruelty that they are and affectively and viscerally consolidates addressees' insight into the devastating harms that human rights abuse inflicts.

For many middle-class people in the locally peaceful, relatively democratic United States and similar locales, threats to human rights seem remote. Yes, excuses for abrogating civil liberties are proliferating. Yes, social and economic rights are routinely trampled. And, yes, sexual violence against women persists at unconscionably high rates. Human rights have certainly not been adequately realized in the United States or anywhere else. Yet, public opinion poll data never detect widespread, serious concern about any of these human rights issues. Perhaps so many of us enjoy such a high degree of security and freedom (and seldom venture outside our protected environs) that we are at risk of losing sight of just how pressing human rights fulfillment is.

Statistical compilations of the types and frequencies of human rights violations leave people cold (Slovic 2007; Wilson & Brown 2009, 19–20). Compacted into a finite set of principles on the UN website or selectively wielded as rhetorical weapons in government officials' foreign policy arsenals, human rights are drained of their human meaning. In contrast, victims' stories bring human rights down from the empyrean of mathematical and moral abstraction, and by sparking empathetic engagement with individuals targeted for human rights abuse, promote awareness of the paramount urgency of securing human rights.

Chapter 5

The Ethics and Politics of Putting Victims' Stories to Work

They asked us to lead them to women who had been raped so they could record their stories. "Tell us what happened—how did you feel?'" Women were so upset after the interviews, we did not know what to do. We never heard from them [the researchers] again— we decided then that we would never work with researchers again. They *stole our stories*. We can gather the stories ourselves from our own people—you can help [with training].

> Women's Group, Thailand, 2003; quoted in Pittaway, Bartolomei, and Hugman (2010), p. 236 (emphasis added)

When I come to these hearings to be a part—to observe the hearings at this Tribunal, I have visualized the brutality of the regime, and when [Civil Party] Robert Hamill put the photo of the person who was seen struggling in a pool of blood, it really shocked me, because I could imagine how difficult life could have been for my husband at that time, and I could not really control my feeling at that time, and [so] I passed out.

> Im Sunthy, Civil Party in the Extraordinary Chambers in the Courts of Cambodia; quoted in Ciorciari and Heindel (2011), p. 128

To get a purchase on ethical ways of using victims' stories, it is worth calling to mind some indisputably unethical uses. For different reasons, both individual consumers and professional users of victims' stories can come in for moral criticism.

Individual consumers of published victims' stories—diaries, memoirs, fundraising appeals, news features, documentaries, research reports, official proceedings, and so forth—can be guilty of using these stories to prop up their self-esteem or to satisfy their perverse fascination with others' misfortune. Along these lines, Elizabeth Spelman decries "spiritual bellhops"—people who want to appear to have had experiences that others actually have had and that they're very glad to have avoided (1997, 119). Their "exploitative sentimentality" and pseudo depth of feeling substitute for and interfere with morally appropriate responses. When they should be paying attention to the differences between their currently safe situation and the storyteller's fearsome one, while at the same time recognizing their common humanity, spiritual bellhops voyeuristically objectify victims and dabble in the unseemly pleasures of observing pain while out of danger.

The four preceding chapters, which reframe the concept of a victim, reject rigid narrative templates, and argue for emotional understanding of and empathy with victims' stories, are intended as antidotes to the vice of spiritual bellhopping. In this chapter I'll examine another way in which consumers of victims' stories can go ethically off the rails. Insofar as people need to believe that their world is basically just, they are at risk of succumbing to victim derogation and blaming when they are exposed to injustices that seem insurmountable (Lerner 1980). Rather than acknowledging the extent of injustice and taking responsibility for doing what they can to remedy it, they take shelter in the thought that there is no wrong that needs to be righted because the victims brought it on themselves. Plainly this is an unethical response to victims' stories (or any other report of human rights abuse), and I'll say something about this defense mechanism and about how media outlets and NGOs, as well as individual audience members themselves, can counteract it (section 1).

Sensationalizing victims' stories, twisting their stories to suit your purposes, using someone's story without consent, interviewing victims in ways that retraumatize them, and publishing stories likely to have harmful consequences for the individuals who provide them are brazenly unethical practices in the public arena. Elizabeth Spelman lays bare a more subtle way in which public actors can misuse victims' stories. Her discussion of US slavery reminds us that nineteenth-century suffragists annexed slave narratives to their cause and used them to equate never-enslaved women's subordination under patriarchy with the degradation and defilement inflicted on chattel slaves. Aiming to link women's rights to the abolition movement and to advance the claim that like slavery, women's suffering is systemic, serious, unjust, and remediable, suffragists usurped the suffering of real female slaves and misappropriated their stories (1997, 113–114). When one human rights campaign misleadingly identifies itself with stories of the abuses others have recounted, thereby pushing another human rights campaign aside, it filches other victims' stories and wrongfully silences their voices.

Amy Shuman spotlights an abiding tension in human rights discourse. On the one hand, victims have ownership rights with respect to their personal stories, and on the other hand, publicized personal stories of abuse can enlarge audiences' concrete understanding of human rights and ground mutual recognition and respect (2005, 149). Thus, all sorts of people who are working in various capacities to redress past abuses of human rights, to avert future abuses, and to build a worldwide culture of human rights must strike a morally delicate balance between the entitlement of prospective storytellers to control their own stories and their practices of circulating victims' stories with the goal of solidifying and expanding human rights protections. Journalists, academic researchers, truth commissioners, the officials of international and domestic courts, and the staffs of UN agencies and NGOs are all at risk of compromising victims' rights and using victims' stories unethically. In this chapter, I'll consider some of the pitfalls of disseminating victims' stories, and I'll sketch some guidelines for human rights professionals to follow in the interest of ensuring respect for victims in their capacity as narrators of their own lives (section 2).

One way to reduce the problem of defensive victim blaming is to provide audiences for victims' stories with avenues through which they can productively express their outrage. For this purpose, the availability of social conduits through which they can help is crucial. Civil society and the vast and growing network of grassroots associations, social movements, and NGOs that it encompasses can play a significant role in transforming empathy for victims' stories into altruistic motivation and channeling volunteer labor and monetary contributions into effective organizations. So I begin by characterizing these different types of civil society groups and reflecting on the ethical issues concerning victims' stories that can arise in each context. But questions remain about ethical relations among civil society groups. Because funding is a particularly vexed issue for NGOs, I'll focus on it. Apart from wealthy foundations such as the Bill and Melinda Gates Foundation and the Ford Foundation, civil society is currently beset by fierce, sometimes counterproductive, competition among NGOs for support. Thus, I argue, an ethic of civil relations among civil society actors is needed in order to ensure the steady and reliable advance of respect for human rights (section 3).

Although tellers of autobiographical stories of abuse can behave unethically by deliberately making up incidents, by claiming to have suffered more than they did, or by monopolizing attention to their own suffering by denying that of others, it seems to me that norms of honesty and decency apply to their conduct and raise no ethical problems that require special treatment. While it might seem that victims have a special obligation to bear witness or supply testimony—in other words, that it's wrong for them to remain silent or hide part of the truth—I am persuaded that recounting your experience of victimization can be revictimizing and that enforced recounting is revictimizing in many contexts. Testifying to sexual violence is a prime case in point, for in many societies being subjected to sexual assault is considered shameful and results in ostracism of the victim or worse. Because the consequences of telling first-person stories of abuse are culturally specific and can be downright cruel, I defer to victims— their understandings of their individual vulnerabilities and their judgments about the extent of their individual obligations. So I'll leave the ethics of telling their stories to their discretion and won't discuss this matter further.

For similar reasons, I won't discuss the ethics of victims-only support groups and political advocacy groups and the possible uses to which they may decide to put their stories. Here, too, it seems to me that victims who have chosen to insulate themselves from the influence of people who don't share their experience are in the best position to judge what organizational aims, structure, and practices are conducive to their recovery and empowerment.[1] I note, though, that one function that such groups can perform is to articulate and enforce adherence to ethical norms regarding the acquisition and use of victims' stories by aid organizations and scholarly investigators (Madlingozi 2010, 222–224).

1. THE PROBLEM OF VICTIM DEROGATION AND BLAMING

Conceivably, consumers of victims' stories could become so enraged by the brutal behavior of the accused perpetrator(s) that they would want to lash out and seek vengeance, rather than pursuing justice within a human rights framework. However, restraining vengeance will not be my focus here because apathy toward and dismissal of victims are far more prevalent and no less counterproductive audience responses to their stories.[2] One of the major problems in using victims' stories to advance human rights is that readers, listeners, and viewers are prone to victim derogation and blaming, especially when they feel powerless to do anything effective to help (Ross and Miller 2002). Thus, I'll analyze how human psychology can block altruistic responses to victims' stories, and I'll suggest some practical solutions that human rights advocates and well-meaning consumers can adopt in order to defuse victim derogation and blaming.

As early as 1966, Melvin Lerner and his associates began publishing studies suggesting that people need to believe in a just world and are willing to derogate and blame victims in order to protect that belief from manifest counterevidence (Lerner and Simmons 1966). Research on the BJW (belief in a just world) and the justice motive (need to believe in a just world) continues to this day and has gained methodological and theoretical refinement over time.

To clarify the importance of these hypotheses with respect to promoting a human rights agenda, it is useful to start with some relatively recent research on the psychological function of the BJW. Carolyn Hafer's studies point to the BJW's contribution to enabling people to pursue long-term goals by socially accepted means (Hafer and Bègue 2005, 144). It wouldn't make sense to pursue extended projects unless you thought the world sufficiently orderly and stable to support planning steps toward your goal, and it wouldn't make sense to confine yourself to measures that fall within social norms unless you thought that the probity of your means would be rewarded along with your achievement. Thus you need to believe that people reliably get what they deserve in order to invest in your future, and the BJW is adaptive. Research by Claudia Dalbert complements Hafer's. According to Dalbert, the BJW promotes well-being by reducing anger in the face of undesirable outcomes that might otherwise be perceived as unfair (Hafer and Bègue 2005, 144). In different respects, Dalbert and Hafer urge that the BJW is personally beneficial to believers (also see Furnham 2003, 806–808).

Assuming that the BJW is advantageous to individuals in these fundamental ways, it is no wonder that they are motivated to hold onto this conviction. Although just-world theory is best known for its revelations about people's willingness to derogate and blame innocent victims, it would be wrong to think that these are the only strategies available to shore up the BJW (Hafer and Bègue 2005, 145). As usual, people have at their disposal an extensive repertoire of cognitive strategies that are non-rational and morally dubious. They include avoiding relevant and accessible information about injustice; reinterpreting seeming injustice by viewing the putative victim as provoking the harm, as having a bad character deserving of harm, or as needing to suffer in order to improve herself; placing the victim in a social world where, unlike in your own community, injustice happens; and pretending to be cynical about justice and disclaiming the BJW. However, two active coping strategies are available that are rational and morally exemplary—working to prevent future injustice and helping to compensate victims of past injustice.

If disseminating victims' stories is to promote human rights, it is clear that the stories must be presented in contexts that neutralize denial coping strategies and that prompt pro-social coping strategies. For this purpose, it is necessary to take into account what is known about why some people opt for constructive responses to injustice, while others resort to victim blaming and other strategies that prolong and sometimes worsen injustice. Students of just-world theory invoke the concept of self-efficacy to explain which direction of response—denial or pro-social—exposure to injustice will elicit. Studies show that individuals prefer pro-social responses if they believe themselves able to bring about a just and lasting outcome at an acceptable cost (Reichle and Schmitt 2002, 128). Beliefs about self-efficacy depend on resources, such as money and power, as well as on personality traits, such as optimism and hope for a more just world. Moreover, people may objectively have ample resources to help but subjectively feel that such resources aren't available to them, and vice versa (Reichle and Schmitt 2002, 129–130).[3] When people don't subjectively register adequate resources and perceived self-efficacy is therefore low, they opt to deny injustice rather than acknowledge and attempt to remedy it.

It is crucial, then, to communicate victims' stories in conjunction with information about how audience members can take ameliorative action and how a small contribution can help a lot. Some NGOs have learned this lesson. In its solicitation materials, Doctors Without Borders, an international organization that sends medical personnel to treat patients wherever humanitarian health crises erupt, informs recipients that a paltry $35 can provide lifesaving treatment to 36 young children infected with malaria. Similarly, City Harvest, a New York organization that collects leftover food from restaurants and markets and gives it to needy people, emphasizes that a mere $36 donation will help feed 20 children for an entire week.[4] For those who have more free time than money, both organizations' websites offer opportunities to volunteer. Likewise, to allay fears that donations end up in the pockets of highly paid executives rather than benefiting people in need, both organizations assure prospective contributors that only a tiny fraction of monies collected goes to administrative costs and tell them where they can check the organization's financial bona fides.

In a similar vein, journalists and documentarians can contextualize stories of human rights abuse and victims' suffering with pertinent information about NGOs that are effectively fighting these wrongs. While advocating contributions to particular NGOs exceeds the purview of investigative journalism (such advocacy belongs in editorial content), factual reportage of human rights issues is incomplete if it omits material about what is being done to combat abuses and support victims.

Barbara Reichle and Manfred Schmitt argue that, in addition to the BJW and self-efficacy, empathy influences willingness to help victims rather than derogate or blame them.[5] In their discussion of their longitudinal studies of the attitudes of ethnic Germans in the West toward East Germans after reunification, foreign migrant workers, and people living in the Global South, Reichle and Schmitt note that the national government established a "solidarity fund" that cost individual West German taxpayers very little and that was dedicated to strengthening the East German economy. By quieting donors' worries about excessive cost and dubious success, this program secured a sense of self-efficacy and reduced the negative effects of the BJW (2002, 143). In addition, Reichle and Schmitt maintain that the ease with which ethnic Germans from West Germany identify with their counterparts in the East who had the misfortune to find themselves stuck in the Soviet sector at the end of World War II diminished the effects of defensive maneuvers to preserve the BJW and worries about whether ameliorative efforts would succeed (2002, 143–144; also see Blader and Tyler 2002, 230, 242). As a result, their pro-social motivation prevailed.

Their work adds a layer of complexity to using victims' stories to advance human rights. In particular, it points to the urgency of presenting victims' stories in ways that offset tendencies to dis-identify with victims from social groups other than your own. Implicit biases based on inaccurate and negative stereotypes are prime culprits in dis-identification. Implicit biases are encoded in cognitive schemas that function subconsciously to generate discriminatory perceptions and conduct. Although the human rights regime is founded on the value of our common humanity, in practice implicit biases divide us into valued and disvalued social groups and subvert our commitment to the value of common humanity. It is imperative, then, that human rights organizations take measures to counteract this invidious dynamic when they invoke victims' stories in their awareness and funding campaigns.

Current research shows that calling attention to the ubiquity of negative stereotypes can reinforce their influence. However, it is possible to incentivize defiance of implicit biases. For example, one study shows that communicating that the "vast majority of people try to overcome their stereotypic preconceptions" sharply reduces the effects of implicit biases (Duguid and Thomas-Hunt 2014, 4, 12). Not only must audience members for victims' stories be made aware that negative stereotypes may affect their judgment, they must also be reminded of the egalitarian convictions they share with their community and the prevalence in their community of efforts to suppress the influence of distorting and damaging stereotypes.

Yet, human rights organizations should not be expected to shoulder the whole burden of managing the deleterious effects of the BJW and implicit biases. There is variation among people regarding how strong their BJWs are. Some people need to believe in a just world less than others, and they exhibit denial responses to a lesser degree. However, little is known about how the BJW takes root in human psychology and why some people get along without strong BJWs. Of interest, though, is evidence of demographic differences in the strength of the BJW. Non-urban residents have stronger BJWs than urban residents; Euro-Americans have stronger BJWs than African-Americans (Furnham 2003, 810). It appears, then, that personal experience may combine with social scaffolding to strengthen or weaken the BJW. If so, contact with a wider range of experiences and altering social scaffolding to present a more accurate picture could moderate the BJW and diminish its unjust consequences.

It is also essential that conscientious individuals hold themselves responsible for taming the less salubrious propensities of their psychic economies. They can seek out experiences of injustice at odds with their own positive experiences of justice—for example, by going out of their way to become acquainted with victims' stories of human rights abuse. Mindful that they may harbor a disposition to react negatively to victims, they can thoroughly scrutinize the evidence, looking for reasons not to despise or accuse the victim and reasons to hold others responsible for the harm that has befallen her (for discussion of this practice of countering misleading intuitions, see Chapter 3, section 5). In addition to pursuing experiences that are likely to curb the excesses of a rigid BJW and that are conducive to open-mindedness about others' suffering, individuals can undertake to disrupt their reliance on inaccurate, negative stereotypes. Virginia Valian suggests several commonsense precautions against implicit biases:

1. Be explicitly aware of them; notice when you're relying on them; entertain alternative views of the case before you.
2. Don't make snap judgments; devote more time to the case.
3. Don't multitask; give your full attention to the case.
4. Regard yourself as accountable; check your judgment against that of someone you know to be less influenced by implicit biases.

(Valian 1998, 306–309)[6]

No one can altogether overcome her cultural inheritance and its stockpile of malign stereotypes, but everyone can be critical and vigilant and take responsibility for confronting social reality less defensively and more fairly.

2. THE ETHICS OF USING VICTIMS' STORIES TO PROMOTE HUMAN RIGHTS

I'll now turn to ways in which professionals can ethically acquire and use victims' stories. In relation to this topic, I'll use the term *professional* broadly. I mean this category to include a wide variety of individuals whose vocations bring them into contact with victims of human rights abuse and give them reason to use victims' stories in their work. Thus, professionals include academic researchers, journalists, practitioners employed by NGOs and UN agencies, immigration attorneys, asylum judges, criminal court judges, and appointees to truth commissions. Also I mean to include only those professionals who support human rights—by building awareness of human rights abuses, working to end outbreaks or entrenched practices of abuse, aiding victims of abuse, expanding respect for human rights, and so forth. I think it's clear, after all, that appropriating victims' stories and using the stories to rationalize the victims' suffering or to argue for narrowing the reach of human rights protections is ethically unacceptable.

As is apparent from the list of human rights professionals given above, victims' stories can be marshaled to support human rights in a wide variety of ways. Not surprisingly, these different uses give rise to commensurately different, though not unrelated, ethical issues. Because the topic of ethically using victims' stories is huge and complex, I need to schematize and simplify a bit here in order to set out some broad guidelines. I start by offering a somewhat artificial and certainly not exhaustive taxonomy of types of users:

1. Justice projects—such as criminal courts and tribunals, truth commissions, and asylum courts;
2. Aid projects—such as domestic and international humanitarian and development NGOs;
3. Research projects—such as academic scholarship, journalism, and watchdog organizations.

Plainly, these human rights projects overlap and sometimes contribute to one another.[7] All of them seek to obtain firsthand knowledge of human rights abuse, and all aim to use that knowledge to promote a human rights agenda. Thus, all of these projects face the ethical question of how to respect victims despite instrumentalizing their stories in pursuit of human rights. Clearly, obtaining informed consent from victims is necessary to respect them, for informed consent ensures that the informant is telling her story voluntarily. As well, ensuring that recording victims' stories won't retraumatize them is necessary to respect storytellers, for protection from retraumatization ensures that no harm is done in the debriefing process. Since respecting free agency and safeguarding personal security are core moral norms, these two requirements—informed consent and non-retraumatization—apply to all three types of projects. However, these projects' means of collecting victims' stories and their methods of using victims' stories differ, and these differences pose distinctive moral questions. I'll begin by exploring the ethics of using victims' stories in aid projects and research projects. Then I'll take up some ethical issues peculiar to justice projects.

A. Aid and Research Projects

In both aid projects and research projects, transparency about the nature of your project—its methods and expected outcomes—is necessary for informed consent (Dang 2013). Moreover, if an interviewer is not going to compensate a victim for telling her story, it is crucial to let her know in advance and to make sure she is not hoping for payment. If an interviewer does intend to compensate the victim in some way, this too should be made clear. For example, NGOs often gather victims' stories to learn what a community needs, and they sometimes recycle the stories to raise funds to supply needed goods or services to that community and others like it. Alternatively, researchers might agree to exchange the information provided by victims for training in preparing advocacy materials that the victims need in order to pursue a self-defined political agenda on their own (Pittaway et al. 2010, 234, 237). Reciprocity, whether between aid workers and victims or researchers and victims, is clearly desirable.[8] In many professional projects, however, reciprocity takes the relatively thin form of disseminating victims' stories to increase domestic or international awareness of their plight or to develop better theories of the causes and consequences of human rights abuse. When expanding knowledge is a project's sole end, it is incumbent on professional users of victims' stories to convey to their subjects what their objective is and why the victims have reason to share that objective.

Other values that are at stake in aid projects and research projects center on ensuring that victim-informants are not revictimized in the participant selection process, in the interview setting, or in the dissemination process. Regarding the identification of interview subjects, bad practices can victimize those who are not chosen. Relying on presumptive, sometimes self-declared, community leaders to speak for others or to designate participants excludes the perspectives of marginalized community members and risks worsening their victimization. By recruiting openly and soliciting testimony from anyone who volunteers her story, aid and research professionals do all they can to prevent victimization by silencing (Pittaway et al. 2010, 233–234).

In regard to the interview setting, it is important that the interview subject have input into the ground rules governing the location where the interview will take place, the form the record of her testimony will take, and the types of questions that may be asked (Dang 2013). By deferring to subjects' wishes concerning these issues, aid and research professionals enable victims to establish arrangements that will shield them from further victimization. In view of this self-protective function, victims' requests ought to be granted, provided that they do not undermine the aims of the aid or research project.

The vulnerability of many victims to professionals' demands for highly specific types of information is another ethical concern. In order not to revert psychologically to the throes of their traumatic experiences, many victims need to tell their whole story—what happened to whom and when, how her relationships were affected, and how the abuse continues to shape her life. For such victims, being compelled to speak only about a narrow topic that happens to interest a human rights professional is revictimizing. Consequently, aid and research professionals must bear in mind that every victim has a unique, multifaceted, temporally extended story, and they must take precautions to make sure that confining a victim-informant to telling a truncated story or supplying isolated facts will not be psychologically damaging. Aid and research professionals should not treat victims merely as sources.

In a related vein, Serene Khader cautions professional users of victims' stories against succumbing to "inadvertent ventriloquism"—the tendency to stereotype your interview subjects, discredit their epistemic standing, and substitute your own beliefs and values for theirs (2011, 742–743). Interviewers, in Khader's view, are well advised to exercise the virtues of a good listener. Among these she includes concrete thinking, loving attention, the transparent self, and narrative understanding.

By loving attention, she means dispensing with typecasting and endeavoring to discern the particularity of the other (2011, 754). By the transparent self, she means the ability to apprehend those of someone else's needs and desires that conflict with your own (2011, 756). Loving attention and the transparent self facilitate accurate perception of the interview subject. Concrete thinking and narrative understanding immerse listeners in the interview subject's circumstances. By fastening on the particulars of the subject's circumstances, concrete thinking enables aid and research professionals to jettison frameworks that distort victims' experience and to better conceptualize what they are hearing (2011, 754). Narrative understanding repudiates a punctate view of moral choice and action and instead places choice and action in a temporal frame that spans the past events leading up to the choice situation and the future that is likely to eventuate because of the choice that's made (2011, 758).

These four virtues press interviewers to be reflexive about who they are and where they come from as they interact with victims. Like consumers of victims' stories, human rights professionals must not allow implicit biases to corrupt their judgment. As well, these virtues press interviewers to respect the expertise their subjects have gained in virtue of their experience. They are, after all, people who, having experienced severe harm at the hands of others, may well have insights into how and why it came about, as well as into what they need now and what a good future would look like for them (Dang 2013). To ethically use victims' stories to advance human rights, professionals must acknowledge the limits of their own expertise and must respect the expertise of victims.

This last point raises issues concerning the dissemination of victims' stories and the hazards of speaking for others. In this regard, a few ethical standards are obvious. If confidentiality has been promised to storytellers, their identities must be shielded to ensure storytellers' privacy and possibly their safety. If storytellers were promised an opportunity to review the use to which their stories will be put, this promise must be honored and their suggestions taken seriously. Under no circumstances is it permissible to portray the tellers of victims' stories as pathetic victims (for the pathetic victim paradigm, see Chapter 1, section 1A).[9] In the words of *Digital Storytelling for Social Impact,* a report commissioned by the Rockefeller Foundation:

> Stories for social impact must show people as active agents of change, who play a central role in creating solutions to the problems they face. This preserves their dignity, encourages empathy, and inspires support from others.
>
> (http://www.rockefellerfoundation.org/uploads/files/41207e9a-d277-425e-85e7-94715846fcfe-digital.pdf, accessed December 21, 2014)

Respecting the integrity and complexity of victims' stories requires that the storytellers not be reduced to passive, helpless, dehumanized cyphers when their stories are used to promote human rights.[10]

In a now-classic paper, "The Problem of Speaking for Others," Linda Alcoff explores the problems with which those who undertake to speak for others must grapple, together with the reasons why it is sometimes morally obligatory to speak for others (2006). Because aid professionals must represent others' needs to donors and because research professionals must represent others' suffering to inform the public or develop theories, both confront the issues that Alcoff considers. After arguing that the impulse to stay silent is based on a wrongheaded epistemology and that political effectiveness sometimes requires speaking for others, Alcoff offers four guidelines designed to prevent professional users of victims' stories and others who have occasion to speak for others from running amok:

1. Don't use speech to dominate others; monitor and suppress speaking to the exclusion of listening.
2. Critically reflect on your reasons for offering the information or ideas that you intend to put forth; beware of implicit biases.

3. Be accountable to those on whose behalf you speak; invite them to critique your representations of them.

4. Analyze the probable effects of what you say; anticipate "where the speech goes and what it does there."

(2006, 87–88)[11]

Complementing Khader's account of the virtues of good listeners, Alcoff's guidelines direct aid professionals and research professionals to keep faith with the stories they collect and the victims who recount them—that is, to use victims' stories in a manner that redeems the trust victims have placed in them by confiding their stories to them (also see and VanHooser and Ackerly 2009).

B. Justice Projects

As I stated earlier, norms of informed consent and non-retraumatization apply to justice projects, as well as to aid and research projects. However, there are several kinds of justice project—punitive, reparative, and sanctuary.[12] Each of these types of justice project raises distinctive ethical issues in regard to compliance with the norms of informed consent and non-retraumatization.

Punitive justice projects include the International Criminal Tribunal for the former Yugoslavia, the International Criminal Tribunal for Rwanda, the Extraordinary Chambers in the Courts of Cambodia, and the International Criminal Court in The Hague. Criminal courts and tribunals are charged with indicting and trying individuals who are accused of crimes against humanity and war crimes. The first order of business for punitive projects, then, is to reach verdicts in the cases brought before them in accordance with procedures that respect the right to a fair trial. Thus, victim-witnesses may be subjected to sharp adversarial cross-examination aimed at impeaching their testimony and acquitting the defendant

(Ciorciari and Heindel 2011,128; Dembour and Haslam 2004, 164, 166). Likewise, guaranteeing a fair trial to defendants restricts what victim-witnesses can be permitted to say. They are required to focus on providing information relevant to determining whether a defendant is guilty (Ciorciari and Heindel 2011, 126; Dembour and Haslam 2004, 156). As a result, the story that's admissible in court frequently doesn't coincide with the story that matters to the victim.

Sanctuary justice projects include settlements for refugees wherever people are displaced by armed conflict or natural disaster and national asylum systems. I won't discuss refugee camps because no special issues about victims' stories arise in connection with them. The UN High Commissioner for Human Rights regards all persons fleeing war or natural disaster who request admittance to a camp as de facto refugees and grants them sanctuary without question (http://www.unhcr.org/509a836e9.html, accessed 12/28/2014).[13] In contrast, asylum-granting sanctuary projects take a skeptical view of the very people the system was erected to serve—namely, victims of human rights abuse seeking resettlement abroad. Asylum courts are charged with deciding whether refugees ought to be granted permanent residence outside their home countries on the grounds that they are subject to persecution in their homeland. Bound by the strictures of national immigration law and sworn to enforce exclusionary immigration policies in the Global North, immigration judges commonly suspect applicants for asylum of trying to migrate for reasons other than the persecution they profess to have endured (Kirmayer 2003, 175–176). Their credibility thrown into doubt, and often obliged to participate in hearings without the benefit of legal counsel, applicants may be subjected to harried, unsympathetic interrogation about minute details of their victimization (Marouf 2010–2011, 423–424, 428–430). Again, there is a disconnect between the purposes of the institution and respect for victims' stories.

Examples of reparative justice projects include South Africa's Truth and Reconciliation Commission, Argentina's National Commission on the Disappearance of Persons, and Chile's National Truth and Reconciliation Commission and National Commission on Political Imprisonment and Torture. As justice projects go, truth commissions provide the most latitudinarian forums for victims to tell their stories. But because they aim at creating a comprehensive record of what happened and sometimes at societal reconciliation as well, rather than at punishment or restitution, victim-witnesses often end up disappointed by these proceedings. Moreover, they don't experience catharsis; they don't forgive their persecutors; and they resent being exhorted to do so (Madlingozi 2010, 214–215; Soyinka 1999, 81–82).

Because the methods and purposes of justice projects are matters of public knowledge, it might seem that these projects bear little responsibility for informing prospective victim-participants about their operations and the harms that may befall victims who engage with them. However, securing informed consent to participation seems no less elusive in justice projects than in other human rights projects. To judge by studies of victim-witnesses in post-genocide or post-tyranny criminal courts and truth commissions, the assumption that they adequately understood what they were getting into is unwarranted. Victims often fail to anticipate how disturbing it can be to be constrained by rules of evidence in a trial setting, nor do they anticipate how humiliating incredulous, pointed legal questioning can be. As well, confronting the defendants on trial or alleged perpetrators in a truth commission and recounting horrific incidents or listening to others recount horrific incidents can reignite a victim's remembered fear and pain.[14] As a result, retraumatization is an ever-present danger, and experts lament the paucity of psychological support services for victim-witnesses (Brounéus 2010; Ciorciari and Heindel 2011; Dembour and Haslam 2004; D. Taylor 2014, 18–20).[15]

Unlike victim-witnesses in punitive and reparative projects, however, refugees have no choice but to appear for asylum hearings, for they risk deportation and resumed persecution if they don't appear. Yet, these hearings, as I pointed out earlier, are seldom conducted in a manner sensitive to the fragility of victims. So the values of informed consent and protection from retraumatization are effectively contravened in this type of sanctuary project.

Legally established institutions carry out most justice projects.[16] Because these institutions assign circumscribed roles to participants and operate according to fixed procedures, there is little room for victim-witnesses to negotiate the terms on which their testimony will be given. Yet, they are so eager to help incriminate their tormenters in criminal courts, so anxious to have their experiences entered into the historical record under the auspices of truth commissions, or so desperate to save their own skin by entering an asylum claim that they may unwittingly risk retraumatization. In setting up these institutions, concerned lawmakers try to accommodate the needs of victim-witnesses who have suffered severe trauma, but the requirements of justice limit what can be done in deference to victims' vulnerabilities. Still, I argue, justice projects—especially punitive and sanctuary projects—have to date done less than ought to be done to secure informed consent and protection from retraumatization for victim-witnesses.

Many victims who have been warned that they may be "harassed during cross-examination" nevertheless want to testify in criminal courts because seeing their persecutors or those who tortured and killed family members convicted and punished is of paramount importance to them (Ciorciari and Heindel 2011, 124–125; Dembour and Haslam 2004, 156, note 18). The high value that victims place on doing their part to see justice done raises the question of what reforms could make testifying in criminal proceedings less hazardous for victims. One possibility would be to educate judges and defense lawyers about the vulnerabilities of victims and train them to elicit testimony with all due consideration for the emotional volatility of traumatic memories (Ciorciari and Heindel 2011, 135; Danieli 2004, 6). Another possibility, already mentioned, would be to provide adequate psychological support for victim-witnesses during and after trials (Ciorciari and Heindel 2011, 136; Dembour and Haslam 2004, 176). It is clearly a mistake to assume that because victims volunteer to give evidence, they won't need psychological counseling to manage revived traumatic symptoms.

Marie-Bénédicte Dembour and Emily Haslam offer a more radical suggestion. Having found that victims' testimony in the *Krstic* trial at the International Tribunal for the Former Yugoslavia mainly served scene-setting functions and didn't speak directly to the actions and guilt of the accused, they question whether victims need to testify to get convictions in these cases. As well, they ask whether technology could provide vehicles for them to testify without risking retraumatization (Dembour and Haslam 2004, 168). To the extent that their analysis of the role of victim-witnesses in the *Krstic* trial is generalizable, their proposal would not undercut defendants' right to a fair trial, and it would be beneficial to victims in two respects. Not only would it spare them the ordeal of appearing in an alienating courtroom setting, but also it would allow many more victims to contribute their stories to the court's record. The latter is important because victims who are not selected to testify often feel that they have failed to discharge an imprescriptible duty to deceased family members (Ciorciari and Heindel 2011, 129; D. Taylor 2014, 17). If victims' truth telling in criminal trials is to be healing for them as well as instrumental in securing rightful convictions—that is, if criminal trials are to be conducted ethically—the concept of participation by victim-witnesses in punitive justice projects must be rethought.[17] Not only must procedures be tailored to do a better job of securing informed consent and protection from retraumatization for victim-witnesses, but also steps must be taken to ensure that judicial officials and support staff understand the reasons for these adjustments and are committed to adhering to these norms.

In the United States, one justice project—the asylum system—makes no concessions whatsoever to victims' needs. Informed consent is presumed, and no provisions are made to prevent retraumatization. Indeed, it is difficult to imagine how a justice project could be less respectful of victims.

Fatma Marouf documents the deplorable arrangements for recruiting US judges and conducting hearings. Immigration judges are Department of Justice civil servants, most of whom previously held positions in the Department of Homeland Security, where hostility toward migrants abounds (Marouf 2010–2011, 429). As a result, many judges adopt an "inquisitorial" posture in hearings (Marouf 2010–2011, 430).[18] In the face of such intimidating dubiety, victim-applicants are encumbered by multiple disadvantages: unnerved by the official setting, retraumatized by recounting their persecution, ill-equipped to finesse cultural differences (Kirmayer 2003, 170). Moreover, when asylum-seekers deliver fragmentary, inconsistent stories, judges who have little knowledge of the psychology of trauma are quick to conclude that they're lying (Kirmayer 2003, 174; for discussion of what I call hybrid victims' stories, see Chapter 2, section 5–7).

To ensure greater impartiality, Marouf recommends separating the appointment of immigration judges from the Department of Justice (2010–2011, 430). However, this reform is insufficient to ensure respect for victims and their stories, for Marouf proceeds to point out that US immigration judges work under appalling conditions. Their calendars of cases are overloaded; they do not have adequate support staff to do legal research; they are expected to deliver oral decisions on the spot (431–433). Given these pressures, implicit biases are apt to thwart even the most fair-minded judges. Marouf's solution is twofold: (1) reduce judges' caseloads and eliminate the rushed schedules they are expected to maintain, and (2) furnish training in how to counteract implicit biases (434, 447). Additionally, it is imperative that asylum judges be educated about trauma and its effects on autobiographical narration if they are to do their part in preventing retraumatization. As in punitive justice projects, appropriate training for asylum judges must be a priority if US asylum courts are to respect victims in their capacity as storytellers.

Finally, it is scandalous that the United States does not mandate legal counsel for indigent asylum-seekers and that 40 percent of asylum applicants appear at their hearings without legal representation (Marouf 2010–2011, 424). Although it is well known that some asylum-seekers are not fleeing persecution, it is indisputable that many are and that the outcome of their hearings is critical to their future well-being, in some cases to their very survival. In light of this fact, the current US asylum system is worse than unethical in its treatment of victims and their stories. The remedy—a corps of state-employed lawyers tasked with assisting asylum applicants who cannot afford representation—is obvious and attainable.

Despite the concerns I have raised about ethically using victims' stories in justice projects, there is compelling reason to work to reform punitive and sanctuary projects and, most especially, to devise procedures through which reparative projects can ensure informed consent and non-retraumatization for victims. Apropos of truth commissions, Margaret Walker argues that victims' truth telling can serve a double normative purpose (2010). First, providing a forum in which victims can tell their stories respects the human right to the truth regarding human rights abuse (2010, 526–528). Second, an exchange of truths between victims and perpetrators can constitute a form of reparation. Truth telling, Walker argues, is reparative when the victims' credibility is secured and perpetrators shed deniability, when those responsible for human rights abuse forthrightly, thoroughly, and accurately state what they have done, and when the truths become part of the publicly acknowledged record and are integrated into popular consciousness (2010, 536–539). When those conditions are met, truth telling reclaims victims' dignity and justifies their hope for enduring respect.

Like most commentators, I focus on truth commissions because they are the justice projects—the officially sanctioned forums—that are specifically tasked with airing victims' stories and generating permanent records of their testimony. Research projects and aid projects do important moral work, but they can't do the same work as reparative justice projects. Nevertheless, each type of project contributes directly or indirectly to respecting the human right to know the truth about past or ongoing wrongs. Provided that victims' stories are ethically acquired and deployed, all of these types of human rights projects play a vital role in the larger project of advancing human rights.

3. ETHICAL POLITICS: CIVIL SOCIETY AND ADVANCING HUMAN RIGHTS

Participation in civil society might seem like a simple solution for the deleterious effects of the BJW—that is, resorting to victim derogation or victim blaming when you feel powerless to achieve a just solution. However, because civil society is arguably a "necessarily contested idea" (Edwards 2011b), gesturing at civil society isn't particularly informative.

Often termed the "third realm," civil society may be conceived as a space of voluntary, non-coercive association—in contradistinction to the family, which is in many respects non-voluntary, and in contradistinction to the state, which wields coercive power (Walzer 2002, 35). So defined, civil society comprises a potpourri of social groups—industry lobbying organizations, trade unions, recreational softball leagues, community-sponsored soup kitchens, the NAACP, Greenpeace, and Amnesty International, to name just a few. However, civil society is sometimes characterized more narrowly as a social realm in which benevolence and other moral motivations take precedence over self-interest, or as a realm of community and commitment to the common good separate from the individualistic realm of business and the pursuit of profit (Cohen and Arato 1992, viii–ix; Seligman 2002, 19, 28–29). According to this view, civil society is the intermediate sector between the private sector, where self-interest is unleashed in competitive markets, and the public sector, where state regulation imposes constraints.[19] Conceived in this way, civil society excludes industry lobbying organizations and trade unions, for they exist solely to advance the interests of their members.

It would take me too far afield to debate the merits of different conceptions of civil society (for alternative views, see Chambers and Kymlicka 2002; Crocker 1998, 500–503; Edwards 2011a).[20] Nor do I consider theoretical issues about civil society in non-liberal, non-democratic states where the aims of civil society must often be fulfilled, if fulfilled at all, in clandestine face-to-face interaction or through secretive social media networking. For my purposes, it suffices that grassroots associations and NGOs dedicated to furnishing the benefits that realized human rights should secure, social movements mustered to protest institutions or policies that neglect or abuse human rights, and NGOs founded to monitor human rights compliance and publicize violations are uncontroversial civil society actors. (Hereafter, when I refer to grassroots associations, social movements, and NGOs, I'll mean those that aim to advance human rights in one way or another.) Although these groups may rely on various state functions—such as guarantees of the rights to free speech and assembly, financing through public contracts, and legal provisions that exempt nonprofits from taxes—they are not state entities. Moreover, they do not engage in commercial activity to reap profits, but rather to promote human dignity and freedom.

Their admirable aims notwithstanding, all of these human rights groups need to be vigilant in ensuring respect for victims and their stories of abuse. In the first part of this section, I examine ethical issues that arise for participants in more loosely organized human rights groups and a possible ethical shortcoming with respect to participation in large-scale, professionalized NGOs. In the second part, I take up a problem endemic to ethical relations among human rights NGOs.

A. Ethical Practices within Human Rights Groups

I didn't discuss grassroots associations and social movements in section 2 because they don't belong in the category of human rights projects that I developed there.[21] Whereas professionals acquire and use victims' stories in those human rights projects, grassroots associations and social movements are not professionalized ventures, and victims' stories play a less salient role in the work of these groups, if they play any role at all.

Some grassroots associations resemble aid projects run by NGO professionals, for they work to make good on unrealized human rights entitlements. In the face of market failures and gaps in the social safety net, neighborhood food banks deliver goods subsumed by the right to an adequate standard of living (International Covenant on Economic, Social, and Cultural Rights, Art. 2, Sec. 1). In the face of worldwide failure to implement the Beijing Declaration clause condemning violence against women, shelters for battered women provide housing and counseling for victims of domestic violence (UN Fourth World Conference on Women, 1995, Para. 29).[22]

However, grassroots associations differ from professionalized NGOs inasmuch as they may not rely on victims' stories to determine what goods or services to furnish or to recruit volunteers and donations. The interests and capabilities of the citizen-friends who found them often determine what work they do, and these volunteers are typically moved by sympathy for suffering neighbors or principled commitments to alleviating misfortune or realizing human rights. Still, nothing prevents a grassroots association from collecting victims' stories in an effort to improve its work. Nor does anything prevent such a group from using victims' stories to solicit funding and labor from the wider community, perhaps eventually hiring employees to run the day-to-day operations of their organization. As the ambitions of a grassroots association grow, the difference between it and an NGO may reduce to whether it remains an informal cooperative effort or incorporates as a nonprofit. Setting aside the classification question, what matters ethically is that the members of a grassroots association adhere to the norms for aid professionals if they gather or publicize victims' stories.

In contrast, some grassroots associations, such as victim support groups, limit their membership to victims of a certain type of abuse. As I said in my introductory remarks, I believe it is not for me to say how victims themselves may ethically use their stories to recover from human rights abuse or to claim their human rights. Presumably, though, norms of confidentiality among group members would apply.

Grassroots associations and social movements often enlist allies in solidarity with victims. For ethical guidance, I would urge those supporters of victims who are entrusted with knowledge of victims' stories in the context of a grassroots association or a social movement to cultivate the virtues that Serene Khader prescribes for listeners and to follow Linda Alcoff's recommendations when speaking for others (section 2). However, grassroots associations and social movements sometimes try to rally support through speak-outs—meetings at which victims publicly tell their stories—or by circulating those stories through traditional or electronic media. Clearly, all victim-participants should have a voice in whether to pursue either strategy, and allies should defer to victims' judgment regarding its advisability. Furthermore, neither fellow victims nor allies should pressure any reluctant victim into public exposure. Here again, I am convinced that respect for victims in their capacity as storytellers entails that each victim be granted discretion over the use of her story.

So far, I have focused on grassroots associations and social movements. However, as I urged in section 1, NGOs can also serve as release valves that subdue BJW defenses. But whereas participants in grassroots associations and social movements are paradigmatically active in a group's ongoing decision-making processes and public activities, participants in NGOs may do nothing more than click an icon on a website and donate money. Theories of civil society that regard civil society groups as indispensable buttresses for democracy see this relatively disengaged participation as ethically flawed, for it bypasses deliberation with others about the organization's direction and leaves contributors isolated from one another. According to this view of civil society, these anonymous NGO donors are not genuine participants, for they lack a sense of common purpose and shared responsibility, and they do not experience the satisfactions of membership in a cohesive community of like-minded friends.

My initial reply to this criticism questions the image of NGOs as global behemoths that shun member participation. In fact, human rights NGOs vary enormously in scale. Some are gigantic organizations that employ cadres of experts and have budgets to match—for example, Amnesty International and Care. However, many aren't. Women Defending Ourselves is a San Francisco NGO providing self-defense training for women as a stopgap against gendered human rights abuse. Your community shelter for battered women and children may also be a local NGO, and it may or may not be affiliated with an umbrella organization, such as the National Coalition

Against Domestic Violence. NGO programs can be local, national, or transnational in impact, and their governance systems can be local, national, or transnational in structure. Moreover, the astounding pro-liferation of NGOs in every region of the world since 1990 suggests that the colossus stereotype is misleading (Brown et al. 2000, 10–12).

For my purposes, though, the most telling reply spotlights how effective giant NGOs often are as advocates for human rights and providers of benefits to which right-holders are entitled (Brown et al. 2000, 19–23; Roth 2014). Consequently, it is rational for individu-als who are conscience-stricken by the lapses and oversights of the international human rights regime to turn to these organizations to represent them in pursuit of a more just world. By making mone-tary donations to these NGOs, individuals know they heighten their influence through consolidation of resources and specialization in advocacy or benefit delivery. If so, there is good reason to grant even the biggest, most professionalized NGOs a role in keeping victim derogation and victim blaming at bay.

Nevertheless, I hasten to add that we are not confronting an either/or predicament. The institutionalized human rights move-ment, with its professional NGO staffing and presence on the world stage, coexists perfectly well with scrappy, agile grassroots associa-tions and social movements that are quick to latch onto novel polit-ical opportunities and take advantage of digital technology and transitory social phenomena to build momentum for their cause (Tarrow 2009, 172). Prominent NGOs do not threaten or obstruct small-scale, seat-of-the-pants activism. But for individuals who lack the time or inclination for traditional modes of civil society partici-pation, contributing to the advance of human rights through dona-tions to large-scale NGOs is clearly an acceptable alternative.

Grassroots associations, social movements, and NGOs all provide outlets for expressing moral concerns about perceived wrongs.[23] Thus they all serve as buffers against toxic BJW defense mechanisms. By augmenting people's sense of empowerment and efficacy, these joint undertakings pacify the tendency to derogate or blame victims. Recent history shows, moreover, that the advent of the Internet and the rise of social media have exponentially enhanced people's ability to improvise collective responses to perceived wrongs.[24] More surely than ever before, then, affirming your helplessness in the face of injustice in today's connected world looks to be a hypocritical excuse, as opposed to a realistic appraisal of your puny power.

B. *Ethical Relations among Human Rights NGOs*

In their discussion of women's transnational human rights networks, Margaret Keck and Kathryn Sikkink quote a Nigerian women's rights activist who reiterates the ethical issue of speaking for others that I discussed in section 2 and diagnoses a new ethical problem that I propose to address now:

> Why should we [local NGOs] link hands [with Global North NGOs]? Local NGOs cannot get support for their work so we have to affiliate with international NGOs. Then we all hold up our hands to the "gates of heaven." When international NGOs arrive at the gate, they drop us and do the talking on our behalf.
>
> (1998, 183; bracketed material added)

The problem of funding that this activist alludes to is multidimensional. As Keck and Sikkink note, few NGOs in the Global South have the staff, time, and know-how to write the elaborate proposals that major funding agencies demand, and so-called pass-through funding—whereby a sponsoring NGO obtains a large grant to distribute to smaller Global South NGOs—is meager (1998, 182–183). At the same time, competition for funding among Global North NGOs has become cutthroat. So fierce and winner-take-all has this competition become that one commentator worries that a Global North NGO "oligopoly" is emerging (Simmons 1998, 88).

Funding issues dominate discussions of the future of NGOs. In Thomas Dichter's words, "[T]he funding pie is shrinking just as the growth of NGOs around the world continues to expand" (1999, 52). Many Global North states are reducing foreign aid budgets, and since personal incomes in the Global North have plateaued, so have individuals' contributions to nonprofits (Edwards 1999, 29). As a result, NGOs scramble for public grants and private donations, and this Hobbesian struggle for survival incentivizes profound changes in the cultures of NGOs. Many adopt private-sector values and hire MBAs to manage money and boost efficiency (Dichter 1999, 53–55). They compete with one another to provide services that garner media coverage, which serves as a surrogate for effectiveness and in turn attracts funding (Salm 1999, 95). This syndrome is plainly inimical to high ethical standards for these civil society actors.

In light of global structural conditions and internal institutional imperatives, urging NGOs to withdraw from this noxious competition might seem naive. Nevertheless, I can't resist pointing out that the World Association of Non-Governmental Organizations (WANGO) embraces this radical injunction in its Code of Ethics and Conduct for NGOs. Although some of the major international human rights NGOs belong to WANGO, I regret to say that alarmingly few of them subscribe to the code of ethics. Still, I think it is worth highlighting a couple of tenets that WANGO's document enunciates:

- Sustainable progress, peace, and justice require that all organizations contribute to the common good. Thus an NGO should integrate self-development and service to others . . . (8)

- NGOs should maintain ethical, cooperative relationships with other NGOs, and should partner where possible and appropriate for the sake of the greater public good (9)

> (http://wango.org/codeofethics.aspx accessed 1/18/2015)

Apparently, the authors of this code believe that the common good is the superordinate value that must guide the conduct of NGOs. NGOs should collaborate to advance the common good, and they should not allow institutional gains to take precedence over advancing the common good. A tall order, it would seem, considering what is actually happening in the world of large-scale, international, professionalized NGOs.

It is necessary to acknowledge the strand of idealism in the WANGO code, but it is no less necessary to notice that its idealistic elements comport with some hardheaded, realistic analyses of how major international NGOs need to change in order to remain relevant and go forward. Consider, for example, the views of Michael Edwards, a former director of the Ford Foundation's Governance and Civil Society Program, whose prior experience spans work at the World Bank and numerous NGOs. Edwards writes:

> NGOs cannot fulfill any of their new roles unless they agree to work together, both with other NGOs in other parts of the world and with other allies in civil society. They need to integrate themselves into wider civil society coalitions and cross-sectoral alliances that can reach further into the economic and political arena.
>
> (1999, 30)

He then entertains two adaptations to changing conditions that are available to NGOs today.

The one Edwards calls the "global marketing strategy" would sink NGOs deeper into the corporate mentality that has already made inroads on their practices. Each NGO could undertake "more aggressive global marketing of the NGO's own brand, in which the agency becomes an openly market-oriented institution intent on building its own position vis-à-vis competitors" (1999, 32). Adhering to this corporatization strategy, NGOs would constantly seek out and expand into new markets while devising ever more marketable services and products. Edwards doubts the tenability of this approach (1999, 33). First, the foreign aid funding that supports NGO projects is declining, with no end in sight. Second, NGOs might find themselves competing unsuccessfully with commercial purveyors of similar services and products offered at lower prices. Third, even if the for-profit sector doesn't jump into this market, some NGOs that adopt this model will fail because market competition weeds out weaker competitors. Fourth, this approach is a formula for compromising NGO values and sacrificing any claim to make a real dent in the social, political, and economic structures that perpetuate poverty, inflame armed conflict, and subvert human rights.

Edwards advocates what I would call the *ethical alternative*. I'll quote him at length:

> In this scenario, Northern NGOs become equal members of emerging international movements, coalescing around common goals and values but working synergistically to achieve and advance them. The priority goes to working in one's own society, and working from it to support the efforts of others— building capacity in different parts of the movement, making space for weaker members to become strong, coming together and breaking apart according to context and circumstance. This is the traditional role of international NGOs, played out much

more forcefully and strategically in the context of globalization and shifting north-south relations. Each member of the movement concentrates on its area of comparative advantage, and has an equal voice in negotiating solutions to the dilemmas of governance, accountability, management, and communications in multilayered international alliances. . . . In this approach, impact comes not from the size or market share of individual NGOs, but from the multiplier effect of working together and leveraging change in much larger structures—markets, businesses, politics, ideas, and attitudes. Legitimacy is derived from the NGO's social roots (its domestic constituency) and from demonstrable adherence to the values that hold the movement together. There is no intention of building up ever-larger NGOs, because the overall objective is to build support for the cause, not the institutions that promote it.

(Edwards 1999, 33)

If Edwards is right (and I think he is), WANGO's ethical imperatives for NGOs coincide with their survival imperatives.

4. CONCLUDING REFLECTIONS

I began this chapter by rehearsing some of Elizabeth Spelman's insights into misuses of victims' stories, and I'll end it by reprising and updating one of her themes. Spelman, recall, condemns the women's suffrage movement in the US for its appropriation and usurpation of the anti-slavery abolitionist movement. As with current trends in the world of international NGOs, suffragists acted as if advancing rights was a zero-sum game that women and blacks could not win together. In hindsight, we know that the second wave feminist movement of the 1960s–1970s also had a monocular agenda. Under the banner of women's rights and women's equality, the interests of women of color, lesbians, and poor women, among others, were shunted aside. Much anguished soul-searching and enmity among women could have been avoided if Spelman's critique, WANGO's principles, and Edwards's collaborative vision had informed the practice of mid-twentieth-century feminism. It is crucial that today's human rights movement adopt the ethical view that Spelman, WANGO, and Edwards propound.

Their view is triply attractive. First, they regard the full panoply of human rights protections as equally important. They do not hierarchize human rights. Second, they respect all right-holders as equals. They do not prioritize some people's claims over those of others. Third, they unite powerful NGOs and popular social movements in the inspiring quest for full realization of human rights. To that end, they enjoin all players to quell fears of losing out, to retreat from clashing initiatives, and to cooperate for the betterment of all right-holders.

Daunting as heeding this counsel may be, doing so is mandatory for organizations dedicated to advancing human rights. Were human rights proponents to adhere to this ethic of solidarity and pursue a strategy of concerted action, there would be reason to hope that the resistance to human rights that's built into national and transnational centers of power would ultimately yield. Anticipating that prospect, I envisage a world in which victimization would cease to exploit people's vulnerabilities and strip them of the humanity they share with everyone else. Victims would neither be despised nor glorified. Their stories would receive the attention and the credibility they deserve. Reports of abuse would routinely kindle vibrant outrage, set in motion thorough inquiries into allegations, and result in fitting remedies for legitimate claimants. But the clamor of new victims' stories would gradually subside, for spotty, grudging implementation of human rights and outright violations of human rights would be roundly condemned. With commitment to the dignity of common humanity firm, the culture of human rights would flourish, thanks in part to the courageous victims who have told their stories.

NOTES

Introduction

1. For a rich treatment of these matters, see Walker (2006).
2. I have decided not to discuss the stories of Holocaust victims for several reasons. First, many other scholars have written insightfully about those stories. Since I do not have anything of great moment to add to these earlier treatments, I do not believe it would serve any useful purpose to recapitulate this work here. Second, because the advent of the international system of human rights in the aftermath of the Holocaust did not put a stop to human rights abuse, I believe it is important to seek out contemporary resources for strengthening commitment to human rights norms and resisting their abrogation. Third, I believe it is crucial to address forms of human rights abuse that took place very recently or that are ongoing today. Human rights abuse is not a thing of the past; it is a horrifically timely issue.
3. I didn't interview victims because as a philosopher I'm not qualified to do so. Rather I rely on published diaries, memoirs, and interviews conducted by journalists and academic researchers.
4. As the editor of Slahi's text, Siems requested a meeting with Slahi to discuss his changes to the manuscript and to make sure that Slahi approved them. The Pentagon turned down this request (2015, xliv–xlv).
5. For this biographical outline, I rely principally on research regarding Slahi's case that Siems presents in his introduction to *Guantánamo Diary*.
6. Official US documents corroborate the allegations of torture at Guantánamo that Slahi makes in his book.

7. For the results of the polygraph test, see Slahi (2015, footnote on p. 309).

8. Guantánamo guards confiscated Slahi's manuscript and transferred it to a high-security depository in Washington, DC. It was kept secret until Slahi revealed its existence during his testimony at a 2005 Administrative Review Board hearing. Years later, litigation and negotiation compelled US authorities to turn the manuscript over to Slahi's attorneys, but only in a declassified, redacted version (Slahi 2015, xv–xvi).

9. On a couple of occasions when he does lose control, he tells us about it (Slahi 2015, 243, 258). For example, in the midst of his "Birthday Party" while "bleeding from [his] mouth, [his] ankles, [his] wrists, and maybe from [his] nose," one of the torturers commands him to say his name, and he screams it back. Slahi comments on this turn of events:

> You could tell I was completely scared. Usually I wouldn't talk if somebody starts to hurt me. . . . This was a milestone in my interrogation history. You can tell I was hurt like never before; it wasn't me anymore, and I would never be the same as before. A thick line was drawn between my past and my future with the first hit [redacted] delivered to me.
>
> (Slahi 2015, 258)

10. I take the scope of human rights protections to be demarcated by the various UN-sponsored treaties that legally implemented the aspirations enunciated in the *Universal Declaration of Human Rights*. Links to the human rights conventions can be found here: http://www.ohchr.org/EN/ProfessionalInterest/Pages/CoreInstruments.aspx (accessed 2/5/15).

11. Although *A Woman in Berlin* was not published until 1954, the author kept her diary during the last days of World War II in Europe. As I stated earlier, my preference is to draw attention to post-1948 human rights abuse. Alas, I could not find a comparably sustained victim's story recounting the abuses that took place in the rape camps that Serbian troops operated in Bosnia during the 1990s wars in the Balkans or similar campaigns of abuse elsewhere. So in order to include sexual violence in armed combat in my treatment of victims' stories, I've made an exception for *A Woman in Berlin*.

Chapter 1

1. Rorty's "we" is comprised of people "in the safe, rich democracies" (1993, 113).

2. Rorty echoes Locke's characterization of offenders, saying that "we" see them as "beasts of prey," and he adds that we see victims, too, as animals—we see them as "cattle" being herded (1993, 113).

3. I'll have little to say about the historical events, institutions, and social forces that subvert Locke's correlation of rights, violations, and victims. Nor will I say

much about the ulterior motives that undoubtedly shore up divisions between rights violations and ascriptions of victimhood.

4. http://www.un.org/en/documents/udhr/ (accessed 8/25/2014)

5. http://www.unhcr.org/3b66c2aa10.html (accessed 8/25/2014).

6. People with disabilities were incarcerated and abused elsewhere.

7. I leave aside SS claims that their victims were really criminals or enemies of the state, as well as controversies about the complicity of the Jewish Elders in the deportation of members of their communities. The former were lies, and the latter overlook the ultimate inescapability of the genocide. With respect to the *kapos* in the camps—Jews recruited to serve the Nazis in exchange for better treatment—see Card (2002, 220–227).

8. It's worth noting that the *OED* tells us that use of the term *victim* to denote someone "who is put to death or subjected to torture by another" or someone "who suffers severely in body or property through cruel or oppressive treatment" precedes applying the term to victims of natural forces—such as disease and "acts of god"—by nearly 150 years. Whereas the pathetic victim paradigm first appeared in English in 1660, victimization by yellow fever did not enter usage until 1803, victimization by earthquakes not until 1890.

9. Paul Ricoeur's account of characters in a narrative seems to echo this polarization of individuals. According to Shaun Gallagher, Ricoeur holds that characters are either agents or sufferers, not simultaneously both agents and sufferers (2003, 12).

10. For a fascinating discussion of a historical exception to this rule, see Didier Fassin and Richard Rechtman's analysis of the politics of victimization following the Viet Nam War. US veterans who had committed war crimes against Vietnamese civilians and enemy soldiers were classified as victims on the grounds that they were suffering from post-traumatic stress disorder (2009, 84–95).

11. For similar representations of Liu in the media, see Nicholas Kristof's *New York Times* column (http://kristof.blogs.nytimes.com/2010/10/08/liu-xiaobo-and-chinese-democracy/?_php=true&_type=blogs&_r=0, accessed 9/6/2014), an unsigned BBC report (http://www.bbc.com/news/world-europe-11499098, accessed 9/6/2014), Tania Branigan's report for the *Guardian* (http://www.theguardian.com/world/2010/oct/08/liu-xiaobo-nobel-chinese-fury, accessed 9/6/2014), and this from *Fox News* (http://www.foxnews.com/world/2010/10/08/chinese-dissident-liu-wins-nobel-peace-prize/, 9/6/2014).

12. Many human rights violations don't imprison or physically restrain people. Rather, they consist of institutionalized discriminatory exploitation or subordination that stops far short of the Third Reich's concentration camps and extermination technologies. For example, until the US Supreme Court's 2015 decision in *Obergefell v. Hodges*, many US states denied same-sex couples the

right to marry, and very few governments elsewhere countenance same-sex marriage. AI advocates for these victims, too. Unfortunately, I do not have space to consider this and other forms of victimization in relation to the two victim paradigms.

13. I defend the claim that severe poverty in an LDDW economy coerces individuals into irregular migration channels in Meyers (2014), and I defend the claim that women who voluntarily migrate with the help of traffickers and who are forced into sex work at their destinations are victims of force and ought to be granted asylum in Meyers (2016).

14. For purposes of the present project and in the interest of space, I limit my discussion to prevalent patterns of vulnerability in parts of the former Soviet Union and trafficking practices within Eastern Europe and into Western Europe.

15. Kelly adds a layer of complexity to the coercive economic forces brought to bear on these women. Many "smuggled" women borrow money from relatives to seek their fortunes in foreign sex industries. If they are deported and return empty-handed, they are unable to repay their debts and feel compelled to submit to retrafficking in the hope of making good on their debts, if not improving family finances (2005, 248).

16. Kara notes that in Central and Eastern Europe, seduction coupled with promises of lifelong romance in the West is another common ploy to lure women into trafficking schemes (2009, 9).

17. For additional discussion of inalienable rights, see section 3A.

18. See Haynes (2006, 440). For discussion of the problem of defining trafficking and distinguishing it from smuggling as a problem in research methodology, see Kelly (2005, 238).

19. See Cudd (2006, 125–126, 198).

20. Evidence of wage or debt bondage in the worldwide trafficking underground is extensive. See, for example, the 2002 Human Rights Watch report on Bosnia and Herzegovina, "Hopes Betrayed: Trafficking of Women and Girls to Post-Conflict Bosnia and Herzegovina for Forced Prostitution" (http://www.hrw.org/legacy/reports/2002/bosnia/Bosnia1102.pdf, accessed 4/12/2009); the 2007 International Organization for Migration report "Assessment of Mobility and HIV Vulnerability among Myanmar Migrant Sex Workers and Factory Workers in Mae Sot District, Tak Province, Thailand" (http://www.iom-seasia.org/resource/pdf/AssessmentofMobilityHIVMyanmar.pdf, accessed 4/12/2009); and Sean O'Neill's 2007 "Crime Gangs 'Expand Sex Slavery into Shires'" (http://www.timesonline.co.uk/tol/news/uk/crime/article2547626.ece, accessed 4/12/2009). Evidence of remittances to sex workers' families is spottier. Laura María Agustín argues that the payments are substantial ("Contributing to 'Development': Money Made Selling Sex," Chapter 2, p. 10, in Sex Work and Money, ed. Melissa Ditmore (http://www.nswp.org/pdf/

R4SW-09.PDF, accessed 4/12/2009). However, testimony concerning wage bondage in Europe leaves the impression that trafficked sex workers there seldom if ever escape from its grip.

21. For a powerful account of how globalization and 1990s International Monetary Fund policies sparked an explosion of sex trafficking, see Kara (2009, 25–30).

22. Not surprisingly, some women tell stories that smack of ambitions to upward mobility rather than escape from poverty (Jacobsen and Skilbrei 2010, 199–200). However, because stories of desperate flights from severe poverty and/or domestic abuse and the need to support family back home predominate, I center my discussion on that background narrative.

23. I thank Michael Kühler for bringing this point to my attention. For relevant discussion, see Held (1989).

24. From another standpoint, what my argument shows is something that many human rights advocates know intuitively—namely, that refusing to recognize all of these women as victims has nothing to do with the authenticity of their victimization. At best, it has only to do with an excessively rigid, yet attractive interpretation of the concept of a victim. At worst, it has to do with a xenophobic politics underwritten by erroneous calculations of crass self-interest on the part of workers and citizens of more affluent societies.

25. 2008 data from Amnesty International confirm that 138 countries—or more than two-thirds of the countries in the world—have abolished the death penalty in law or in practice (http://www.amnesty.org/en/death-penalty/abolitionist-and-retentionist-countries, accessed 3/31/2009).

26. In light of the evidence I presented in section 1A that Europeans also conceive pathetic victims as innocent in virtue of their passivity, it is an interesting question why the European Union's ban on capital punishment is not seen as controversial. Unfortunately, I cannot pursue this issue here.

27. With Governor Pat Quinn's signing of the death penalty repeal bill passed by the Illinois legislature, the moratorium has been converted into a permanent prohibition (http://www.suntimes.com/4225981-417/gov.-pat-quinn-signs-bill-repealing-illinois-death-penalty). New Mexico, New Jersey, Connecticut, New York, Nebraska, and Maryland have also abolished capital punishment in recent years (http://www.deathpenaltyinfo.org/states-and-without-death-penalty, accessed 7/3/2015).

28. The Innocence Project and the Center for Wrongful Convictions at the Northwestern University Law School are affiliated. Unlike the Innocence Project's website, which does not express approval for abolishing the death penalty, the website of the Center for Wrongful Convictions states that "the only sure way to avoid executing an innocent person is to abolish the death penalty" (http://www.law.northwestern.edu/wrongfulconvictions/aboutus/, accessed 1/3/2009). This statement is better than silence on the issue of

abolition, but it stops well short of asserting that the death penalty is a violation of human rights.

29. Of course, a case can be made that no crime can justify cruel and inhuman punishment. Although that approach to rejecting the death penalty complements my argument concerning the two victim paradigms, I won't pursue it here.

30. I borrow this language from Schaffer and Smith (2004, 186).

31. I thank Florian Zimmermann for prompting me to develop this line of thought.

32. Although Locke sets limits on the severity of punishment, his doctrine that offenders forfeit their rights comports with this mistaken view that rightly convicted prisoners cannot be victims of human rights violations.

33. For valuable discussion of the victim–perpetrator polarity in human rights discourse and its malign impact on prisoners' rights, see Schaffer and Smith (2004, 160–186).

34. It is worth noting that the scope of this argument is extremely broad. If it is sound, it follows that no one can consent to doing sex work, whether or not she or he has been trafficked and regardless of the conditions of work.

35. See, for example, http://www.nytimes.com/2002/04/22/opinion/stopping-the-use-of-child-soldiers.html;
http://www.nytimes.com/2007/05/13/nyregion/13soldier.html?pagewanted=all;
http://www.nytimes.com/2007/04/29/weekinreview/29gett.html?pagewanted=all;
http://www.nytimes.com/2005/05/08/magazine/08UGANDA.html?sq=May%208,%202005&st=cse&scp=4&pagewanted=all;
http://www.hrw.org/reports/2007/burma1007/2.htm#_Toc180812702.
Also see Beah (2007), especially Chapters 13 and 16.

36. For documentation of confiscated passports, see, for example, http://www.nytimes.com/1998/01/11/world/contraband-women-a-special-report-traffickers-new-cargo-arge-slavic-women.html?sec=&spon=&scp=5&sq=trafficking%20victims%20confiscated%20passport&st=cse&pagewanted=all;
http://www.nytimes.com/2008/07/10/nyregion/10nurse.html?scp=6&sq=trafficking%20victims%20confiscated%20passport&st=cse;
http://www.hrw.org/en/news/2000/02/21/international-trafficking-women-and-children.
For evidence of the use of photographs, see: http://www.bloomberg.com/apps/news?pid=20601109&sid=amKSCFA_Fm3s&refer=home;
http://www.europarl.europa.eu/workingpapers/libe/pdf/109_en.pdf, p. 13.

37. In the case of child victims, the measures aren't merely too costly. Rather, children don't have the agentic capacities that would make it sensible to expect them to take any action whatsoever.

38. For related discussion of the role of variable social expectations in ascriptions of responsibility, see Smiley (1992).

39. Coercion is the most controversial of these three concepts. Questions about whether a proposal should be considered a coercive threat or a legitimate offer raise the issue of whether submitting to the proposal would make someone worse off than she otherwise would be as judged by her actual circumstances or as judged by her rightful circumstances. This is the question about whether the proposal recipient's baseline should be empirical or moralized. As well, there are debates about whether coercion is necessarily wrong and whether offers as well as threats can be coercive. Important contributors to these debates include Robert Nozick (1974), Alan Wertheimer (1987), David Zimmerman (1981), and Scott Anderson (2008a, 2008b).

40. That so many prisoners worldwide—"detainees" in the "war on terror"—are now dragooned into this no-rights zone is all the more cause for alarm. For related discussion, see my discussion in the Introduction of Mohamedou Ould Slahi's *Guantánamo Diary*.

41. For documentation of the case, see http://www.justfamilies.org/roundup/ and http://www.nytimes.com/2014/08/30/us/victim-of-domestic-violence-in-guatemala-is-ruled-eligible-for-asylum-in-us.html (both accessed 9/9/ 2014). This development both surprised and pleased feminist asylum experts, for the United States is not a State Party to the Convention on the Elimination of All Forms of Discrimination Against Women.

42. For an elegant critique of morally innocent persons, as opposed to moral innocence with respect to actions, see Wolgast (1993). Along similar lines, Soderlund comments that in the United States innocence has become a "criterion for public sympathy. . . . But it is a nearly impossible standard against which to hold living, breathing human beings, except perhaps children" (2005, 81).

43. See, for example, Ackerly (2008), Nickel (2007), Beitz (2001), Shue (1980), Griffin (2008), and Pogge (2007).

44. http://www.ohchr.org/EN/ProfessionalInterest/Pages/CoreInstruments. aspx (accessed 9/14/2014).

45. Here, I am suggesting that Fjellstrom's impotence criterion is too strong, that it is absolutist in a way that resembles the innocence-as-passivity criterion (2002, 112–113). For helpful, related discussion of human dignity and the "simplistic contrast between agency and passivity," see Nussbaum (2001, 405–414).

46. John Braithwaite points out that Richard Cheney and some other Western leaders opposed releasing "Mandela the terrorist" from prison (Braithwaite 2006, 435). Braithwaite condemns the "stupidity" of their position, and I would argue that the two paradigms I set out underwrite this stupidity (Braithwaite 2006, 435). Although I think many people now regard Mandela as a heroic victim despite the fact that he committed and advocated violence to end apartheid, he seems to be the exception that proves the rule. Both because apartheid was so indisputably abominable and because Mandela turned out to be such

an exemplary leader after his release, people endorse this exception without modifying the paradigm.

47. Following Schaffer and Smith and Brown, it might be argued that the trouble with our conception of a victim is not the simplistic views of innocence that are in play but rather that victimhood is construed as a personal identity, as opposed to a transitory position vis-à-vis a certain event. I think there is something to this point. Perhaps some experiences of victimization counterproductively congeal into identities. Yet, over-identifying with victimization would not be so harmful if it didn't mean identifying with passivity. I hasten to add, however, that some forms of victimization seem all but impossible to "get over," perhaps shouldn't be "gotten over"—genocide is an obvious case in point. For these victims, acknowledgment of their agency in the midst of horror can be pivotal to psychological survival.

Chapter 2

1. Nelson (now Lindemann) (2001) and Danto (1985) are exceptions to this trend. In characterizing narratives, neither cites normative features.

2. I'm not sure whether Amsterdam and Bruner would contest my point. They claim that their definition is "austere" and that it specifies "what is necessary to make a story," which suggests that they do not regard their account as stipulative or as explicating one of many possible narrative structures (2000, 113). If this is their position, I think it's too restrictive.

3. Along similar lines, Susan Slyomovics documents the inhibition of women's testimony about rape in post-Apartheid South Africa and after the death of King Hassan II in Morocco (Slyomovics 2005, 81, 85, 87).

4. For discussion of the need for this kind of contextualization in subversive narratives, see Ewick and Silbey (1995, 218–220). In a situation with interesting parallels to and departures from Shepler's case, Schaffer and Smith analyze how the stories of women who were abducted by the Japanese and turned into "comfort women" during World War II lost relevant contextual information (2004, 134–146).

5. For valuable discussion of controversies concerning traditional justice and transitional justice, see "Reparations, Truth, and Reconciliation" (in Soyinka 1999). For discussion of the premium placed on forensic or factual truth and the relative neglect of narrative truth—the narrative arc, emotional tenor, and rich detail of victims' stories—in the official report of the South African Truth and Reconciliation Commission, see Wilson (2001, 36–38).

6. For doubts about the necessity of closure, see Rimmon-Kenan (2006).

7. A narrative along the lines I sketch here would satisfy Noël Carroll's condition of narrativity, which is that the events depicted participate in a causal network (2001, 126).

8. This narrative would satisfy J. David Velleman's condition of narrativity, which is that the events depicted participate in an emotional arc (2003, 17).

9. See Chapter 4 for discussion of the rhetorical devices employed in another victim's story of sexual predation and the compromises that mass rape led her to make.

10. At the time of its publication, however, it did not gain a wide readership, in part because its appearance was eclipsed by the beginning of the Civil War (Yellin 2000, xxvi).

11. On the issue of comprehensiveness, Strejilevich observes that such narratives are "incapable of exhibiting all the horror," and she rejects demands for "total exposure" (2006, 207). Thus, some victims' stories do not measure up to one of the presumed advantages of chronicles over annals.

12. For helpful discussion of the difference between core events and peripheral details in asylum-seekers' stories, see Herlihy et al. (2002).

13. In arguing that closure is an artifact of narrative and doesn't exist in the real world, White assumes that closure consists of a final ending (1987, 23–24). Pointing out that events don't come to an end, he urges that closure can only be moral and that morality is a function of the imagination, not a feature of the world.

14. I adopt the term *rapport* here, following Montesquieu, who, according to Hannah Arendt, defines laws as *rapports* (Arendt 1998, 190). For related discussion of narrative necessity in autobiographical stories and the dangers of narrative fixity, see Westlund (2011, 396–397).

15. Put another way, definitive moral closure amounts to repudiating what Ronald Dworkin calls the "interpretive attitude" (1986, 47–52). Adopting the interpretive attitude toward social and legal norms authorizes individuals and public officials to reconsider norms in light of the purpose they are supposed to serve.

16. In my view, White exaggerates the finality of narrative closure when he is arguing that moral closure is the only possible form of narrative closure, but he concedes that no closure is definitive when he is arguing that the annals and chronicle forms more accurately represent reality.

17. For rhetorical analysis of some women's testimony in the first few days of the South African TRC, see Ross (2001, 260–266). I'll have more to say about the rhetoric in which victims' stories are couched in Chapters 3 and 4.

18. I note, though, that a hybrid victim's story that achieves narrative moral closure in the sense I present here may, but need not, facilitate psychological closure for the victim.

19. I leave aside psychological ignorance and poor interpretative skills.

20. See Mullin (2002) for helpful suggestions about moral imagination in relation to literary works that represent morally problematic states of affairs.

Chapter 3

1. I have learned a great deal from Nussbaum's work on emotion and emotional understanding of literature (1990, 2001). However, principally for reasons of space, but also because her work has already received extensive comment in the literature, I won't take up her thinking in this chapter.

2. For a similar view in legal theory, see Dershowitz (1996).

3. For useful comment on this claim, see Goldie (2003, 310 n13).

4. Ironically, Cheryl Misak provides an epistemological defense of Velleman's own use of storytelling and his invocation of the personal experience it encodes in "A Right of Self-Termination?" (2008).

5. Shlomith Rimmon-Kenan (2006) suggests a minimalist view of narrative:

   I would characterize narrative by two necessary features, plus an additional, dynamic and variable cluster of optional characteristics. In my view, a "discursive formation" (Kreiswirth's term) is a narrative when double temporality and a transmitting (or mediating) agency are dominant in it. As I suggested in the final chapter composed for the 2002 edition of my *Narrative Fiction* (orig. 1983), narratives are governed by a dual time-scheme owing to the ontological gap between the succession of signs and the temporality of the events (in whatever expanded definition). As distinct from that edition of the book, however, I substitute "transmitting agency" for "narrator" here in order to make room for phenomena like film, characterized not by a narrating voice but by a composite mediating agency: scriptor, director, producer, director of photography, editor, etc. Optional characteristics, resemblances that are often mentioned in discourse about narrative, are: beginnings-middles-and-ends, closure, coherence, causality, addressee. In the absence of either double temporality or a transmitting agency, or in case of a predominance of optional over necessary features, I would prefer to speak of "narrative elements" rather than "a narrative." (17)

6. For influential discussions relating narrative to selfhood, see Taylor (1989); Schechtman (1996, 2007, 2008); Lindemann Nelson (2001); Mackenzie (2008); Goldie (2012).

7. For relevant work on this topic, see Goldie (2003a, 2003b) and Carroll (2001, 215–235, 306–316).

8. Robinson cites the empirical work of Robert Zajonc (1980, 1984, 1994) and Richard Lazarus (1991) to support her account of affective appraisals. Although Robinson maintains that affective appraisals are noncognitive because they "occur without any conscious deliberation or awareness" and "do not involve any complex information processing," I regard her reasons for denying these appraisals cognitive standing as unduly restrictive (2005, 45). If there is such a thing as nonconceptual or nonpropositional knowledge, and I think there is, then there is no reason not to count "affective appraisals" as cognitive. That feeling need not have a cognitive dimension does not entail that it never does.

9. For work on emotion that complements Robinson's account in important ways, but that argues against the role of conceptual or propositional participation in the constitution of emotion, see Prinz (2004, 57). Other work that complements Robinson's account but that argues for less separation between bodily appraisal and arousal on neurological grounds includes Colombetti and Thompson (2007) and Colombetti (2010).

10. Iris Young maintains that narrative capitalizes on the "erotic dimension of communication," that the rhetorical devices that stories employ "pull on thought through desire" (1997, 71). Her observation raises complex issues that I can't address here, but I want to point out that Robinson's account of emotion as an agency-guiding faculty that is also integral to narrative understanding brings her view into close proximity with Young's claim about the link between narrative and desire. For discussion of Young's view, see Chapter 4, section 6.

11. Robinson develops this line of thought as a critique of Noël Carroll's (2001, 225–233) theory of "criterial prefocusing" in literature. Against Carroll's view that fiction determines how readers will respond emotionally by embedding the necessary and sufficient conditions for particular emotions in the plotline, Robinson points out that "many of the shifting states that are evoked in the ongoing experience of reading do not have neatly categorizable names" (2005, 182).

12. The accuracy of Beah's account has been questioned in press reports. Journalists for the *Australian* have turned up testimony to the effect that Beah is mistaken about some dates and therefore about the age at which he first sought refuge in the rain forest and other events. These investigations have escalated into broad charges about the truthfulness of Beah's narrative, and these allegations have been covered by *Slate* and other publications (http://www.slate.com/id/2185928/).

    I am in no position to adjudicate this controversy. However, two points seem noteworthy to me. First, there can be no doubt that UNICEF workers took Ishmael Beah into custody and sent him to Benin Home for detoxification treatment, counseling, and aid in locating his only living blood relative in Sierra Leone. Presumably substantiated by official records, the UNICEF website affirms the organization's role in extricating Beah from the Sierra Leone army (http://www.unicef.org/voy/takeaction/takeaction_3264.html). Likewise, it seems indisputable that Beah was selected to represent Sierra Leone at a UN conference on the problems of children and that he met Laura Simms while in New York City participating in the conference. Second, in one respect, his account of the war in Sierra Leone is remarkably restrained. To the best of my recollection, his book only once mentions one of the most ghastly practices known to have characterized the warfare there during the 1990s— the RUF often terrorized villagers by using machetes to amputate the limbs, lips, ears, etc., of their supposed enemies (Beah 27). Had Beah's aim been to produce a sensational account that would fictionalize his work but maximize book sales, it seems likely that he would have played up this practice.

13. I say "roughly" because different websites, including UNICEF's and NPR's, give divergent dates for his age at the time he was first affected by the war. In light of everything that happened to him subsequently, it's easy to understand how his memoir might err about precisely when his village first came under rebel attack and to forgive a bit of inexactitude.

14. In a rare mention of imagination, Robinson's discussion of how compassion for Anna Karenina is aroused cites Lawrence Blum's claim that "dwelling imaginatively on the condition of the other person" is necessary for compassion (2005, 110).

15. For her discussion of the role of ethical impropriety in imaginative resistance, see Gendler (2006, 154–156).

16. See, for example, Ovuga, Emilio, Thomas O Oyok, and E. B. Moro (2008). (http://www.ncbi.nlm.nih.gov/pmc/articles/PMC2583264/, accessed 10/14/2014) and Thabet, Abdel Aziz, and Panos Vostanis (2008). (http://www.ncbi.nlm.nih.gov/pubmed/18365135, accessed 10/14/2014).

17. Experts on children's rights point out that well-meaning Americans can be over-zealous in pursuing them. For example, they may throw their support behind closing or boycotting carpet factories that employ child labor, only to find those children forced into prostitution instead (Basu and Van 1998).

18. Hayden White's account of narrative history suggests another way to weave human rights abuse into stories (see Chapter 2, section 3). Narratives of the process of recognizing and implementing a right or of challenges to and changes in orthodox understandings of a right could incorporate affectively moving vignettes recounting victimization. The conceptual apparatus that frames the larger narrative of social, political, or legal history would cue readers to generate rights-congruent interpretations of their affective appraisals.

19. His book raises a number of questions about whether the emotional understandings that readers gain from it can be extended to other realms. For example, how is PTSD related to moral responsibility? Does suffering from PTSD reduce your moral responsibility if you're an adult soldier, say, in Iraq? Does the emotional understanding I reached from his memoir depend on the lethal trio of childhood, addiction, and PTSD? What if Beah hadn't succumbed to PTSD but was a vulnerable child who became addicted to cocaine and opiates? Is the setting of war necessary to excuse Beah's crimes? Writing in the *New York Times*, James C. McKinley, Jr., reports on thirteen-year-old children from poverty-stricken Laredo, Texas, whom a Mexican drug ring recruited to form an assassination squad and paid in luxurious housing, cash, and cocaine (June 23, 2009, 1, 18). These boys are now in prison serving life terms for murder. Why aren't they serving as UN ambassadors for the rights of children, as Beah now does? These questions are left unanswered by the story of a single victim. Moreover, they raise questions

about what is needed to resolve them. No doubt we need more victims' stories and affective understanding, but surely we also need a theory of responsibility.

Chapter 4

1. For discussion of Stueber's simulationist view of empathy in relation to imaginative resistance, see Chapter 3, section 4

2. The other prongs are cognitive empathy—representing others' mental states using Theory of Mind—and motor empathy—mirroring the movements of others (2005, 699; 2008, 159–160). These forms of empathy bear most directly on the philosophy of mind; whereas emotional empathy is an explicitly moral conception.

3. Developmental psychologist Martin Hoffman is a prominent exception to this claim. By equating empathic distress with a pro-social motive, he builds a desire to help into his definition of empathy (2011). Thus, the target of his studies is altruistically motivating empathetically shared feelings.

4. I've altered Goldie's terminology in the interests of gender parity.

5. Goldie is aware that his account partitions off a number of other senses of the term *empathy* (2007, 70–71; 2011, 303–305).

6. So his remarks in earlier work to the effect that empathy may deepen and strengthen sympathy must be set aside (2000, 180, 214).

7. Goldie's position on thinking about others from the external perspective resembles Iris Young's (1997, chapter 2) account of asymmetrical reciprocity, wonder, and enlarged thought in several respects. Among other things, both invoke the trope of gift giving to develop their views, and each affirms that it is logically impossible for one person to assume another's identity in some way that empathy requires.

8. I acknowledge, though I don't discuss, merely conventional utterances of sympathetic formulae and corrupt pretenses of sympathy deployed to manipulate or maintain power over others.

9. What I am describing here resembles what Goldie calls "emotional sharing" (2000, 193). His examples are feeling the same emotion as his spouse when their child is in danger and feeling the same emotion as other members of a theater audience. Unlike what I have described above, Goldie's emotional sharing is not a response to the person or people with whom you are sharing the emotion but rather to a third thing. What I am describing also resembles what he calls "emotional identification" in which your sense of your own identity "to some extent *merges*" with your sense of the other's identity (2000, 193). I'm not sure I understand Goldie's conception of a partially merged identity. For me, his examples—for example, "ecstatic religious identification," a "hypnotic subject's identification with the hypnotist," a "child's

identification with a doll or puppet," or a "mother's identification with her child"—don't point to a single type of experience (2000, 194). His second metaphor, "draining away of the boundaries of cognitive and sensory identity" (2000, 193), convinces me that he is not talking about what feminist philosophers term a "relational self" and leads me to believe that the form of sympathy I describe differs from emotional identification. What I am talking about is a way of interacting with another person, possibly an intimate, not a loss or fusing of self.

10. Goldie also considers the possibility of mingling your characteristics with those of the other, but that possibility isn't relevant to my line of argument (2000, 200).

11. Stephen Darwall calls this type of interpersonal engagement "projective empathy" (1998, 266–270). I find Goldie's terminology more perspicuous, however, because this type of imagining represents the other's subjectivity only insofar as it happens to coincide with your own. As such, it accesses another person's situation without accessing that individual's distinctive experience of it.

12. Goldie disagrees with this claim. He holds that giving advice on the basis of empathy merely replicates what the person "would decide on without our involvement" (2007, 82). I reject his position for two reasons. First, people usually seek out advice when they are overwhelmed by events and confused about their feelings. It's because they don't know what course of action to pursue and fear that they may go wrong that they ask others for advice. In other words, there is no predetermined determinate decision for empathy to discover. Second, what empathy accomplishes overlaps with what Goldie recommends doing when asked for advice, which is analyzing the person's desires, typical patterns of response, and so forth. As will become clear later, I doubt that strictly maintaining a third-person perspective on the other is the best way to fully grasp her particular identity and life trajectory. Consequently, I doubt that Goldie's external analytical approach is the best strategy for offering helpful advice.

13. Stephen Darwall refers to what Goldie and I simply call "empathy" as "proto-sympathetic empathy" (1998, 270–271). I'll have more to say about his account in section 3.

14. For a study of how botox disables this automatic facial mimesis, thereby undermining perception of others' emotions, see Neal and Chartrand 2011.

15. I leave aside his 2011 claim that empathy—or, more precisely, the kind of empathy that he thinks simulationists must embrace—is conceptually impossible because I assume that people are referring to something when they attribute empathy to someone.

16. My view is in line with some psychological studies of empathy. Psychologists Hodges and Wegner describe empathy as a "hard and effortful" task that may bring cognitive and emotional capabilities into play (1997, 312–313, 320).

According to DeTurk, relational empathy proceeds through "a series of successive approximations to the other's point of view" (2001).

17. Likewise, Darwall asserts that empathy "can be consistent with the indifference of pure observation or even the cruelty of sadism" (1998, 261; for a similar position, see Nussbaum 2001, 331).

18. Two recent papers by Pierre Jacob (2011) and Frédérique de Vignemont and Pierre Jacob (2012) seem to adopt a position similar to mine, for they argue that a caring condition is necessary for empathy. However, I'm not sure the similarity is genuine. Jacob maintains that the caring condition rules out the possibility that empathy is the default response to noticing another person's affective state (2011, 523–524). De Vignemont and Jacob argue that the caring condition ensures that empathy is other-directed—that is, not egoistic (2012, 307). On my reading of this work, though, they are not using the terms *care* and *other-directed* in a moral or even a proto-moral sense, for they distinguish empathy from sympathy. Thus, they seem to be saying that in order to empathize you must take an interest in the other, not that you must take a humane interest in the other.

    Sonia Kruks incorporates concern into her conception of respectful recognition in a way that is closer to my view (2001, 155). Although she says that sympathy, compassion, affinity, and empathy "approximate" what she means by "respectful recognition," she denies that any one of them captures what she has in mind (2001, 156).

19. Readers conversant with James Blair's work on empathy in psychopathic persons and autistic persons might find this proposal questionable (2005, 2008). Blair distinguishes cognitive empathy (the ability to mind-read) from affective empathy (the ability to care about others' feelings). In philosophical terms, he identifies one concept of empathy for philosophy of mind and another for ethics. He maintains that persons with autism have impaired cognitive empathy and unimpaired affective empathy, whereas psychopathic people have unimpaired cognitive empathy and impaired affective empathy. I do not doubt the importance of Blair's findings for understanding and perhaps helping the populations he studies. However, I do not think that moral philosophy would be well served by adopting his definitions of empathy. In the ethics literature the distinction between empathy and sympathy is well established, and in ordinary speech the distinction between empathy and sizing people up is well established. Moreover, as I will bring out in section 3A, it is far from clear that empathy promotes pro-social action. All in all, I am convinced that preserving these distinctions not only supports lucid descriptions of moral psychology but also conduces to rigorous philosophical argumentation.

20. There is an extensive psychology literature on the relation between empathy and altruistic behavior, and it is worth noting that these studies seldom

mark the distinctions I have sketched in this section (e.g., Coke, Batson, and McDavis 1978; Handgraaf et al. 2008).

21. In the same vein, Barbara Montero's claim that proprioception is an aesthetic sense that enhances appreciation of dance performances relies on our off-line corporeal response capabilities—that is, the priming of neuromuscular responses that stops short of activating movement (2006).

22. It's possible that when Mackenzie and Scully laud moral imagination, they mean only that you should think creatively about the other in a problem-solving mode in order to decide how best to interact with her. Goldie sometimes seems to favor this view. However, nothing in their paper suggests that they would be receptive to eliminating acentrally imagining-how-it-is for others from their account of intersubjectivity.

23. See Bartky (1997).

24. Neither Goldie nor Kruks distinguishes empathizing with a flesh-and-blood person from empathizing with a literary representation of a person. Kruks switches from an account of meeting up with a battered woman in person to an account of reading about genital cutting in autobiographical narratives. Victims sometimes corporeally communicate their experience directly, as in Kruks's encounter at the battered women's shelter, but often they recount their stories in oral testimony (which may be taped or transcribed), written memoirs, or videos. Since this is so, it would be useful to have psychological studies of how the presence of a manifestly wrongfully injured person affects perceivers compared with the impact of live testimony from the same victim after the fact. As well, it would be useful to learn how non-victimized people are differentially affected by victims' stories couched in different media. However, reaching any general conclusions about these matters would be greatly complicated not only by issues of credibility but also by differences in victims' skill in using the media they choose to express themselves.

25. In some cultural groups that practice female genital cutting, the procedure is similar to what Mandela describes. Teenage girls gather for a period of seclusion and preparation, and the cutting symbolizes their advancement to the status of womanhood and creates a lifelong bond among the women who have been cut together (Robertson 1996). I haven't come across a diary or other extended first-person account of undergoing female genital cutting in this type of setting, but it would be of great interest to read one. If the report didn't present the moment of cutting and the aftermath as abhorrent, would Kruks or I be able to suspend our reflexive protection of our own genitals and resist projecting our own feelings and values onto the initiate?

26. My aversion includes the heads/faces of non-human mammals, but I can't take up moral relations between people and other animals here. I refer readers to Gruen (2015) for discussion of empathizing with different species of nonhuman animals.

27. I take it that boxing fans are able to suppress their empathetic capacities or that their empathetic responses are overpowered by the excitement of the contest, with an assist from norms of masculine aggression. While some empathetic nullification may be necessary to carry out valuable social functions, such as medical care for severely injured victims of natural disasters and armed combat, a case can be made that the desensitization of the legions of boxing enthusiasts is deplorable.

28. A similar claim can be inferred from a recent newspaper article on an organization that provides therapy in Jordan for victims of torture in Iraq. Discussing her response to the stories told by clients, many of whom are men, therapist Muriel Genot states, "Sometimes I feel almost physical pain when I listen to a detailed explanation of what happened. I feel it at the level of the skin, almost like my skin is being stretched or removed" ("Tugging at Threads to Unspool Stories of Torture," by Denise Grady, New York Times, May 2, 2011, http://www.nytimes.com/2011/05/03/health/03torture.html?_r=0, accessed 10/7/2015).

29. There are professional female boxers, but their numbers are tiny compared to males (http://www.wbanmember.com/trends-in-professional-female-boxing-and-world-title-fights-1993-to-2012, accessed 2/12/2015).

30. Jenefer Robinson points out that "understanding a text is necessarily a matter of *filling in the gaps*" because no text is without gaps (2005, 117; see Chapter 3, section 2, for additional discussion). However, the nature and extent of the gaps vary from text to text, and victims' stories must navigate between effectively guiding and obnoxiously propagandizing their audience. See Chapter 2, section 4 and Chapter 3, section 7 for discussion of victims' need to morally guide their audience and the liabilities of overt propagandizing.

31. In correspondence, Kruks has assured me that she agrees with this claim and that she was pointing to the ease of empathetic understanding between similarly embodied individuals and tendencies to misperceive and downplay the seriousness of a differently embodied person's suffering. My line of thought in this section accents the extent of unimpeded intercorporeal communication in order to head off the possibility that anyone might adopt overblown beliefs about corporeal isolation despite Kruks's carefully qualified remarks.

32. Out of respect for the author's lifelong wish not to be identified, I refer to her as "Anonymous," although her identity has been revealed on many websites.

33. Along these lines, Merleau-Ponty maintains that a long feather on a woman's hat can be integrated into her body image and hence into her agentic self ([1962]2004, 165). Conversely, Fernando Botero's suite of paintings based on the torture of prisoners held by the US military at Abu Ghraib makes a visual case for the dehumanizing effects of forced exposure (Marlborough Gallery, 2006).

34. For an equally riveting description of abuse of an empathetically compelling element of common humanity, see Ishmael Beah's account of burying a group of enemy soldiers alive (discussed in Chapter 3, section 3).

35. For treatment of the invisibility of rape in discourse and society, see Franco (2006).

36. Haidt et al. argue that disgust is a common category of experience, that body products are among the elicitors of disgust, and that "core disgust" is encoded in "embodied schemata" that can be elaborated in culturally variable ways (1997). Their psychological studies could account for the visceral intelligibility of Anonymous's image despite gendered bodily differences. See Kristeva for a theory of the role of abjection in the consolidation of individual identity that accounts for the power of Anonymous's depiction of this incident (1982). However, see Nussbaum for discussion of the how "hypertrophic" disgust projected onto othered groups of people endangers equal respect for persons and obstructs compassion (2001, 220–223). Whereas Nussbaum's suggestions about the role of disgust in misogyny help to explain the vilification of Anonymous when her book was first published in German in 1960, her insistence that such projections of disgust "are not inevitable" makes way for an empathetic reception of Anonymous's text today (2001, 221–222, 346–349).

37. Here I take exception to Jesse Prinz's claim that "*any* focus on the victim of a transgression should be avoided, because of potential bias" (2011a, 228; also see 2011b, 229). While I agree with him that individualizing a victim's story runs the risk of alienating readers/auditors by arousing their prejudices, I argue that empathetic engagement with victims of human rights abuse would be short-circuited and insight into the human meaning of human rights abuse greatly shrunken without attention to the individual victim.

38. Note the similarity between Anonymous's strategy for minimizing her vulnerability to sexual assault and the one Harriet Jacobs ascribes to Linda Brent (Chapter 2, section 4).

39. Discussions of imaginative resistance help illuminate different individuals' empathetic receptivity to or repudiation of diverse victims' stories. See, for example, Gendler (2006), Goldie (2003a), Driver (2008), and Stueber (2011).

40. Goldie claims that it is possible to empathize with a type, and he illustrates this possibility as follows. While hiking in the Pyrenees, he came upon an ancient Roman road and proceeded to centrally imagine being a Roman foot soldier marching through that terrain (2000, 204). It strikes me as dubious to classify this harmless "let's pretend" exercise as an instance of empathy. It fits better with Goldie's account of "in-his-shoes" imagining.

41. For evidence that the persuasive power of narrative depends on "psychological transportation" and that poor literary craft sabotages transportation, see Green and Brock (2005).

42. Yet, nothing prevents men from directly feeling with the pain and humiliation of forced male-on-male anal intercourse, and such visceral imagining would surely be relevant to understanding the harm that sexual assault inflicts on women. Maybe most heterosexual men never contemplate that possibility—because of anxiety about homosexuality or because it's so unlikely that it will happen to them—but that's another matter.

Chapter 5

1. For a valuable account of the founding and evolution of the post-Apartheid South African organization, Khulumani Support Group, see Madlingozi (2010, 213–224).
2. I don't mean to imply that issues about vengeance are unimportant. The problem of honor killings is a very serious one. However, it is outside the scope of my project.
3. As is well known, people who are objectively poor give a higher percentage of their resources to charity than people who are objectively affluent (http://www.nytimes.com/2010/08/22/magazine/22FOB-wwln-t.html?_r=0).
4. Presumably school lunch programs also contribute to meeting children's nutritional needs in New York City.
5. Reichle and Schmitt are using a minimalistic conception of empathy at variance with the one I advocate in Chapter 5.
6. Also see Crouch and Schwartzman (2012).
7. I regard what I am calling "aid projects" as social justice projects that seek to realize social and economic human rights. However, since there remains considerable controversy about this understanding of justice, and since this is not the place to defend my view, I reserve the category of "justice projects" for formal institutions devoted to punishing wrongdoers or enforcing the rights of victims.
8. For valuable discussion of the proposal to treat victims' stories in an intellectual property rights framework, see Colvin (2006). Colvin notes the tension between storytellers' ownership of their stories and the contributions their stories can make to public debates. While stressing the importance of respecting victims, he argues that the consequences of commodifying victims' stories would be harmful overall.
9. For critique of using photographic images purporting to show helpless, passive victims in fundraising campaigns, see Bell and Carens (2004, 326–328).
10. For critique of the Oxfam report "Listening to the Displaced" on the grounds that it renders its subjects "speechless and without agency," see Rajaram (2002).
11. For a skeptical treatment of "transitional justice entrepreneurs," the production of disempowered victims, and responsibility to victims' stories, see Madlingozi (2010).

12. Readers familiar with the work of the UN Human Rights Council's Special Rapporteur on the Promotion of Truth, Justice, Reparation, and Guarantees of Non-recurrence may note a discrepancy between the categories he uses and the categories I propose. In his 2012 report to the General Assembly, the rapporteur, Pablo de Greiff, addresses four issues: truth-seeking (establishing an accurate historical record of human rights abuse), justice initiatives (prosecuting perpetrators of human rights abuse), reparation (making amends to victims), and guarantees of non-recurrence (reforming institutions and social practices to prevent future human rights abuse) (http://www.ohchr.org/Documents/HRBodies/HRCouncil/RegularSession/Session21/A-HRC-21-46_en.pdf, accessed 12/30/2014).

Whereas de Greiff's mandate concerns transitional justice in the broadest sense, I am concerned specifically with justice issues in which victims' stories play a salient role. Thus, our categories overlap to some extent. What he calls "justice initiatives," I call "punitive projects." What he divides between "truth-seeking" and "reparation," I partially discuss under the category of "reparative projects." Insofar as truth telling counts as a type of reparation, it falls within my concerns. However, inasmuch as reparation might require restitution of property or compensatory damages, it falls outside the bounds of my concerns. Another respect in which the scope of de Greiff's interests is broader than mine is non-recurrence. He addresses the problem of preventing future abuse, but I do not. Although victims' stories can play a role in guiding social consciousness so as to prevent recurrence (see Schaffer 2008), I do not take up this matter because legal guarantees are pivotal to non-recurrence and because the dissemination of victims' stories, insofar as it plays a role in securing non-recurrence, merely amplifies the work of truth-seeking. In another respect, my interests are broader than his. I address sanctuary projects, but he does not. He doesn't take up this matter because sanctuary projects do not contribute to transitional justice. I do take it up because one type of sanctuary project hinges on the stories victims tell.

13. Of course, aid projects operate within refugee camps, and aid workers in refugee camps are obligated to observe the ethical strictures I discuss for that type of project.

14. Because justice projects are usually public proceedings, it is seldom appropriate to promise victim-storytellers confidentiality. Although anonymous witnesses should be allowed to testify when their subsequent safety cannot be guaranteed, the right to a fair trial mandates that criminal courts and tribunals be governed by a presumption in favor of publicity.

15. A caveat: Every study I have consulted concerning the psychological impact on victim-witnesses of participating in criminal trials or truth commissions calls for more empirical research on this topic.

16. Refugee camps are an exception. Some are built and run by governments, others by the UN or humanitarian organizations, such as the Red Cross.

17. For helpful discussion of an array of conceptions of victim participation in transitional justice projects, see D. Taylor (2014, 22–27).

18. Lawrence Kirmayer reports that a similarly adversarial spirit and poor preparation for interaction with traumatized victims prevails in Canadian asylum proceedings (2003, 170, 176). Didier Fassin and Richard Rechtman describe a similar regime of suspicion toward refugees in France (2009, 256, 273–274).

19. For valuable feminist critique of these conceptualizations of civil society and analysis of feminist ambivalence about this realm, see Phillips (2002), Rosenblum (2002), and Okin (2002).

20. For discussion of the status of truth commissions with respect to their position vis-à-vis civil society, see Crocker (1998, 505–506).

21. For an account of how these diverse types of groups become integrated into "advocacy networks" with international clout, see Keck and Sikkink (1998).

22. http://www.un.org/womenwatch/daw/beijing/platform/declar.htm, accessed 1/17/2015; also see the Platform for Action, Part D, http://www.un.org/womenwatch/daw/beijing/platform/violence.htm, accessed 1/17/2015.

23. Note that BJW can have harmful consequences for victims as well as bystanders. For example, victims of sexual assault are prone to blaming themselves for decisions that might have put them in danger, rather than becoming angry with and blaming their attackers (Brison 2002, 73–77). Participation in victim support groups can help victims direct their feelings and reproaches at more appropriate targets.

24. For a theoretical treatment of and practical suggestions for transnationalizing civil society via the Internet, see Ackerly (2006). For analysis of diverse types of domestic/transnational activism and a guardedly optimistic assessment of their ability to promote human rights, see Tarrow (2010).

REFERENCES

Aaltola, Elisa. 2014. "Affective Empathy as Core Moral Agency: Psychopathy, Autism, and Reason Revisited." *Philosophical Explorations* 17 (1): 76–92.

Ackerly, Brooke A. 2006. "Deliberative Democratic Theory for Building Global Civil Society: Designing a Virtual Community of Activists." *Contemporary Political Theory* 5 (2): 113–141.

Ackerly, Brooke A. 2008. *Universal Human Rights in a World of Difference.* Cambridge, UK: Cambridge University Press.

Alcoff, Linda. 2006. "The Problem of Speaking for Others." In *Theorizing Feminisms: A Reader.* Ed. Elizabeth Hackett and Sally Haslanger. New York: Oxford University Press.

Amsterdam, Anthony G., and Jerome Bruner. 2000. *Minding the Law.* Cambridge, MA: Harvard University Press.

Anderson, Scott. 2008a. "Of Theories of Coercion, Two Axes, and the Importance of the Coercer." *The Journal of Moral Philosophy* 5: 394–422.

Anderson, Scott. 2008b. "How Did There Come to Be Two Kinds of Coercion?" Chapter 1 in *Coercion and the State.* Ed. David Reidy and Walter Riker. New York: Kluwer/Springer, 17–30.

Anonymous. 2005. *A Woman in Berlin: Eight Weeks in the Conquered City.* Trans. Philip Boehm. New York: Henry Holt.

Appiah, Kwame Anthony. 2010. "Why I Nominated Liu Xiabo." *Foreign Policy* (Oct. 8, 2010). (http://www.foreignpolicy.com/articles/2010/10/08/why_i_nominated_liu_xiaob, accessed 9/6/2014).

Arendt, Hannah. 1998. *The Human Condition.* Chicago: University of Chicago Press.

Aristotle. 1947. *Poetics.* In *Introduction to Aristotle.* Ed. Richard McKeon. Trans. Ingram Bywater. New York. Modern Library

Baker, Joanne. 2010. "Claiming Volition and Evading Victimhood: Post-Feminist Obligations for Young Women." *Feminism and Psychology* 20 (2): 186–204.

Banner, Francine. 2000–2001. "Rewriting History: The Use of Feminist Narratives to Deconstruct the Myth of the Capital Defendant." *N.Y.U. Review of Law and Social Change* 26: 569.

Bartky, Sandra Lee. 1997. "Sympathy and Solidarity: On a Tightrope with Scheler." In *Feminists Rethink the Self*. Ed. Diana Tietjens Meyers. Boulder, CO: Westview Press.

Basu, Kaushik, and Pham Hoang Van. 1998. "The Economics of Child Labor." *American Economic Review* 88 (3): 412–427.

Bauby, Jean-Dominique. 1997. *The Diving Bell and the Butterfly*. Trans. Jeremy Leggatt. New York: Vintage.

Baumgartner, Frank R., Suzanna L. De Boef, and Amber E. Boydstun. 2008. *The Decline of the Death Penalty and the Discovery of Innocence*. Cambridge, UK: Cambridge University Press.

Beah, Ishmael. 2007. *A Long Way Gone: Memoirs of a Boy Soldier*. New York: Farrar, Straus, and Giroux.

Beitz, Charles R. 2001. "Human Rights as Common Concern." *American Political Science Review* 95 (2): 269–282.

Bell, Daniel A., and Joseph H. Carens. 2004. "The Ethical Dilemmas of International Human Rights and Humanitarian NGOs: Reflections on a Dialogue between Practitioners and Theorists." *Human Rights Quarterly* 26 (2): 300–329

Bennett, W. Lance. 1997. "Storytelling in Criminal Trials: A Model of Social Judgment." In *Memory, Identity, Community: The Idea of Narrative in the Human Sciences*. Ed. Lewis P. Hinchman and Sandras K. Hinchman. Albany: State University of New York Press.

Blader, Steven, and Tom Tyler. 2002. "Justice and Empathy: What Motivates People to Help Others?" In *The Justice Motive in Everyday Life*. Ed. Michael Ross and Dale T. Miller. Cambridge, UK: Cambridge University Press.

Blair, R. J. R. (James). 2005. "Responding to the Emotions of Others: Dissociating Forms of Empathy through the Study of Typical and Psychiatric Populations." *Consciousness and Cognition* 14: 698–718.

Blair, R. J. R. (James). 2008. "Fine Cuts of Empathy and Amygdala: Dissociable Deficits in Psychopathy and Autism." *Quarterly Journal of Experimental Psychology* 61 (1): 157–170.

Braithwaite, John. 2006. "Narrative and 'Compulsory Compassion.'" *Law & Social Inquiry* 31 (2): 425–446.

Brickman, Philip, Dan Coates, and Ronnie Janoff-Bulman. 1978. "Lottery Winners and Accident Victims: Is Happiness Relative?" *Journal of Personality and Social Psychology* 36 (8): 917–927.

Brison, Susan J. 2002. *Aftermath: Violence and the Remaking of a Self*. Princeton, NJ: Princeton University Press.

Brounéus, Karen. 2010. "The Trauma of Truth Telling: Effects of Witnessing in the Rwanda Gacaca Courts on Psychological Health." *Journal of Conflict Resolution* 54 (3): 408–437.

Brown, L. David, et al. 2000. "Globalization, NGOs, and Multi-Sectoral Relations." Working Paper #1, Hauser Center for Non-Profit Organizations, http://ssrn.com/abstract=253110 or http://dx.doi.org/10.2139/ssrn.253110 (accessed 1/15/2015).

Brown, Wendy. 1995. *States of Injury: Power and Freedom in Late Modernity.* Princeton, NJ: Princeton University Press.

Bruner, Jerome.1990. *Acts of Meaning.* Cambridge, MA: Harvard University Press.

Bruner, Jerome. 2003. *Making Stories: Law, Literature, Life.* Cambridge, MA: Harvard University Press.

Bunch, Charlotte, and Niamh Reilly. 1994. *Demanding Accountability: The Global Campaign and Vienna Tribunal for Women's Human Rights.* New Brunswick, NJ: Center for Women's Global Leadership, http://www.cwgl.rutgers.edu/docman/coalition-building-publications/283-demand-accountability/file (accessed 7/1/2015).

Calhoun, Cheshire. 1994. "Separating Lesbian Theory from Feminist Theory." *Ethics* 104 (3): 558–581.

Card, Claudia. 2002. *The Atrocity Paradigm: A Theory of Evil.* New York: Oxford University Press.

Cavell, Stanley. 1979. *The Claim of Reason.* New York: Oxford University Press.

Carroll, Noël. 2001. *Beyond Aesthetics: Philosophical Essays.* Cambridge, UK: Cambridge University Press.

Chambers, Simone, and Will Kymlicka. 2002. *Alternative Conceptions of Civil Society.* Princeton, NJ: Princeton University Press.

Chapkis, Wendy. 2003. "Trafficking, Migration, and the Law: Protecting Innocents, Punishing Immigrants." *Gender and Society* 17: 923–937.

Ciorciari, John D., and Anne Heindel. 2011. "Trauma in the Courtroom." *Cambodia's Hidden Scars.* Ed. Beth Van Schaack, Daryn Reicherter, Youk Chhang, and Autumn Talbot. Documentation Center of Cambodia.

Code, Lorraine. 1991. *What Can She Know? Feminist Theory and the Construction of Knowledge.* Ithaca, NY: Cornell University Press.

Cohen, Jean L., and Andrew Arato. 1992. *Civil Society and Political Theory.* Cambridge, MA: MIT Press.

Coke, Jay, Daniel Batson, and Katherine McDavis. 1978. "Empathic Mediation of Helping: A Two-Stage Model." *Journal of Personality and Social Psychology* 36 (7): 752–766.

Colombetti, Giovanna. 2010. "Enaction, Sense-making and Emotion." In *Enaction: Towards a New Paradigm for Cognitive Science.* Ed. John Stewart, Olivier Gapenne, and Ezequiel Di Paolo. Cambridge, MA: MIT Press.

Colombetti, Giovanna, and Evan Thompson. 2007. "The Feeling Body: Towards an Enactive Approach to Emotion." In *Developmental Perspectives on Embodiment and Consciousness.* Ed. Willis Overton, Willis F. Overton, Ulrich Mueller, and Judith Newman. New York: Lawrence Erlbaum.

Colvin, C. J. 2006. "Trafficking Trauma: Intellectual Property Rights and the Political Economy of Traumatic Storytelling." *Critical Arts: A South-North Journal of Cultural & Media Studies* 20 (1): 171–182.

Coplan, Amy, and Peter Goldie. 2011. "Introduction." In *Empathy: Philosophical and Psychological Perspectives.* Ed. Amy Coplan and Peter Goldie. Oxford: Oxford University Press.

Cover, Robert M. 1983. "Nomos and Narrative." *Harvard Law Review* 97 (4): 4–68.

Crocker, David A. 1998. "Transitional Justice and International Civil Society: Toward a Normative Framework." *Constellations* 5 (4): 492–517.

Crouch, Margaret, and Lisa Schwartzman. 2012. "Gender, Implicit Bias, and Philosophical Methodology." A Special Issue of *Journal of Social Philosophy* 43 (3).

Cudd, Ann. 2006. *Analyzing Oppression.* New York: Oxford University Press.

Dahl, Gudrun. 2009. "Sociology and Beyond: Agency, Victimisation and the Ethics of Writing." *Asian Journal of Social Science* 37 (3): 391–407.

Dang, Minh. 2013. "Putting the Human into Human Trafficking Reporting: Tips for Interviewing Survivors." Presented at Reporting Sex Trafficking: A Local Problem with Global Dimensions, A McCormick Specialized Reporting Institute, University of North Carolina, Chapel Hill.

Danieli, Yael. 2004. "Victims: Essential Voices at the Court." *Victims' Rights Working Group Bulletin* Issue 1 (Sept. 2004): 6.

Danto, Arthur C. 1985. *Narration and Knowledge.* New York: Columbia University Press.

Darwall, Stephen. 1998. "Empathy, Sympathy, Care." *Philosophical Studies* 89: 261–282.

Darwall, Stephen. 2011. "Being With." *Southern Journal of Philosophy* 49 (Spindel Supplement): 4–24.

Daley, Suzanne. 2010. "Rescuing Young Women from Traffickers' Hands." *New York Times,* http://www.nytimes.com/2010/10/16/world/europe/16romania.html?_r=1&emc=eta1, originally published 10/15/2010 (accessed 12/21/2010).

Debes, Remy. 2015. "From Einfühlung to Empathy: Sympathy in Early Phenomenology and Psychology." In *Sympathy: A History.* Ed. E. Schliesser. New York: Oxford University Press.

Delgado, Richard. 1989. "Legal Storytelling: Storytelling for Oppositionists and Others: A Plea for Narrative." *Michigan Law Review* 87: 2411.

Dembour, Marie-Bénédicte, and Emily Haslam. 2004. "Silencing Hearings? Victim-Witnesses at War Crimes Trials." *European Journal of International Law* 15 (1): 151–177.

Dershowitz, Alan M. 1996. "Life Is Not a Dramatic Narrative." In *Law's Stories: Narrative and Rhetoric in the Law.* Ed. Peter Brooks and Paul Gewirtz. New Haven, CT: Yale University Press.

DeTurk, Sara. (2001). "Intercultural Empathy: Myth, Competency, or Possibility for Alliance Building?" *Communication Education* 50 (4): 374–384.

Dichter, Stephen. 1999. "Globalization and Its Effects on NGOs: Efflorescence or a Blurring of Roles and Relevance." *Nonprofit and Voluntary Sector Quarterly* 28 (4) Supplement: 38–58.

Dotson, Kristie. 2012. "A Cautionary Tale: On Limiting Epistemic Oppression." *Frontiers* 33 (1): 24–47.

Driver, Julia. 2008. "Imaginative Resistance and Psychological Necessity." *Social Philosophy and Policy* 25 (1): 301–313.

Duguid, Michelle, and Melissa Thomas-Hunt. 2014. "Condoning Stereotyping?: How Awareness of Stereotyping Prevalence Impacts Expression of Stereotypes." *Journal of Applied Psychology* 100 (2): 343–359. http://dx.doi.org/10.1037/a0037908.

Dunn, Jennifer L. 2005. "'Victims' and 'Survivors': Emerging Vocabularies of Motive for 'Battered Women Who Stay.'" *Sociological Inquiry* 75 (1): 1–30.

Dworkin, Ronald. 1986. *Law's Empire.* Cambridge, MA: Harvard University Press.

Edwards, Michael. 1999. "International Development NGOs: Agents of Foreign Aid or Vehicles for International Cooperation?" *Nonprofit and Voluntary Sector Quarterly* 28 (4) Supplement: 25–37.

Edwards, Michael. 2011a. *The Oxford Handbook of Civil Society.* New York: Oxford University Press.

Edwards, Michael. 2011b. "Conclusion: Civil Society as a Necessary and Necessarily Contested Idea." In *The Oxford Handbook of Civil Society.* Ed. Michael Edwards. New York: Oxford University Press.

El Sadaawi, Nawal. 1980. *The Hidden Face of Eve: Women in the Arab World.* Trans. Sherif Hatata. London: Zed Books.

Ewick, Patricia, and Susan S. Silbey. 1995. "Subversive Stories and Hegemonic Tales: Toward a Sociology of Narrative." *Law and Society Review* 29: 197–226.

Fassin, Didier, and Richard Rechtman. 2009. *The Empire of Trauma: An Inquiry into the Condition of Victimhood.* Princeton, NJ: Princeton University Press.

Feinberg, Joel. 1979. "The Nature and Value of Rights." In *Rights.* Ed. David Lyons. Belmont, CA: Wadsworth.

Felman, Shoshana. 2002. *The Juridical Unconscious: Trials and Traumas in the Twentieth Century.* Cambridge, MA: Harvard University Press.

Fjellstrom, Roger. 2002. "On Victimhood." *Sats: Nordic Journal of Philosophy* 3 (1): 102–117.

Franco, Jean. 2006. "Rape and Human Rights." *PMLA* 121 (5): 1662–1664.

Fricker, Miranda. 2007. *Epistemic Injustice: Power and the Ethics of Knowing.* New York: Oxford University Press.

Furnham, Adrian. 2003. "Belief in a Just World: Research Progress over the Past Decade." *Personality and Individual Differences* 34: 795–817.

Gallagher, Shaun. 2003. "Self-narrative, Embodied Action, and Social Context." In *Between Suspicion and Sympathy: Paul Ricoeur's Unstable Equilibrium (Festschrift for Paul Ricoeur)*. Ed. A. Wiercinski. http://pegasus.cc.ucf.edu/~gallaghr/gallonline.html.

Gendler, Tamar Szabó. 2006. "Imaginative Resistance Revisited." In *The Architecture of the Imagination*. Ed. Shaun Nichols. Oxford: Oxford University Press.

Gendler, Tamar Szabó. 2009. "Imaginative Resistance." In *A Companion to Aesthetics*, 2nd edition. Ed. Stephen Davies et al. Malden, MA: Blackwell.

Goldie, Peter. 2000. *The Emotions*. Oxford: Oxford University Press.

Goldie, Peter. 2003a. "One's Remembered Past: Narrative Thinking, Emotion, and the External Perspective." *Philosophical Papers* 32 (3): 301–319.

Goldie, Peter. 2003b. "Narrative, Emotion, and Perspective." In *Imagination, Philosophy, and the Arts*. Ed. Matthew Kieran and Dominic McIver Lopes. London: Routledge.

Goldie, Peter. 2007. "Dramatic Irony, Narrative, and the External Perspective." In *Narrative and Understanding Persons*. Ed. Daniel Hutto. Cambridge, UK: Cambridge University Press.

Goldie, Peter. 2011. "Anti-Empathy." In *Empathy: Philosophical and Psychological Perspectives*. Ed. Amy Coplan and Peter Goldie. Oxford: Oxford University Press.

Goldie, Peter. 2012. *The Mess Inside: Narrative, Emotion, and the Mind*. Oxford: Oxford University Press.

Goldman, Alvin I. 1992. "Empathy, Mind, and Morals." *Proceedings and Addresses of the American Philosophical Association* 66: 17–41.

Goldman, Alvin I. 2011. "Two Routes to Empathy: Insights from Cognitive Neuroscience." In *Empathy: Philosophical and Psychological Perspectives*. Ed. Amy Coplan and Peter Goldie. Oxford: Oxford University Press.

Govier, Trudy. 1993a. "Trust and Testimony: Nine Arguments on Testimonial Knowledge." *International Journal of Moral and Social Studies* 8 (1): 21–39.

Govier, Trudy. 1993b. "When Logic Meets Politics: Testimony, Distrust, and Rhetorical Disadvantage." *Informal Logic* 15: 93–104.

Govier, Trudy. 2005. "Truth and Storytelling: Some Hidden Arguments." In *Uses of Argument: Proceedings of a Conference at McMaster University*. Ed. David Hitchcock. McMasters University. Hamilton: Ontario Society for the Study of Argumentation.

Green, Melanie C., and Timothy C. Brock. 2005. "Persuasiveness of Narratives." In *Persuasion: Psychological Insights and Perspectives*. Ed. Timothy C. Brock and Melanie C. Green. London: Sage Publications.

Griffin, James. 2008. *On Human Rights*. Oxford: Oxford University Press.

Gruen, Lori. 2009. "Attending to Nature: Empathetic Engagement with the More than Human World." *Ethics and the Environment* 14 (2): 23–48.

Gruen, Lori. 2015. *Entangled Empathy: An Alternative Ethic for Our Relationships with Animals*. Brooklyn, NY: Lantern Books.

Hafer, Carolyn, and Laurent Bègue. 2005. "Experimental Research on Just-World Theory: Problems, Developments, and Future Challenges." *Psychological Bulletin* 131 (1): 128–167.

Haidt, Jonathan, et al. 1997. "Body, Psyche, and Culture: The Relationship between Disgust and Morality." *Psychology and Developing Societies* 9 (1): 107–131.

Handgraaf, Michel J., et al. 2008. "Less Power or Powerless? Egocentric Empathy Gaps and the Irony of Having Little versus No Power in Social Decision Making." *Journal of Personality and Social Psychology* 95 (5): 1136–1149.

Hatzfeld, Jean. 2006. *Life Laid Bare: The Survivors in Rwanda Speak*. Trans. Linda Coverdale. New York: Other Press.

Haynes, Dina Francesca. 2006. "Used, Abused, Arrested, and Deported: Extending Immigration Benefits to Protect the Victims of Trafficking and to Secure the Prosecution of Traffickers." In *Women's Rights: A Human Rights Quarterly Reader*. Ed. Bert B. Lockwood. Baltimore, MD: Johns Hopkins University Press.

Held, Virginia. 1989. "Birth and Death." *Ethics* 99: 362–388.

Herlihy, Jane, Peter Scragg, and Stuart Turner. 2002. "Discrepancies in Autobiographical Memories—Implications for the Assessment of Asylum Seekers: Repeated Interviews Study." *BMJ* 7: 324–327.

Herman, Judith. 1992. *Trauma and Recovery*. New York: Basic Books.

Hodges, S., and D. M. Wegner. 1997. "Automatic and Controlled Empathy." In *Empathic Accuracy*. Ed. W. J. Ickes. New York: Guilford, 311–339.

Hoffman, Martin. 2011. "Empathy, Justice, and the Law." In *Empathy: Philosophical and Psychological Perspectives*. Ed. Amy Coplan and Peter Goldie. Oxford: Oxford University Press.

hooks, bell. 1997. "Sisterhood: Political Solidarity between Women." In *Feminist Social Thought: A Reader*. Ed. Diana Tietjens Meyers. New York: Routledge.

Jacob, Pierre. 2011. "The Direct-Perception Model of Empathy: A Critique." *Review of Philosophy and Psychology* 2 (3): 519–540.

Jacobsen, Christine M., and May-Len Skilbrei. 2010. "Reproachable Victims? Representations and Self-Representations of Russian Women in Transnational Prostitution." *Ethnos* 75 (2): 190–212.

Johnston, Mark. 2001. "The Authority of Affect." *Philosophy and Phenomenological Research* 113 (1): 181–214.

Kahneman, Daniel, Paul Slovic, and Amos Tversky. 1982. *Judgment under Uncertainty*. Cambridge, UK: Cambridge University Press.

Kara, Siddharth. 2009. *Sex Trafficking: Inside the Business of Modern Slavery*. New York: Columbia University Press.

Keck, Margaret E., and Kathryn Sikkink. 1998. *Activists beyond Borders: Advocacy Networks in International Politics*. Ithaca, NY: Cornell University Press.

Kelly, Liz. 2005. "'You Can Find Anything You Want': A Critical Reflection on Research on Trafficking in Persons within and into Europe." *International Migration* 43 (1–2): 235–265.

Khalili, Laleh. 2008. "On Torture." *Middle East Report* 249 (Winter): http://www.merip.org/mer/mer249/khalili.html (accessed 4/12/2009).

Khader, Serene J. 2011. "Beyond Inadvertent Ventriloquism: Caring Virtue for Anti-paternalist Development Practice." *Hypatia* (Special Issue on *Responsibility and Identity in Global Justice.* Ed. Diana Tietjens Meyers) 26 (4): 742–761.

King, Deborah K. 1997. "Multiple Jeopardy, Multiple Consciousness: The Context of Black Feminist Ideology." In *Feminist Social Thought: A Reader.* Ed. Diana Tietjens Meyers. New York: Routledge.

Kirmayer, Laurence J. 2003. "Failures of Imagination: The Refugee's Narrative in Psychiatry." *Anthropology and Medicine* 10 (2): 167–185.

Kristeva, Julia. 1982. *Powers of Horror.* Trans. Leon S. Roudiez. New York: Columbia University Press.

Kruks, Sonia. 2001. *Retrieving Experience: Subjectivity and Recognition in Feminist Politics.* Ithaca, NY: Cornell University Press.

Kupperman, Joel J. 1999. *Value and What Follows.* New York: Oxford University Press.

Lazarus, Richard. 1991. *Emotion and Adaptation.* New York: Oxford University Press.

Lerner, Melvin J. 1980. *The Belief in a Just World: A Fundamental Delusion.* New York: Plenum.

Lerner, Melvin, and Carolyn Simmons. 1966. "Observer's Reaction to the 'Innocent Victim': Compssion or Rejection?" *Journal of Personality and Social Psychology* 4 (2): 203–210.

Leydesdorff, Selma. 2011. *Surviving the Bosnian Genocide: The Women of Srebrenica Speak.* Trans. Kay Richardson. Bloomington: Indiana University Press.

Liao, Yiwu. 2013. *For a Song and a Hundred Songs.* Trans. Wenguang Huang. Boston, MA: Houghton Mifflin Harcourt.

Locke, John. [1690]1980. *The Second Treatise of Government.* Indianapolis, IN: Hackett.

MacIntyre, Alasdair. 1984. *After Virtue,* 2nd edition. Notre Dame, IN: University of Notre Dame Press.

Mackenzie, Catriona. 2006. "Imagining Other Lives." *Philosophical Papers* 35 (3): 293–325.

Mackenzie, Catriona. 2008. "Imagination, Identity, and Self-Transformation." In *Practical Identity and Narrative Agency.* Ed. Kim Atkins and Catriona Mackenzie. New York: Routledge.

Mackenzie, Catriona, and Jackie Leach Scully. 2007. "Moral Imagination, Disability, and Embodiment." *Journal of Applied Philosophy* 24 (4): 335–351.

MacKinnon, Catharine A. 1989. *Toward a Feminist Theory of the State.* Cambridge, MA: Harvard University Press.

Madlingozi, Tshepo. 2010. "On Transitional Justice Entrepreneurs and the Production of Victims." *Journal of Human Rights Practice* 2 (2): 208–228.

Mandela, Nelson. 1994. *Long Walk to Freedom: The Autobiography of Nelson Mandela.* Boston: Little, Brown.

Marouf, Fatma E. 2010-2011. "Implicit Bias and Immigration Courts." *New England Law Review* 45: 417–448.

McKinley, James C., Jr. 2009. "Drug Cartels in Mexico Lure American Teenagers as Killers." *New York Times,* June 23, 2009, 1, 18.

Merleau-Ponty, Maurice. [1962]2004. *Phenomenology of Perception.* Trans. Colin Smith. New York City: Routledge.

Meyers, Diana Tietjens. 1986. *Inalienable Rights: A Defense.* New York: Columbia University Press.

Meyers, Diana Tietjens. 1994. *Subjection and Subjectivity: Psychoanalytic Feminism, and Moral Philosophy.* New York: Routledge.

Meyers, Diana Tietjens. 2014. "Corporeal Selfhood, Self-Interpretation, and Narrative Selfhood." *Philosophical Explorations* 17 (2): 141–153. doi: 10.1080/13869795.2013.856933.

Meyers, Diana Tietjens. 2014. "Rethinking Coercion for a World of Poverty and Migration." In *Poverty, Agency, and Human Rights.* Ed. Diana Tietjens Meyers. New York: Oxford University Press.

Meyers, Diana Tietjens. 2016. "Victims of Trafficking, Reproductive Rights, and Asylum." In *Oxford Handbook of Reproductive Ethics.* Ed. Leslie Francis. New York: Oxford University Press.

Mills, Charles. 1998. *Blackness Visible: Essays on Philosophy and Race.* Ithaca, NY: Cornell University Press.

Minow, Martha. 1993. "Surviving Victim Talk." *UCLA Law Review* 40: 1411–1445.

Misak, Cheryl. 2008. "Experience, Narrative, and Ethical Deliberation." *Ethics* 118: 614–632.

Montero, Barbara. 2006. "Proprioception as an Aesthetic Sense." *The Journal of Aesthetics and Art Criticism* 64 (2): 231–242.

Mullin, Amy. 2002. "Evaluating Art: Morally Significant Imagining versus Moral Soundness." *Journal of Aesthetics and Art Criticism* 60 (2): 137–149.

Narayan, Uma. 1997. *Dislocating Cultures.* New York: Routledge.

Neal, David T., and Tanya L. Chartrand. 2011. "Embodied Emotion Perception: Amplifying and Dampening Facial Feedback Modulates Emotion Perception Accuracy." *Social Psychological and Personality Science* 2 (6): 673–678.

Nelson, Hilde Lindemann. 2001. *Damaged Identities; Narrative Repair.* Ithaca, NY: Cornell University Press.

Nickel, James W. 2007. *Making Sense of Human Rights,* 2nd edition. Malden, MA: Blackwell.

Nozick, Robert. 1974. *Anarchy, State, Utopia.* New York: Basic Books.

Nussbaum, Martha C. 1990. *Love's Knowledge.* New York: Oxford University Press.

Nussbaum, Martha C. 2001. *Upheavals of Thought: The Intelligence of Emotions.* Cambridge, UK: Cambridge University Press.

Okin, Susan Moller. 2002. "Comment on Nancy Rosenblum's 'Feminist Perspectives on Civil Society and Government.'" In *Civil Society and Government.* Ed. Nancy L. Rosenblum and Robert C. Post. Princeton, NJ: Princeton University Press.

Ovuga, Emilio, Thomas O Oyok, and E. B. Moro. 2008. "Post Traumatic Stress Disorder among Former Child Soldiers Attending a Rehabilitative Service and Primary School Education in Northern Uganda," http://www.ncbi.nlm.nih.gov/pmc/articles/PMC2583264/ (accessed 10/14/2014).

Peach, Lucinda Joy. 2006. "Victims or Agents: Female Cross-Border Migrants and Anti-Trafficking Discourse." *Radical Philosophy Today* 4: 101–118.

Pheterson, Gail. 1989. *A Vindication of the Rights of Whores.* Seattle, WA: Seal Press.

Phillips, Anne. 2002. "Does Feminism Need a Conception of Civil Society?" In *Alternative Conceptions of Civil Society.* Ed. Simone Chambers and Will Kymlicka. Princeton, NJ: Princeton University Press.

Pineda, Jaime A. 2009. *Mirror Neuron Systems: The Role of Mirroring Processes in Social Cognition.* New York: Humana Press.

Piper, Adrian. 1991. "Impartiality, Compassion, and Modal Imagination." *Ethics* 101 (4): 726–757.

Pittaway, Eileen, Linda Bartolomei, and Richard Hugman. 2010. "Stop Stealing Our Stories': The Ethics of Research with Vulnerable Groups." *Journal of Human Rights Practice* 2 (2) (July 01): 229–251.

Pogge, Thomas. 2007. "Severe Poverty as a Human Rights Violation." In *Freedom from Poverty as a Human Right: Who Owes What to the Very Poor?* Ed. Thomas Pogge. Oxford: Oxford University Press.

Prinz, Jesse. 2005. "Are Emotions Feelings?" *Journal of Consciousness Studies* 12 (8–10): 9–25.

Prinz, Jesse. 2011a. "Is Empathy Necessary for Morality?" In *Empathy: Philosophical and Psychological Perspectives.* Ed. Peter Goldie and Amy Coplan. Oxford: Oxford University Press.

Prinz, Jesse. 2011b. "Against Empathy." *Southern Journal of Philosophy* (Spindel Supplement) 49: 214–233.

Rajaram, Prem Kumar. 2002. "Humanitarianism and Representations of the Refugee." *Journal of Refugee Studies* 15 (3): 247–264.

Reichle, Barbara, and Manfred Schmitt. 2002. "Strategies for Restoring Belief in a Just World: Evidence from Longitudinal Change Analyses." In *The Justice Motive in Everyday Life.* Ed. Michael Ross and Dale T. Miller. Cambridge, UK: Cambridge University Press.

Reilly, Niamh. 1994. *Testimonies of the Global Tribunal on Violations of Women's Human Rights.* Highland Park NJ: Plowshares Press, http://www.nuigalway.ie/soc/documents/online_publications/reilly_testimonies_1994.pdf (accessed 7/1/2015).

Rimmon-Kenan, Shlomith. 2006. "Concepts of Narrative." In *The Travelling Concept of Narrative: Studies across Disciplines in the Humanities and Social Sciences*. Ed. Matti Hyvärinen, Anu Korhonen, and Juri Mykkänen. Helsinki: Helsinki Collegium for Advanced Studies, https://helda.helsinki.fi/bitstream/handle/10138/25747/001_03_rimmon_kenan.pdf.txt;jsessionid=5EB-7FA9B4ABAA95571E368A648C0E976?sequence=2 (accessed 10/5/2015)

Rizzolatti, Giacomo, and Laila Craighero. 2004. "The Mirror Neuron System." *Annual Review of Neuroscience* 27: 169–192.

Robertson, Claire. 1996. "Grassroots in Kenya: Women, Genital Mutilation, and Collective Action, 1920–1990." *Signs* 21 (3): 615–642.

Robinson, Jenefer. 2005. *Deeper Than Reason: Emotion and Its Role in Literature, Music, and Art*. Oxford: Oxford University Press.

Rogers, Gerry. 1994. *The Vienna Tribunal*, http://www.wmm.com/filmcatalog/pages/c172.shtml.

Rorty, Richard. 1986. "Freud and Moral Reflection." In *Pragmatism's Freud*. Ed. Joseph H. Smith and William Kerrigan. Baltimore, MD: Johns Hopkins University Press.

Rorty, Richard. 1993. "Human Rights, Rationality, and Sentimentality." In *On Human Rights: The Oxford Amnesty Lectures 1993*. Ed. Stephen Shute and Susan Hurley. New York: Basic Books.

Rosenblum, Nancy L. 2002. "Feminist Perspectives on Civil Society and Government." In *Civil Society and Government*. Ed. Nancy L. Rosenblum and Robert C. Post. Princeton, NJ: Princeton University Press.

Ross, Fiona C. 2001. "Speech and Silence: Women's Testimony in the First Five Weeks of Public Hearings of the South African Truth and Reconciliation Commission." In *Remaking a World: Violence Social Suffering and Recovery*. Ed. Veena Das et al. Berkeley: University of California Press.

Ross, Michael, and Dale T. Miller. 2002. *The Justice Motive in Everyday Life*. Cambridge, UK: Cambridge University Press.

Roth, Kenneth. 2014. "The End of Human Rights?" *New York Review* LXI (16): 72–74.

Rousseau, Jean-Jacques. [1762]1979. *Emile, or On Education*. Trans. Allan Bloom. New York: Basic Books.

Salm, Janet. 1999. "Coping with Globalization: A Profile of the NGO Sector." *Nonprofit and Voluntary Sector Quarterly* 28 (4) Supplement: 87–103.

Schaffer, Kay. 2008. "Testimony, Nation Building, and the Ethics of Witnessing: After the Truth and Reconciliation Commission in South Africa." *Pathways to Reconciliation: Between Theory and Practice*. Aldershot, UK: Ashgate.

Schaffer, Kay, and Sidonie Smith. 2004. *Human Rights and Narrated Lives: The Ethics of Recognition*. New York: Palgrave.

Schechtman, Marya. 1997. *The Constitution of Selves*. Ithaca, NY: Cornell University Press.

Schechtman, Marya. 2007. "Stories, Lives, and Basic Survival." In *Narrative and Understanding Persons*. Ed. Daniel Hutto. Cambridge, UK: Cambridge University Press.

Schechtman, Marya. 2008. "Staying Alive: Personal Continuation and a Life Worth Having." In *Practical Identity and Narrative Agency*. Ed. Kim Atkins and Catriona Mackenzie. New York: Routledge.

Seligman, Adam B. 2002. "Civil Society as Idea and Ideal." In *Alternative Conceptions of Civil Society*. Ed. Simone Chambers and Will Kymlicka. Princeton, NJ: Princeton University Press.

Shepler, Susan. 2002. "Les Filles Soldats: Trajectoires d'apres-guerre en Sierra Leone." *Politique Africaine* 88: 49–62 (my citations refer to the English language version of this article in manuscript, for which I thank Susan Shepler).

Shepler, Susan. 2006. "Can the Child Soldier Speak?" Conference on Humanitarian Responses to Narratives of Inflicted Suffering. University of Connecticut, Storrs. October 13–15, 2006.

Sherman, Nancy. 1998. "Empathy, Respect, and Humanitarian Intervention." *Ethics & International Affairs* 12 (1): 103–119.

Shue, Henry. 1980. *Basic Rights: Subsistence, Affluence, and U.S. Foreign Policy*. Princeton, NJ: Princeton University Press.

Shuman, Amy. 2005. *Other People's Stories: Entitlement Claims and the Critique of Empathy*. Urbana: University of Illinois Press.

Simmons, P. J. 1998. "Learning to Live with NGOs." *Foreign Policy* 112 (Autumn): 82–96.

Slahi, Mohamadou Ould. 2015. *Guantánamo Diary*. Ed. Larry Siems. New York: Little, Brown.

Slote, Michael. 2007. *The Ethics of Care and Empathy*. London: Routledge.

Slovic, Paul. 2007. "'If I look at the mass I will never act': Psychic Numbing and Genocide." *Judgment and Decision Making* 2 (2): 79–95.

Slyomovics, Susan. 2005. "The Argument from Silence: Morocco's Truth Commission and Women Political Prisoners." *Journal of Middle East Women's Studies* 1 (3): 73–95.

Smiley, Marion. 1992. *Moral Responsibility and the Boundaries of Community*. Chicago: University of Chicago Press.

Soderlund, Gretchen. 2005. "Running from the Rescuers: New U.S. Crusades against Sex Trafficking and the Rhetoric of Abolition." *Feminist Formations* 17 (3): 64–87.

Soyinka, Wole. 1999. *The Burden of Memory, the Muse of Forgiveness*. New York: Oxford University Press.

Spelman, Elizabeth V. 1997. *Fruits of Sorrow: Framing Our Attention to Suffering*. Boston, MA: Beacon Press.

Srikantiah, Jayashri. 2007. "Perfect Victims and Real Survivors: The Iconic Victim in Domestic Human Trafficking Law." *Boston University Law Review* 87: 157–211.

Strejilevich, Nora. 2006. "Testimony: Beyond the Language of Truth." *Human Rights Quarterly* 28 (3): 701–713.

Stueber, Karsten R. 2010. *Rediscovering Empathy: Agency, Folk Psychology, and the Human Sciences.* Cambridge, MA: MIT Press.

Stueber, Karsten R. 2011. "Imagination, Empathy, and Moral Deliberation: The Case of Imaginative Resistance." *Southern Journal of Philosophy* (Spindel Supplement) 49: 156–180.

Tarrow, Sidney. 2010. "Outsiders Inside and Insiders Outside: Linking Transnational and Domestic Public Action for Human Rights." *Human Rights Review* 11 (2): 171–182.

Taylor, Charles. 1989. *Sources of the Self.* Cambridge, MA: Harvard University Press.

Taylor, David. 2014. "Victim Participation in Transitional Justice Mechanisms: Real Power or Empty Ritual?" Impunity Watch. Utrecht: The Netherlands, http://www.impunitywatch.org/docs/IW_Discussion_Paper_Victim_Participation1.pdf (accessed 12/29/2014).

Thabet, Abdel Aziz, and Panos Vostanis. 2008. "Exposure to War Trauma and PTSD among Parents and Children in the Gaza Strip," http://www.ncbi.nlm.nih.gov/pubmed/18365135 (accessed 10/14/2014).

Universal Declaration of Human Rights (UDHR). 1948. http://www.amnestyusa.org/human-rights/universal-declaration-of-human-rights/page.do?id=1031003 (accessed 3/9/2009).

Trout, J. D. 2009. *The Empathy Gap: Building Bridges to the Good Life and the Good Society.* New York: Viking.

Valian, Virginia. 1998. *Why So Slow? The Advancement of Women.* Cambridge, MA: MIT Press.

VanHooser, Sarah, and Brooke Ackerly. 2009. "Global Feminisms Collaborative Research Ethics Statement," http://brookeackerly.org/for-research (accessed 1/5/2015).

Velleman, J. David. 2003. "Narrative Explanation." *Philosophical Review* 112 (1): 1–25.

Velleman, J. David. 2006. *Self to Self: Selected Essays.* Cambridge, UK: Cambridge University Press.

Velleman, J. David. 2009. *How We Get Along.* Cambridge, UK: Cambridge University Press.

Walker, Margaret Urban. 1998. *Moral Understandings: A Feminist Study in Ethics.* New York: Routledge.

Walker, Margaret Urban. 2003. "Truth and Voice in Women's Rights." In *Recognition, Responsibility, and Rights.* Ed. Robin N. Fiore and Hilde Lindemann Nelson. Lanham, MD: Rowman and Littlefield.

Walker, Margaret Urban. 2006. *Moral Repair: Reconstructing Moral Relations after Wrongdoing.* Cambridge, UK: Cambridge University Press.

Walker, Margaret Urban. 2010. "Truth Telling as Reparations." *Metaphilosophy* 41 (4): 525–545.

Vignemont, Frédérique De, and Pierre Jacob. 2012. "What Is It Like to Feel Another's Pain?" *Philosophy of Science* 79 (2): 295–316 (HAL ID: ijn_00686106).

Walzer, Michael. 2002. "Equality and Civil Society." In *Alternative Conceptions of Civil Society*. Ed. Simone Chambers and Will Kymlicka. Princeton, NJ: Princeton University Press.

Waugh, Louisa. 2007. *Selling Olga: Stories of Human Trafficking and Resistance*. London: Orion Books.

Wertheimer, Alan. 1987. *Coercion*. Princeton, NJ: Princeton University Press.

Westlund, Andrea. 2011. "Narrative Necessity and the Fixity of Meaning in a Life." *Narrative Inquiry* 21 (2): 391–398.

White, Hayden. 1987. "The Value of Narrativity in the Representation of Reality." In *The Content of the Form: Narrative Discourse and Historical Representation*. Baltimore, MD: Johns Hopkins University Press.

Wilson, Elizabeth, and Günther Knoblich. 2005. "The Case for Motor Involvement in Perceiving Conspecifics." *Psychological Bulletin* 131 (3): 160–173.

Wilson, Richard Ashby. 2001. *The Politics of Truth and Reconciliation in South Africa: Legitimizing the Post-Apartheid State*. Cambridge, UK: Cambridge University Press.

Wilson, Richard Ashby, and Richard D. Brown. 2009. "Introduction." In *Humanitarianism and Suffering: The Mobilization of Empathy*. Ed. Richard Ashby Wilson and Richard D. Brown. Cambridge, UK; New York: Cambridge University Press.

Wolgast, Elizabeth. 1993. "Innocence." *Royal Institute of Philosophy* 68 (265): 297–307.

Yellin, Janet Fagan. 2000. "Introduction." In *Incidents in the Life of a Slave Girl, Written by Herself* (enlarged edition). Ed. Janet Fagan Yellin. Cambridge, MA: Harvard University Press.

Young, Iris Marion. 1997. "Communication and the Other: Beyond Deliberative Democracy." In *Intersecting Voices*. Princeton, NJ: Princeton University Press.

Zagefka, Hanna, et al. 2010. "Donating to Disaster Victims: Responses to Natural and Humanly Caused Events." *European Journal of Social Psychology* 41 (3): 353–363. doi: 10.1002/ejsp.781.

Zajonc, Robert. 1980. "Feeling and Thinking: Preferences Need No Inferences." *American Psychologist* 35: 151–175.

Zajonc, Robert. 1984. "On the Primacy of Affect." *American Psychologist* 39: 117–129.

Zajonc, Robert. 1994. "Evidence for Nonconscious Emotions." In *The Nature of Emotion*. Ed. Paul Ekman and Richard J. Davidson. New York: Oxford University Press.

Zimmerman, David. 1981. "Coercive Wage Offers." *Philosophy and Public Affairs* 10: 121–145.

INDEX